© Canpolat/Connors

About the Author

SICHAN SIV was nominated a United States ambassador to the United Nations by President George W. Bush in October 2001, and was unanimously confirmed by the Senate. From 1989 to 1993, during the administration of George H. W. Bush, Siv served as deputy assistant to the president for public liaison and deputy assistant secretary of state for South Asia. Ambassador Siv holds a Master of International Affairs from Columbia University. He and his wife divide their time between San Antonio, New York, and Asia.

GOLDEN
BONES

GOLDEN BONES

An Extraordinary Journey
from Hell in Cambodia
to a New Life in America

SICHAN SIV

HARPER PERENNIAL

NEW YORK • LONDON • TORONTO • SYDNEY • NEW DELHI • AUCKLAND

HARPER ● PERENNIAL

A hardcover edition of this book was published in 2008 by HarperCollins
Publishers.

HarperCollins books may be purchased for educational, business, or
sales promotional use. For information please write: Special Markets
Department, HarperCollins Publishers, 10 East 53rd Street, New York,
NY 10022.

All photographs courtesy of the Siv Collection unless otherwise noted.

FIRST HARPER PERENNIAL EDITION PUBLISHED 2009.

Designed by Emily Cavett Taff

Library of Congress Cataloging-in-Publication Data is available upon
request.

ISBN 978-0-06-137541-5

13 WBC/RRD 10 9 8 7 6 5 4 3

To Mae,
who gave me life, love, and hope

To Martha,
who continues to give me happiness

Contents

CONTENTS

Second Episode:
AMERICA

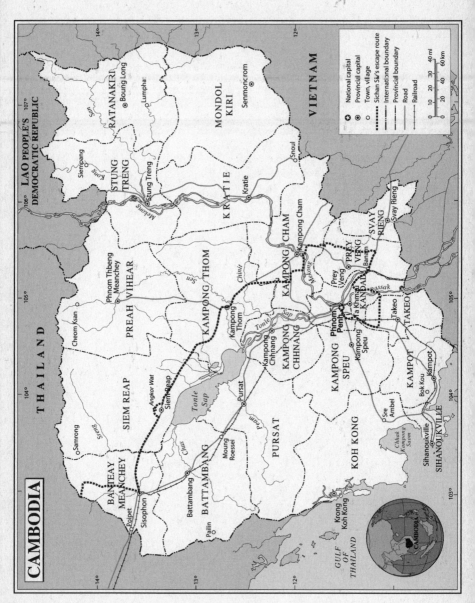

Based on a United Nations map.

Preface

It took me thirty years to write *Golden Bones*.

After my arrival in America on June 4, 1976, each time I introduced myself, people asked me if I was going to write a book. Then the question became *when*. Some even asked *where* they could get a copy. I occasionally joked that I was waiting for a few more chapters.

At the beginning I was very reluctant. I did not want to revisit a painful past. I was looking forward to building a new life. However, during my travels around the country and the world, the questions persisted. As time went by, I started to realize that the benefits of sharing the story would outweigh any temporary sadness. On March 1, 2006, I began to put pen to paper.

Golden Bones starts and ends in 2006. Although it covers some 2,000 years of history, the main story takes place in the second half of twentieth century and the first decade of the twenty-first. The book has two episodes: Cambodia and America. The first episode, "Cambodia," is divided into parts with a time frame, to reflect memory. The second episode, "America," has no time frame, to project timelessness.

As you go through the pages of *Golden Bones*, whatever you do and wherever you are, I trust you will find something that you can relate to. After all, it is a human story.

I look forward to seeing you again in the near future. Until then, may your mind be full of dreams, your heart be full of hopes, and your head make everything a reality.

Sichan Siv
San Antonio, June 4, 2008

GOLDEN BONES

Two Thousand Six

The First Month and Seventeenth Day
Boston, Philadelphia, London, Paris, and Phnom Penh seemed to have something in common on January 17, 2006. It was Benjamin Franklin's 300th birthday.

Born in Boston, Franklin distinguished himself in Philadelphia as a printer, postmaster, scientist, and statesman. He became the only American involved in all the major historic documents during the nation's birth. He had gone to London as a colonial agent and to Paris as the United States' first ambassador. Celebrations of his historic anniversary took place simultaneously. In Philadelphia, the National Constitution Center, next to Independence Hall, opened its exhibition "Benjamin Franklin: In Search of a Better World," which would travel to St. Louis, Houston, Denver, and Atlanta, before ending up in Paris.

Phnom Penh?

The United States did not exist when Franklin was born in 1706. England and France were the only two global powers. Cambodia, once a powerful empire itself, had been in steady decline for a few hundred years.

On Franklin's 300th birthday, my wife, Martha, and I were in Phnom Penh as guests of honor at the dedication of the new U.S. embassy there. The first post-9/11 "standard embassy design," on which all future embassies would be based, stood across the street from Wat Phnom, a most sacred site where the Cambodian capital was founded in 1432, sixty years before Christopher Columbus came to America.

During the inaugural ceremony, my memory flashed back—first to my previous visit to Cambodia.

It was in October 2004, the week before the U.S. presidential election between George W. Bush and John Kerry. Martha and I had been in our hotel room in Lexington, Kentucky, when the phone rang. The State Department Operations Center put through two calls from Washington. My senior colleagues recommended that I go to Cambodia to attend the coronation of the new king.

His Majesty Preah Bat Samdech Preah Norodom Sihanouk of Cambodia, who ascended to the throne in 1941 when Franklin Roosevelt was in the White House, had just abdicated, owing to poor health. The Crown Council elected his youngest son Sihamoni to be the next monarch. In the Throne Hall, while watching rituals that dated back to the tenth century, I felt privileged to be the only dignitary invited to attend from a foreign capital. Other countries were represented by their ambassadors accredited to Cambodia. The reverberations of the enormous Cambodian drums transported my memory even farther back.

To my childhood.

First Episode:

CAMBODIA

Once upon a time in a remote corner of the planet Earth, there was an ancient land blessed with fertile soil and abundant water. Its people were builders who created the world's largest preindustrial city at the beginning of the first millennium. For 1,000 years, from the sixth to the sixteenth centuries, they produced more arts than any other civilization. They became a powerful empire, which was the economic, cultural, and political center of the region.

In the fifteenth century the empire began to lose its influence. For the next 500 years, it struggled to survive between two increasingly stronger neighbors.

Colonization by a European power in the nineteenth century saved the country from being completely swallowed up. It took another ninety years before the ancient land became a new independent nation.

An old prophecy foretold that the new country would go through a series of turmoil and upheavals so violent that before it could get back on the road to its glorious past, the level of blood would reach an elephant's belly.

Three years after the end of World War II, a boy was born to the daughter of a governor and her husband—a police chief—in a small village of the ancient land. This baby was the youngest of their children. It was the Year of the Boar, 2490. And the moon was full.

The astrologer informed the happy parents that the boy's Boar was carrying a crystal ball in his mouth. Legend had it that the ball would allow the Boar to walk on water, climb over mountains, and travel to the farthest and highest places, as long as he kept the ball in his mouth at all times. Otherwise, there could be great hardships. But because his mother's milk was dear, the boy would grow up to be a man of golden bones!

That boy was me.

PART I:

DREAMS AND HOPE, 1948–1970

No matter what happens, never give up hope.

—Mae (1913–1975)

CHAPTER 1

POCHENTONG

At the end of World War II, Pochentong, Cambodia, was a small sleepy village of about 100 people. The lush and tranquil world of my boyhood was also the district headquarters of Phnom Penh and the kingdom's major airport. Cambodia was divided into provinces (*khet*), districts (*srok*), communes (*khum*), and villages (*phum*). The civilian chiefs of our district usually became governors of Kandal (to which the district belonged) and later members of the king's cabinet. Some of them ended up as prime ministers. Assignments to Phnom Penh and Kandal were the route to ultimate power in Cambodia in the 1940s and 1950s.

Pochentong had no running water or electricity. Water was fetched from a nearby pond and sometimes delivered by tanker trucks. We used candles and kerosene lamps at night.

My father, Siv Chham (Cambodians put their family name, or surname, first), was born in 1909 in Tonle Bati, a *srok* in the southern province of Takeo. He was the chief of police, known at the time as *garde provinciale*, of *srok* Phnom Penh. My mother, Chea Aun, was born on the Cambodian new year (April 13), 1913. Her father, Sok Chea, my grandfather, was the *chauvay khet* (governor) of Kampong

Som. She recalled that when he was transferred to another post, they would travel for days by elephants. She was of medium height, wore her hair short, and had a serene look on her face, which reflected a lot of love and compassion. My parents, for some reason, decided to give their children names beginning with the Khmer letter *saw*, or S in English. The practice was later followed by the younger generations.

Our family was small by Cambodian standards. I was the youngest of four. The elder of my two sisters, Sarin, was born on March 21, 1933. I do not remember my second sister Sarun's birthday in 1935. My brother, Sichhun, was born on October 31, 1941. It was the year that eighteen-year-old Prince Sihanouk was crowned king of Cambodia; he would eventually become the most famous Cambodian of the twentieth century. Incidentally, the king and my brother shared a birthday. I was born in the Cambodian Year of the Boar, 2490. Because our traditional year usually goes from April 13 to April 12, I was born on March 1, 1948, on the western calendar.

In 1953 I was sent to Pochentong Primary School. That year, my second sister, Sarun, at age eighteen, was married to an official at the finance ministry. Two years later, Sarin, at age twenty-two, was married to an army officer. Both marriages were arranged—a practice that is still going on, although to a lesser extent.

Life in Pochentong seemed like paradise. With protective parents and a loving upper-middle-class family, I simply had no worries. School and play always went hand in hand. I grew up with children from all walks of life: their parents were peasants, merchants, military people, police, and civil servants. My grade-school pals and I went swimming in ponds, chasing ducks near the railroad station or the airport runway. The one who caught the duck was the winner, until the duck got away. I remember that one day, I got the duck and began to run, naked and barefoot, down the dusty road, followed by screaming children. I came on my brother, who was playing soccer in a nearby field with his friends. "Hey, Kanee! Where are you going with your little friend dangling between your legs?" I immediately stopped to look down at what was dangling, and the duck got away. My brother was one of the few people who called me by my nickname, which had no meaning but sounded cute in Khmer. The others included my parents, sisters, brothers-in-law, uncles, and aunts. I would not respond to any voices other than theirs when I heard my nickname.

My friends and I created our own toys. We used clay to make animals (elephants and horses), fruits (bananas, oranges, mangoes, and pumpkins), buses, trucks, and slingshot bullets. We made our own slingshots from the fork of a guava branch and practiced shooting at trees and stray animals, before getting into a real good-versus-evil fight. We play *jor-kinh* (thief and detective) games, the Cambodian version of cops and robbers or cowboys and Indians. As the son of a police chief, I naturally wanted to play the detective—the good guy. But my friends wanted me to be the bad guy, the ugly barbarian, on the wrong side of the law and society, who had to run and hide behind big trees and bushes. When found, he would have to defend himself, in a slingshot war with the good guys, until he ran out of clay bullets and surrendered. Somehow, I usually managed to evade the pursuers until they gave up.

We competed in flying kites. As we grew older, the kites became more complicated to build. We stopped short of trying to produce *kalaeng aek*, the enormous musical kites that take a few adult males to fly. Once airborne, they fly at very high altitude for hours, sometimes all night, and produce a smooth, soothing sound from the vibrations of a very thin "tongue" of bamboo attached to the head of the kite. The sound was carried far away from one village to another, depending on the direction of the wind.

In the evening, we listened to the national radio, which broadcast news and music a few hours a day.

During the 1950s, Cambodia received many world leaders who were coming to visit this newly independent kingdom, and especially the architectural wonders of its former royal capital Angkor: Dag Hammarskjöld, Jawaharlal Nehru, Sukarno, Zhou Enlai, and others. Each time there was a state visit, the boys and girls of my school were herded to the airport. We were usually among the first to welcome the foreign dignitaries. We wore our standard uniforms: khaki pants and white shirts for boys; navy blue skirts and white blouses for girls. We were at the airport and along the road from the terminal to our village to wave flags, clap our hands, shout greetings, and hold banners. It was always fun to be away from the classroom.

After everyone left the airport, my buddies and I immediately engaged in our favorite activity: avian ball. We took off our uniforms and plunged into the muddy water naked, chasing any bird we could find. Living less than a mile from the airport, I developed an affinity for airplanes. The noise of an approaching aircraft was a cue for my group to sprint to the airfield. We tried to run alongside the plane when it landed. We were usually the first unofficial welcoming committee.

As I went through my six years of primary education, I learned more about the history of Cambodia. While I was in first grade, Vice President and Mrs. Richard Nixon toured Angkor on October 30, 1953, a memorable trip which he would recall forty years later. Under King Sihanouk's leadership, Cambodia gained its independence from France ten days after Nixon's visit. Cambodia's association with France went back a century earlier.

In 1841, Ang Duong was crowned king of Cambodia; he was then in his forties. Cambodia was relatively peaceful during his reign, after many years of turbulence when the Siamese and Annamese were fighting over its control. In November 1853, Ang Duong, fearing that Cambodia would be swallowed by its two powerful neighbors, began making contact with Napoléon III to seek the protection of France. He died before getting any reply from France. His eldest son, Norodom, succeeded him in 1859. It took the French ten years to respond to Ang Duong. In August 1863, Cambodia became a protectorate of France.

Actually, France was not the first European power to reach Cambodia. A Portuguese Dominican monk, Gaspar da Cruz, arrived in the Cambodian capital of Longvek in 1555, toward the end of the reign (1515–1566) of King Ang Chan I. He stayed for one year and then left. The last quarter of the sixteenth century saw more Europeans in Cambodia. Only two, however, remained long enough to provide support to King Satha (1576–1596). The Portuguese Diego Veloso and the Spaniard Blas Ruiz were made governors of Baphuon and Treang, respectively, in recognition of their loyal service to the king.

In the early seventeenth century, Gabriel Quiroga de San Antonio, a Spanish missionary, was so impressed with Cambodia's *kampong* (river ports) that he advised King Philip II to colonize the southeast Asian kingdom. When I came to this part of history, I marveled at the thought that I might have grown up speaking Spanish instead of French. Chey Chetha II (r. 1618–1628) established his royal palace at Udong, which remained Cambodia's capital for nearly 200 years, until 1817. This king was married to an Annamese princess, and in 1623 he allowed the court of Hue to resettle its people in fertile Lower Cambodia (Kampuchea Krom) of the Mekong Delta. By the time Chey Chetha died, the region from Prey Nokor (Saigon) to the old border with Champa was totally occupied by Annamese. In 1636, a Dutch embassy headed by Hendrik Hagenhaar arrived at Udong. His was the first European diplomatic mission.

In the eighteenth century, Cambodia was making its final fights for survival. Successive rulers were paying tribute to either Siam or Annam, and so there were endless reprisals and revenge within the Cambodian courts until the middle of the nineteenth century. In order to save everyone's face, Ang Duong was asked to pay tribute to both Bangkok and Hue. The Annamese returned all the royal regalia, including the sacred sword, as well as other members of the royal family whom they had kept as prisoners in Hue and Prey Nokor. A peace treaty was signed in 1846, and Ang Duong's coronation took place the following year in the presence of representatives of the king of Siam and the emperor of Annam. The French arrived and saved Cambodia from being under dual control of these two expansionist neighbors.

Norodom's younger brother Sisowath reigned from 1904 to 1927. His successor was his eldest son Monivong, who was crowned in 1927. Monivong's reign was marked by Cambodia's second involvement in a world conflict on the side of France. With France's surrender to Germany in 1940, Japan occupied Cambodia but left the Vichy French administration intact. Monivong died in 1941 in the hill resort of Bokor. His body was clandestinely transported back to the royal palace in Phnom Penh, where his death was officially announced. He left behind three children. The eldest, a daughter, Kossomak, was married in 1920 to Suramarit, a grandson of King Norodom; Sihanouk was their 18-year-old son. The Monivong's other two sons were Monireth and Monipong. In principle, the throne would have gone to Monireth. But the French wanted someone easy to manipulate and selected Sihanouk. To France, he was the perfect choice, a product of the two major branches of the royal family. He was the great-grandson of Norodom through his father, and of Sisowath through his mother.

In 1953, 100 years after his great-great-grandfather Ang Duong had requested France's protection from Siam and Annam, Sihanouk succeeded in getting rid of French colonialism. The government in Paris was trying to get out of French Indochina altogether. The following year, a few months after the bloody fifty-five-day battle at Dien Bien Phu, the Geneva Conference guaranteed Cambodia's neutrality and divided Tonkin, Annam, and Cochin China at the seventeenth parallel into North and South Vietnam. In 1955, Sihanouk abdicated in favor of his father, Suramarit, in order to play a more active political role. Unlike other monarchies, modern Khmer kingship is not hereditary but elective. The constitution of 1947, modeled on France's Fourth

Republic, stated that all male descendants of King Ang Duong were eligible to ascend to the throne.

With his prestige as a former king and father of Cambodia's independence, Sihanouk established the Sangkum Reastr Niyum (SRN), which he called a rally of parties. The SRN would win successive elections over the Democratic Party and other opponents. In 1955, Cambodia was admitted to the United Nations along with Albania, Austria, Bulgaria, Ceylon, Finland, Hungary, Ireland, Italy, Jordan, Laos, Libya, Portugal, Romania, and Spain.

CHAPTER 2

PARADISE LOST

I n early 1957, my sister Sarun died unexpectedly, leaving three daughters behind. My mother immediately took over their upbringing. My father, who had been sick, gave instructions for the funeral arrangements from his bed. He watched speechlessly as the body of his daughter was carried away to be cremated. His health suddenly began to deteriorate. As a young child, I did not know what sickness my second sister and my father had suffered from.

We invited Buddhist monks to our house every night to give blessings. We bought a lot of Buddhist books to offer to the monks and other friends as a good deed on the 2,500th anniversary of Buddha's birthday. The whole kingdom joined in the festivities. Prince Sihanouk had brought some of Buddha's relics from Ceylon on May 4. They would be laid in the Preah Sakyamuni Chedey, a specially built funerary monument in front of the Phnom Penh railroad station. It still stands at the same location.

On June 24 my father died after a long illness. My mother, whose eyes had not been dry since Sarun's death, was filled with grief again. Losing a daughter a few months earlier was bad enough, and now she was a widow at age forty-four. My sister Sarin was pregnant with her first child. Sarin was tall, slender, and beautiful, with shoulder-length hair, just as Sarun had been.

I was a little bit confused at what was going on around me. As the younger son, I was the official mourner of the family. I did not know how this tradition began, except that perhaps the grown-ups did not want to shave.

My head and eyebrows were shaved and I was draped in white cotton cloth, the color of mourning. My father's body was bathed clean and dressed in new clothing. His hands were joined together on top of his chest to hold three unburned sticks of incense and candles. A silver coin was put in his mouth before he was covered with a white sheet. He was later put into a specially built coffin. At six feet three inches, he had been extremely tall, probably one of the tallest Cambodians of his time. I remember seeing some of his group pictures: his French colleagues came up to his chest. His important social rank at Pochentong required an elaborate funeral service.

My parents had built our Khmer-style house—on stilts, with wooden walls and tile roof—in 1950. It had a special feature—a concrete water tank. The gutters all around the house collected rain and poured it into the tank. During the rainy season from May to October, we amassed enough water to share with neighbors. Our house was just across the street from the main gate of Wat Pothisataram, Pochentong's Buddhist monastery, where the cremation was to take place. The funeral procession, however, had to go to the market and circle the main square before entering the temple. The longer route was taken in order to let people bid a final farewell to my father.

I was told to sit in front of my father's coffin on the decorated funeral truck. I held some flowers, three unburned candles, and incense in both hands, which I kept in front of my chest. Between me and the coffin was hung my father's uniform with all his decorations and medals. My brother Sichhun and male cousins dressed in white were honorary pallbearers and stood around the coffin. There were two funeral bands that preceded an open truck carrying Buddhist monks who kept chanting and saying prayers. The funeral vehicle was surrounded by police officers forming a symbolic protective cordon with their rifles pointing to the ground.

My family members, dressed in white, walked immediately behind the funeral vehicle. They were followed by former colleagues of my father and friends of the family, including hundreds of villagers. Everyone had a small bouquet of flowers with candles and incense sticks. When we passed in front of the district headquarters, the sentry in his ceremonial uniform stood at attention and saluted my father. Other people gave a *sampeah*. This is the traditional Cambodian greeting with the two hands joined in front of the chest, the lips, or the forehead. The level of the hands indicates the degree of respect. The higher the hands, the more respectful the greeting.

At the monastery, the coffin was carried around the crematorium clockwise three times before it was put on the pyre. After many Buddhist chants, the abbot ignited the pyre to burn the coffin and my father's body. The funeral band of percussion instruments, including two big drums, performed the last heartbreaking music while my mother, Sarin, and other female relatives cried and wept. Their voices and tears tore my heart. I did not cry, because to do so would show weakness, which should not be part of a male's emotions. But inside, I was uncontrollably sad. After more Buddhist blessings, the funeral ceremony was over. We later collected my father's ashes, which we cleaned by pouring coconut juice over them, and put them in a silver urn.

The cremation procedure seemed to have some Hindu and French influence that Cambodians had adapted to their own Buddhist version. The family normally paid for the funeral, with contributions from neighbors and friends.

At nine years old, then, I became fatherless. But as a Khmer saying goes, "It's better to lose a father than a mother; it's better to have a shipwreck than a fire." The government asked my mother whether she wanted to be supported monthly by my father's pension or receive a lump sum. She chose the latter and began a struggle to bring up on her own two sons; three granddaughters, whom she had adopted; and a few nephews and nieces. Our lifestyle changed completely. We went from being a well-to-do family to surviving at a subsistence level.

Adoption in Cambodia was more a moral obligation than a legal matter. One could adopt almost anybody: friends' children, relatives, cousins, etc. My three orphaned nieces became members of my immediate family, joined later by Sarin's eldest daughter, Samnang, when she became a toddler. And my mother, who was their grandmother, became their mother too. Like us, they called her *Mae*, "mother" in Khmer.

My mother had also adopted her baby brother—my uncle—Sa-Orn. I eventually learned that my grandfather Sok Chea was a *chauvay khet* (provincial governor) under King Sisowath. He and my grandmother Cheuy Larch died when Sa-Orn was a baby. Sa-Orn was only a few years older than my sister Sarin. My parents then adopted him, making him a Siv. They cared for him, brought him up, and found him a wife.

After the death of our father, I and my brother Sichhun—seven years older than I, taller, and stronger—worked harder to help with the heavy chores. During the not-so-rainy season from October to May, we carried water from a big pond near the temple and split dead trees to make firewood. We watered our big garden, from which we sold flowers to people who needed them for offerings to Buddha and the monks at the temple.

I was the errand boy of the family and was constantly at my mother's side. I helped her with everything, including putting thread into a needle when she sewed and giving her massages. Sichhun was studying at the prestigious lycée Sisowath, the Phillips Andover Academy of Cambodia. Sisowath was the first secondary school in the nation, founded in 1936 within a former palace of the king, who gave the school his name. Sisowath would produce all the best and brightest of Cambodia before and after independence.

In 1958, when I was ten, I entered my last year (sixth grade) at Pochentong Primary School. Education became more arduous. Schools around the kingdom competed for the largest number of students to pass the Certificat d'Études Primaires Complémentaires (CEPC), the exam that marked the successful completion of primary education. It was a source of great prestige for the school and the community. Our teacher, a strict disciplinarian, had a lot of rattan sticks which he used to whip students who did not know the right answers. The rest of the class had to literally climb the latticed walls to avoid the punishment. He gave our class additional tutoring at night. Our school was near a Chinese cemetery. I was the smallest and youngest in my class and was scared of ghosts. But my strong desire to pass the CEPC overcame my fear. I said a few prayers, closed my eyes, and ran fast in the dark street.

In 1959, at the end of the school year, I successfully completed my primary education. As a present, my mother took me to Siem Reap in the northwestern part of Cambodia, where the world-renowned former capital, Angkor, is located. For Cambodians, a trip to Angkor is like a pilgrimage. They usually go there during the Khmer new year in April: "After you have seen Angkor, you may die and go to heaven."

We took the trip with my other uncle, Chea Thuy. He had a beautiful daughter named Sophal, who had been "reserved" for me. Cambodians, like many other Asians, have a tradition of arranging marriages for their children, especially between colleagues, friends, and relatives. Some young people have been matched since they were babies. Brides and grooms might hardly know each other before their marriage, but they would have an obligation to their parents for having given them life. Amazingly enough, it seemed that more often than not, the young couples would fall in love after the wedding and live happily ever after. The divorce rate was low. Although legal, divorce was generally seen as bringing shame on the whole family.

My siblings' marriages had been arranged by my parents, but for me, unlike them, the concept did not work. After my uncle died in 1963, his wife was in a hurry to marry off her daughter. I was still a teenager and busy studying. It was not going to be a workable match, and the idea was called off.

CHAPTER 3

ANGKOR

The day of the big trip, my mother and I got up at four o'clock in the morning to take the first Pochentong–Phnom Penh bus. The Cambodian capital was a charming city filled with the tropical scents of the flowering trees that lined its boulevards. It had a mixture of Cambodian and French colonial architecture. France continued to have a strong influence on the kingdom, especially in education and culture. We loved everything that was French, and France symbolized the outside world for us. The Khmer word for "foreigner" is *baraing*, meaning "French."

My uncle and his family picked us up on Monivong Boulevard in their Peugeot 203. We went north toward the ferry at Praek Kadam, south of the former royal capital of Udong. We crossed the Tonle Sap River and took national route 6 toward Kampong Thom, about halfway between Phnom Penh and Siem Reap. We stopped there to have lunch by the Saen River. We reached Siem Reap in the late afternoon and went directly to the magnificent architectural masterpieces, to enjoy their beauty. Angkor—especially its showcase temple, Angkor Wat—has remained the embodiment of the 2,000-year history of the Khmer people.

During our few days in Siem Reap, I saw some of the 600 monuments within the sixty-square-mile capital of Cambodia's golden age. Most of them were built from the beginning of the ninth century, when Jayavarman II established kingship for the Khmer empire in 802 at Phnom Kulen. At the height of the Khmer civilization, Angkor was the most powerful cultural, economic, and political center of Southeast Asia. At eleven, I was face-to-face with Cambodia's glorious past.

THE WONDERS

Angkor Wat, one of the world's wonders, was built during the reign of Suryavarman II, the "sun king" (r. 1113–1150). It was to be his funeral temple, in which he was to be deified as Vishnu, a Hindu god. As such, Angkor Wat was the only major temple facing west, the direction of death in Hinduism. It is the world's largest religious monument, has remained the centerpiece of Khmer architecture, and has continued to be featured on the national flag, regardless of political regimes. The lotus bud towers represent Mount Meru, the spiritual universe of the gods. The central complex has a base of 717 by 620 feet and is surrounded by galleries measuring 5,000 by 4,000 feet. The outer walls measure 2.5 miles and are bordered by an enormous moat 200 yards wide.

Angkor Wat's galleries tell the Hindu epics of Ramayana and Mahabharata, and the struggle between good and evil. Other important scenes include the myth of the "churning of the sea of milk" and life in heaven and hell. As I stood on the main causeway looking eastward, with the sun setting behind me, the beauty of Angkor Wat was breathtaking. This monument is the ultimate symbol of human achievement in twelfth-century architecture.

Succeeding the sun king in 1150, his cousin Dharanindravarman II became the first Buddhist monarch, although Buddhism and Hinduism had both arrived in Cambodia at about the beginning of the first millennium. Transitions between the two religions sometimes produced violent reactions, including the desecration of temples.

Dhanarindravarman II inherited and continued the war against the kingdom of Champa, to the east. He appointed his twenty-five-year-old son commander in chief of his armed forces. The son was fighting against Champa when he learned of his father's death and the coronation of Yasovarman II (r. 1160–1166). Out of loyalty to the new king, Dharanindravarman II's son continued to fight, sacking many central provinces of Champa. In Angkor, Yasovarman was assassinated by a court mandarin who proclaimed himself king in 1166. During the mandarin's reign, the son of Dharanindravarman II lived in hiding in Cambodia while Champa attacked Angkor and occupied the capital for five years. At the death of the usurper, he organized a rebellion against Champa's occupation forces. He set ambushes before engaging in direct confrontation with the enemy. He managed to put a fleet together and, with a naval victory, ended Champa's occupation in 1181. He came to the throne as Jayavarman VII and would reign as one of Cambodia's greatest kings until his death in 1215. During his reign, the kingdom became more influenced by Buddhism.

The concept of *devaraja* (god-king) was at its peak under Jayavarman VII. The king was considered an intermediary between heaven and earth, between gods and people. He was Cambodia's master builder. He built more than any other king: about 100 hospitals, rest houses, and numerous temples. Six of his masterpieces were: Banteay Kdei; Bayon; Neak Porn; Ta Prohm (1186), dedicated to his mother; Preah Khan (1191), dedicated to his father; and the great city of Angkor Thom. These magnificent monuments provide an extraordinary description of life in Angkor, in tens of thousands of figures depicted in miles of freizes. No chronicles give the names of the architects and engineers who designed and built the great temples. The monuments were described as having been built by the monarchs of the period. That practice con-forms to the Khmer concept of reserving the title of supreme builder for the god-kings.

Angkor, with a population of over 1 million, was the largest me-tropolis of the preindustrial world. It was a huge civilization and an inexhaustible center of information and learning. A sophisticated network of waterways, irrigation canals, and moats brought together necessity and beauty. In the heart of the city is the famous temple of Bayon, characterized by fifty-four unique four-faced towers. Unfortu-nately, when Jayavarman VII, the last great king of Angkor, died, he took with him the glory of Cambodia's golden age. Without a strong leader, the Khmer empire slowly began to decline.

In 1296, the Mongol emperor Kublai Khan's grandson Timur Khan sent to Cambodia an embassy headed by Zhou Daguan. The Chinese diplomatic mission arrived at Angkor during the reign of Indravarman III (1295–1308), when Cambodia was moving steadily toward Buddhism. Zhou lived in Angkor for a year and provided the most detailed account of life in thirteenth-century Cambodia. He described the city of Angkor Thom as having a wall about five miles in circumference, and said that the royal palace, official buildings, and homes of the nobles faced east. Ministers, generals, and all sorts of functionaries were given insignias and attendants according to their rank in the hierarchy. The highest officials were carried in palanquins resembling sedan chairs, with golden shafts and four parasols with handles of gold. Buddhist monks had their heads shaved, wore yellow robes with a knotted strip of yellow cloth around the waist, and traveled barefoot. Festivities for the new year included night-time rockets and firecrackers. The king, surrounded by his court and for-eign ambassadors, watched from a stand in front of the royal palace. There were astronomers who could predict eclipses of the sun and the moon. There were three or four crops a year and plenty of products: veg-etables, fish and reptiles, salt, vinegar, soy, chariots, palanquins, and boats. Women were in charge of trade. And yet despite their advanced civilization, Zhou Daguan, believing in China's superiority, referred to the Cambodians as barbarians.

I n the fourteenth century Cambodia's supreme power in Southeast Asia started to erode. Its cult of *devaraja* ended in 1336 with the accidental death of King Jayavarman IX, who sneaked up on a gardener to test the man's vigilance and was killed by him. Siamese forces began to intensify their harassment of the Khmer empire. They managed to bring back to Sukhothai and Ayuthaya a wealth of goods and knowledge. In 1431, they finally succeeded in sacking Angkor. King Ponhea Yat moved the capital to Phnom Penh. In 1434 Angkor was looted of all its resources. Architects, engineers, artists, dancers, men of letters, scholars, and scientists were brought to Siam as prisoners and bounties. The Siamese began to learn more about arts and sciences from their captives. It was a situation similar to that of the Romans and the Greeks: the students (the captors) ended up doing better than their teachers (the captives).

By the nineteenth century, Khmer princes and scholars were being sent to Siam to study what the Siamese had learned from their ancestors four centuries earlier. During those 400 years Cambodia struggled to survive between Siam and Annam, which later became Vietnam. The latter had already destroyed the Islamic kingdom of Champa in the central part of present-day Vietnam in 1792. Cambodia's territory continued to shrink, to the benefit of its two aggressive neighbors, when the French arrived in 1863 with their *mission civilisatrice*.

THE PILGRIMAGE

Once in a long while, a single trip can become very memorable. My pilgrimage to Angkor was one. Siem Reap was to become my favorite Cambodian city; there, ten years later, I would spend one or two weekends a month relaxing and rejuvenating myself.

Before returning to Phnom Penh, we spent half a day at the Siem Reap market, known for its handicrafts. We selected all the best rattan and wicker bags and baskets and had the Chinese merchants wrap them for us. They let us leave our purchases overnight with them. The following morning we picked up our souvenirs and returned happily to the capital. It was one of the most satisfying trips I had ever made with my mother. At home, everybody was excited to get a present from our pilgrimage. But when we opened the wrappings, we were shocked to find that the merchants had cheated us and replaced our purchases with inferior products.

THE SEA

Another memorable trip with my mother was to the seaside in 1959. Someone in the village chartered a bus for people who wanted to travel on a new road all the way to the ocean. The United States had just finished building the first highway in Cambodia. It linked Phnom Penh to the seaport of Sihanoukville and crossed three provinces: Kandal, Kampong Speu, and Kampot. The bus, filled with our neighbors, left Pochentong before dawn and traveled on the impeccably smooth highway. It snaked through a variety of scenery: rice fields and villages in Kandal and Kampong Speu; forests, mountains, and valleys in Kampot. When we approached our destination, my mother told me that the sound of the waves and the smell of the sea reminded her of her childhood. The maritime areas held many happy memories for her. We visited the port, the downtown market, and the famous beaches at O Cheuteal. After spending a few hours at Sihanoukville, we went via Ream to Kep, another beautiful seaside resort, and spent the night at the provincial capital of Kampot. It was the first time I had been in a hotel. At all these stops, we indulged ourselves in delicious seafood.

Within a short time, I had traveled to two different sides of Cambodia: the ancient cultural center at Angkor and a modern society of highway and seaport.

THE RIVER

One of the most popular events was a three-day Water Festival, *bonn om touk* in Khmer, usually held at the end of the rainy season, in October or November. The rising of the Mekong River caused the great lake of Tonle Sap to double its size. Fish would deposit their eggs in underwater forests and shrubs. When the water retreated, a multitude of fish (some 180 species) got caught in the trees. These unusual features make Tonle Sap the freshwater lake with the most abundant fish per square mile in the world. The festival, which marks the beginning of the fishing season, celebrates the reverse course of Tonle Sap, with hundreds of boats racing in pairs the one-mile course southward following the current of the river. They represent the mythical *nagas* (serpents) that return to the sea after having made the plains fertile during the rainy season.

Bonn om touk, the most exuberant of Khmer festivities, begins when the moon is full in the month of Kadeuk. Unlike the new year in April, when Cambodians leave the capital and provincial cities to visit their families in the villages, the Water Festival brings thousands of people in from the countryside. They come to cheer for the teams they sponsor and support. The long, narrow boats measuring sixty to seventy feet carry forty to sixty oarsmen who row in extremely precise coordination, sitting down or standing up. In some boats, half the oarsmen sit and the other half stand.

Tens of thousands of spectators along the banks of the river must train their ears to tell by the sound of the judge's drums which boat wins. The race is believed to commemorate a naval victory over Champa in 1177.

CHAPTER 4:

FOUR B'S

W hen I was about twelve, although still young, I was old enough to travel alone away from home. The early 1960s was a period of new discoveries for me when I realized that life was a combination of friends, food, and fun.

THE BOWL

Serey Soporn, also known as Svay Sisophon or simply Sisophon, is a major crossroad in the northwest where national routes 5 and 6 merge toward Thailand. My sister Sarin's husband, San Chhuon, was born there, in Battambang province. It was a very fertile region, known as Cambodia's rice bowl. In the late 1950s, Chhuon, who spoke and read Thai fluently, was sent to a garrison in his birthplace. I traveled alone to Sisophon during school breaks to visit my sister and her family. I usually took an express train called the *autorail* in French. I remember its slogan, *Jamais en retard* ("Never late").

The express train, with only two cars, left Phnom Penh at six AM. Including stops, it took about eight hours to cover the whole line of

239 miles. This one-track railroad had been built by French and Cambodian engineers between 1930 and 1940. The first station after Phnom Penh was my native village, Pochentong.

My trips to Serey Soporn allowed me to enjoy the great diversity of Cambodia: green rice fields, tall palm trees, dense jungles, graceful mountains, and beautiful villages with colorful shining roofs of Buddhist temples appearing above treetops. At each station, people sold all kinds of things to eat and drink: coconut and palm juice, sugarcane, steamed rice, grilled chickens, stuffed frogs, fried beetles, crickets, spiders, skewered eels and snakes, fresh and cooked vegetables, and delicious fruits. Some westerners may get sick at the thought of eating insects and snakes, but these were common delicacies in Asia.

Trade at the stations had to be transacted very quickly and was based on pure trust. While bargaining was still going on, the sellers would give their products to the passengers at the windows as the train started moving. The buyers would then throw money to the merchants, who ran alongside the train. Not once did I see anybody cheating: the buyers never took produce without paying, and the sellers never took money without giving merchandise. As a boy traveling alone, I was quite fascinated by these scenes, which would repeat themselves everywhere in Cambodia at bus stations, ferry crossings, and river ports.

My mother was an excellent cook. I enjoyed being with her in the kitchen, where she made me the family's official taster. One of my favorite dishes was *samlaw kawko* (mixed vegetable stew). There was no more pleasing experience for me than to watch *Mae* stir the family hearth-pot, full of delicious food. We normally ate sitting on the floor on colorful mats, in a circle surrounding the main dishes: a big bowl of soup and plates of grilled fish, meat, and vegetables. There were always small portions of fish and soy sauces, and chili pepper to enhance the flavors. Each of us had a dish of rice and a spoon. Cambodians do not eat with chopsticks, except when they have the traditional *noom bantiok*, a noodle dish. Forks and knives arrived only with the French in the nineteenth century. In the villages most people ate with their fingers. My mother loved eating that way. She said, "It tastes better." She also liked to chew bones, especially fish bones. We ate everything on a fish, from the head to the tail. I was told to eat the tail if I wanted to learn how to swim. Those who said this wanted to save the head and body of the fish, especially the cheeks, for themselves, as these were considered the most delicious parts.

During meals, my mother taught us some important Buddhist principles: honesty, love for your neighbor, and respect for all living things. She held us together with her love and strong will, as we endured the loss of our father and moved on with our lives.

Khmer food is similar to Thai and Indian food, but with less spice. Lemongrass and coconut milk are regularly used for a distinct taste. It was a normal practice to share special dishes with neighbors: Chinese, Indian, Vietnamese. So I grew up having what the Cambodians called *mort mian liap* (a lucky mouth), tasting various delicious ethnic foods.

Desserts did not play a big role in my early years. Khmer desserts needed additional preparation, and we made them only for special occasions. Sometimes, we bought them ready to eat in the market. Fruits remained an integral part of our desserts.

THE BEAR

My brother-in-law San Chhuon commanded an army company at Kaup, an area west of Sisophon inhabited by Cambodians of Laotian ancestry. I went to see him once, walking for about an hour from the Kaup railroad station to his military base. One day he found a baby sun bear abandoned under a tree. It was black with a white nose and mouth and a yellow V-shaped spot on the front of the neck. He brought the cub to his barracks, where it was breast-fed by his soldiers' wives. He later sent the cub to us in Pochentong, and it became my first and only pet.

The Khmer word for sun bear is *kla kamoom* ("honeybee tiger"). So I named my new pet Kamoom. I had no idea how to raise a sun bear, but I heard that they liked honey; they must eat everything that is sweet. So every day I fed Kamoom rice mixed with palm sugar or condensed milk. I also let him drink milk. It was quite expensive to raise such an animal as a pet. I was thinking of giving him to a zoo but did not know how to do it. On the other hand, I wanted to show people that I was a responsible teenager and I was proud to be probably the only person in the kingdom to have a bear as a pet.

Our house was on the road to the airport and had no fence. This seems to reflect an old Khmer saying, "There is no need to build a fence; good neighbors make better protection." One day, I heard screaming and ran in the direction of the noise. A group of girls from Phnom Penh who were coming to welcome one of the state visitors had walked in to ask for some drinking water. They were frightened to see a little animal standing up on two feet with milk drooling from his mouth.

"It's OK. He is very friendly. See?" I tried to calm the girls by hugging Kamoom, who began to lick my face.

"Wow! What is it?" asked one of the girls.

"It's a *kla kamoom*!"

"What?"

"A sun bear! Come and pet him." After some hesitation, my visitors approached us slowly and touched Kamoom's fur.

"Wow. He's very soft."

"Yes. He is also very sweet!" I stopped short of saying, "Like you."

I became more attached to my pet, and was always eager to get home to see him. I bathed him, combed him, and walked him regularly. I took care of him until he died. Cambodians believed that a

bear's paws bring luck. After saving the paws, I buried Kamoom myself.
It was another severe loss in my early life. It was a deeply felt grief for
a child. And I never again had another pet.

THE BAGUETTES

Unlike my mother's parents, who were high in the government hierarchy, my father's parents (Tieng Siv and Sok Mum) and their ancestors
were farmers and peasants. My family owned some land that was culti-
vated by our relatives in Tonle Bati. As a lease payback, we would receive some rice during the new harvest. I was sent to visit my relatives
and collect the rice. I always looked forward to these trips because I
was always treated like a little king.

The trip to Tonle Bati—about twenty-two miles—took half a day
in the 1950s and 1960s. I had to get up early to take a bus to the capital
and then walk by the central market to a different station. Early morning in Cambodia is the best time to enjoy a market. Having no refrig-
erators, Cambodians went shopping every morning to get fresh produce
from the countryside to prepare their daily meals. The central market,
known in Khmer as *Pasa Tamey* ("new market") has been the major
center of daily commercial activities in the capital since 1927. It took
me nearly thirty minutes to walk through the maze of stands from the
station for the maritime province buses (including Pochentong buses)
to the one for those that went to the south, the southeast, and the
Vietnamese border. At the second station, I had to find the bus that
went to Takeo and Tonle Bati. Buses in those days had benches facing
the front. Each bench had a small door on the right side to allow passengers to get on and off. The back and top of the bus were usually reserved for cargo. At the windows and doors, the bus had shades that
could be easily pulled down when it rained.

My mother sent a lot of goodies to our relatives: batteries, candles,
incense, candies, condensed milk, fabrics, salt, sauces (fish and soy),

soaps, sugar cubes, toothbrushes, toothpaste, pens, and pencils—there was something for everybody. Regularly, she would add some beautiful, colorful silk material to be made into *sampots*, sarongs, and *kramas*. (A *sampot* is a woman's skirt. A sarong, simply draped cloth similar to a skirt, is usually worn at home. A *krama* is a multipurpose scarf.) These things were quite heavy, but the excitement of traveling to see my relatives in the countryside, where I would be pampered, outweighed the burden.

My mother always reminded me to get as many baguettes as I could when the bus stopped in Takamau. In the early afternoon, I arrived at the village of Hanuman in Tonle Bati, where my grandmother Mum and other relatives lived. The bus stopped in front of her house and I suddenly heard, "Sichan is here! Sichan is here!" Seconds after I managed to get out of the overcrowded bench, my cousins were catching my bags, which were dropped from the rooftop. Sometimes it took longer for the bus attendant to find my belongings, as he had to move around those passengers who had paid less to sit on the roof. Grandmother Mum kissed me and hugged me hard enough to suffocate me. I was her favorite grandson.

"Have you eaten?" Grandmother Mum asked me. This is a traditional Cambodian greeting. There is always something in the kitchen that can be put together to feed the visitor. Of course I said no, and somebody immediately went to the kitchen.

As my grandmother held my hand tight for fear of my getting away, we sat on the split bamboo bed under the house on stilts. I gave her all the goodies to share with everyone.

I was in charge only of distributing the baguettes, of which I brought enough for everybody, including the children. I watched with great joy as they took slow bites of what remained France's most important culinary influence. The French bread had become part of our diet. There was at least one bakery in every *srok*. Baguettes were made in enormous clay ovens that had been brought to maximum temperature with firewood or charcoal.

Baguettes were among the first items that appeared in the markets early in the morning. They were also sold by mobile merchants on bicycles. These merchants rode around and through the villages, from one neighborhood to another, blowing a horn and shouting *Noom paing! Noom paing!* ("Bread! Bread!"). Children and adults would run to surround the traveling salesman. After slitting the baguettes open in the middle, the seller either spread sugar or poured condensed milk evenly inside, depending on the customer's choice. Some customers would just buy the baguettes plain.

Next for me was playtime. I went to the rice fields with my cousins. Depending on the season, they would let me hold the plowshare handle, plant rice, ride buffalo or oxen, and drive the oxcart back to the hamlet. For a farmer, this was all hard work, day in and day out. I found it a lot of fun, but I did not have to do it every day.

France's culinary influence on Cambodia was so strong that even Chinese restaurants were creating French dishes, such as *cervelet du porc au beurre noir* (pig's brain with black butter). If you think this is strange, just wait until Chapter 9!

THE BALLS

At Sisowath Secondary School, the students' backgrounds were mixed. The poor kids got in because they passed the very competitive entrance examination, and they stayed on because they studied hard. I belonged to this group. As I moved to higher grades, the group began to lose members. They were leaving to get jobs to help their parents. Suddenly, my class was full of children of rich and powerful people. Their parents were provincial governors, mayors, cabinet members, wealthy businessmen, and members of the royal family. A son of Prince Sihanouk, Ravivong; and a granddaughter of King Monivong, Sisowath Sovethvong; were in my class. I rode my bike from Pochentong six miles away four times a day; the rich boys came on new motorcycles

and the girls in chauffeured cars. Many of them had already been to
France a few times. They talked about the Champs-Élysées, Boulevard
Saint-Germain, and the Côte d'Azur. But not one had traveled to re-
mote areas of Cambodia like me.

Almost half of the class of forty students were girls—beautiful
girls. I had no illusions about spending the rest of my life with any of
them. Soon enough, each girl would be married off to some guy whom
she had never met who had just returned from France. I was just a silent admirer. I was what the Cambodians called "a rabbit who can only
admire the beauty of the moon." This idea was immortalized by the
song "Apsara" composed by Prince Sihanouk. The rabbit can never
reach the moon, unless the moon lowers itself to the rabbit's level:
hence the Khmer concept of *"Tunsaye + Preah Chan."* The rabbit and
the moon! They can live together only in the sense of being in the
same universe, but not as a couple. They can be good friends, just like
my classmates and me.

April was ball season. We celebrated the Khmer new year on April
13. For me, this was a time of double happiness: it is also my mother's
birthday. Most offices had their annual party around this time. The
medical school had the best ball among university institutions. Sisowath came up at the top among the secondary schools. We managed
to get "Apsara," the most popular young band at the time, to perform
at our ball. They played the Beatles, the Bee Gees, the Platters, the
Rolling Stones, and of course Paul Anka, Elvis Presley, and Frank Si-
natra. These alternated with French songs (Salvatore Adamo, Charles
Aznavour, Dalida, Françoise Hardy, Enrico Macias, Johnny Halliday,
and Sylvie Vartan). There were always compositions by Prince Sihanouk, an accomplished musician who played the saxophone. Ballgoers
dressed up: business suits for the men, never mind that April is quite
hot and humid; and women wore their beautiful silk *sampots* with silver threads and diamond and gold jewelry. Everyone seemed to be
competing to be the best dressed. We danced until early morning to all

the modern tunes as well as the Khmer *roamwong, roam kabach,* and *sarawan.* Cambodians dance these in a circle with men following women, spreading their fingers like a fan and moving forward in short steps. My royal friend Sovethvong was one of my *cavalières,* dancing partners. It was one night a year when everybody seemed to be floating on air.

CHAPTER 5

THE SIXTIES

THE SECONDARY SCHOOL

In 1960 King Suramarit, Prince Sihanouk's father, died of diabetes at age sixty-four. He had been on the throne for only five years. Cambodia became a kingdom without a king. Queen Kossomak remained the symbol of the throne but did not reign. Prince Sihanouk became head of state after parliamentary approval.

In Cambodia, the best schools were government-run. They were older than private schools, and all of them were free. The competition to get in was quite tough. Secondary education was a seven-year program, with three major degrees at the end of the fourth, sixth, and seventh years—the equivalents of grade ten, grade twelve, and freshman year of college in the United States.

The first degree was *Diplome d'Études Secondaires du Premier Cycle* (DESPC). This is the point at which most students, in their late teens or early twenties, left school to find jobs, start a new career, or start a family. Fewer would stay for two more years in school to get the first baccalaureate. The ultimate degree was the second baccalaureate, given at the end of the seventh year (*classe terminale*). Students had to choose between philosophy, experimental sciences, and elementary mathematics. This "thirteenth grade" (counting from the beginning of schooling) was a grueling year. Administered at the end of secondary education, the second baccalaureate would determine a student's future in terms of finding a good job or continuing at a university.

At the time of their graduation from secondary school, Cambodian students were usually between nineteen and twenty-two years old. Older students were from farming and merchant backgrounds. They had to help their families for a few years before or between schooling. Grading was twenty points over twenty, with ten as the average. Results of exams were given with a *mention: passable* for ten to twelve points; *assez bien* ("not bad" or "good enough") for twelve to fifteen; *bien* ("good") for fifteen to seventeen; and *très bien* ("very good") for eighteen to twenty.

After passing the CEPC, at age twelve or thirteen, we all had to take a *concours d'entrée* (entrance examination) to get into a lycée (secondary school). I failed the *concours* and was sent to private schools. At age eleven, I spent my first secondary school year (seventh grade) in Kampong Cham, the capital of the province of the same name, about 92 miles northeast on the west bank of the Mekong River. My mother's youngest sister was my favorite aunt. Her name was Chandee, and she was married to the *yokabat* (deputy district chief) of Koh Sotin, headquartered in Cheehae, about one hour by boat downstream from Kampong Cham. They had a house in Kampong Cham where her two oldest boys and two adopted sons were living and going to school. Their schools included the lycée Sihanouk, which was among the best in the provinces.

I joined this household of teenagers as the youngest. My older cousins, Panha and his brother, belonged to Sichhun's generation. They were in tenth grade and busy studying for the DESPC. Most of their topics of conversation were usually too advanced for me. They talked about their first jobs, having a family, producing children, where to live—and these matters were above my thinking capacity. But over time, I began to absorb and understand their thoughts.

One of the adopted sons and I were in the same class. We were in charge of preparing meals. Each day, whoever got out of the school first would go to the market and buy enough vegetables and fish or meat to make two meals. Panha, the number two cousin, gave whoever was going to cook ten riels a day. The rate of exchange was thirty-five riels to one U.S. dollar, and it is mind-boggling to think that we were able to feed five hungry boys every day for a little over a quarter of a dollar.

I spent my free time writing home, riding my bike around town, or swimming in the Mekong. I looked forward to spending the weekends at Cheehae with my aunt and her family. Two of her sons were about my age. One of their sisters, Vann, known by her nickname Peou, had been "reserved" for my brother Sichhun since both were babies. She was one of the most beautiful girls I had ever seen.

Although I hated to be away from my mother, my year at Kampong Cham taught me some new values in life: mainly, how to adjust to a new environment and make the most of it. It was this adaptability that would keep me alive fifteen years later when I was trying to survive under the Khmer Rouge. Without saying a word to me, my mother had begun to train my mind and soul to cope with unusual and hostile circumstances, to stay alive, and always to have hope.

In 1960 I returned to Pochentong after developing some skills in cooking, swimming, and writing. I began to read more about what was happening overseas. The first political news I learned was the race between the Democratic candidate John F. Kennedy and the Republican Richard M. Nixon for the American presidency.

Sichhun passed his DESPC and began looking for a job. After a stint at the merchant marine school, he was admitted to the royal police academy, which had been built by the United States in Tuol Kork, an elegant residential area of Phnom Penh. At his graduation, he chose Prey Veng, on the east bank of the Mekong bordering South Vietnam, for his first assignment. It did not hurt his career that the governor was once our father's boss. Sichhun was sent to command the Police Royale of Kampong Trabaek. The district, which ranked second in rice production in the country, was located on national route 1 on the way to Vietnam.

After Sichhun left home, I had to double up on my work to help my mother. First, she sold lotus leaves at the Pochentong market. In the afternoon, she went on a small boat to cut the leaves from a pond behind the village Buddhist temple. After I got out of school, I went to help her wash the leaves and put them together in sets of five. I folded them only once in bundles of five sets each. I got up early in the morning and went to the market to distribute them to my mother's customers. Lotus leaves were used as the basic wrapping material for all kinds of fresh produce.

Later, my mother sold some kinds of Khmer breakfast called *baw-baw trey kaw*, porridge served with small fish and vegetables. I got up every morning at four with my mother and helped her make the fire for cooking. Sometimes I fell asleep again until everything was cooked. I put all the pots, pans, plates, and spoons in a cart and pushed it to the market. I set up the stand for my mother and returned home to get ready to go to school.

Mother's next business was a catering service. We called it *bye kae* ("monthly meals"). Most of her customers were in the military. The Royal Khmer Air Force had its major base at Pochentong. Nearby, there were two airborne battalions. Many officers and troops did not like their canteen food. So they used my mother's *bye kae*. We delivered their meals twice a day in Cambodian food boxes called *charn srak*, a set of four or five round lidded metal containers, one on top of another, secured by a handle.

In addition to catering meals for a living, my mother was known as a *tiong pheou*, a chef. She volunteered or was called on to cook for a great number of people, especially at weddings, funerals, or *bonn* (Buddhist festivals). At these events, she used enormous pots to cook many dishes at the same time. It was quite an experience to watch my mother prepare so much food for so many people with the help of a number of *sous-chefs* cutting, chopping, and stirring.

Mae had inherited a small transportation business from my father. He was a part owner of two passenger and cargo buses that ran between Phnom Penh and Samrong, about ten miles west. We had thirty percent of the shares. The majority of the shares were owned by a local businessman. After Sichhun left Pochentong, it fell on me to take care of our business interests. I was everything: bookkeeper, business manager, minority owner. When one of the buses went for repairs, I had to check all the invoices, and I came to know various technical terms, parts, and bus jargon. After a few years, we sold the interest in the company to the majority partner.

Whenever my mother needed additional capital, she resorted to the Cambodian *tontine*, a classic way to raise funds. It is "played" like this. The person who needs the money brings together a number of people to be members. Let's say there are twelve members in a *tontine* of 100 riels per share. The fund-raiser, known as the head or president of the group, gets 1,200 riels. Actually, he gets only 1,100, excluding his own contribution. The second month every member is required to give 100 to the president, making the total capital 1,200. Members are allowed to bid to use the monthly capital. The person who needs the money most will bid highest. Each share will be reduced by the amount of the winning bid. If the highest bid is forty riels, then each member will contribute only sixty. The winner will get only 720 riels, instead of 1,200 (or 1,100). In the following months, the amount of the winning bid will decrease and the monthly capital will increase. At the end of the "game"—the twelfth month—the last member to get money will get 1,100 riels, just like the president of the *tontine*.

The only difference between the president and the last bidder is that the president gets the money first. But he has to do all the paperwork, getting everyone to sign copies of the agreement and distributing them to all. At the opening, the month when the share is collected, the president gives each member a present; usually this is something to eat like bananas, oranges, or *noom ansawm* (traditional Khmer cakes), in appreciation of the members' willingness to participate in the fund-raiser. The leader has to gather all the members every month, preside over the opening of the sealed envelopes that contain the bids, and be sure that all members make appropriate contributions. If a member deserts or does not pay the share in time, it is the president's responsibility to ensure that the missing contribution is replaced. That is why it is important to get trustworthy people to be members of the "game." I did all this constantly for my mother. Sometimes we would have two *tontines* that overlapped each other. Now, as in Kampong Cham, I was put in a situation much above my level. But again, I managed to adapt.

After passing both the DESPC and the French *Brevet d'Études du Premier Cycle* (BEPC), I was admitted to the famous Sisowath lycée, from which my brother Sichhun had graduated earlier.

I was chosen to be a *majeur*, responsible for arranging for chalk and the class roster every day, and keeping the classroom clean. I drew up a cleaning schedule, which everyone was supposed to follow.

Our physics teacher was a very severe Frenchman, Monsieur Le Prince. One day he walked in and we stood up, as we always did to salute the teachers. Oh, no! I noticed that the classroom had not been cleaned. The blackboard was dirty, and there were pieces of paper lying around the teacher's platform. Le Prince was furious. He called me to the front of the classroom. He pointed to the blackboard, the dust on his desk, the scrap paper. He pointed at me, and said, "*Cela ne vous creve pas les yeux?*—Are you blind?"

I dared not glare at him: it was very impolite to look somebody of higher rank in the eyes. Besides, I wanted to avoid his angry gaze. Some of my lazy classmates who did not perform their cleaning duties had been telling me not to worry. When we were children, we used to believe that the French could not see clearly, because their eyes were not black like ours. I could hardly refrain from laughing at the joke that the French could not see well. But Le Prince had nothing wrong with his eyes. I responded softly:

"*Je suis désolé, Monsieur!*—I am sorry, sir!"

Le Prince banged the desk and shouted, "*Vous êtes désolé? À quoi ça sert?*—You are sorry? What good does that do?"

He threw his arms into the air, walked back and forth kicking the papers on the floor, and rolled his eyes. After a pause, he lowered his voice, and with his mouth close enough to bite my face, he said slowly, "*Regardez-moi, M'sieur Sichan. Et mettez ça dans votre petite tête. Si la prochaine fois je trouve une classe si sale, vous et vos copains n'auront pas de physique avec moi; et je vais rapporter le problème à monsieur le surveillant. Vous m'entendez?*—Look at me, Mr. Sichan." (Cambodians are addressed by their first name.) "And get it into your little head. The next time I find such a dirty classroom, you and your pals will not have physics with me; and I am going to report the problem to the superintendent. You hear me?"

"*Oui, Monsieur.*"

"*Retournez à votre place.*—Go back to your seat.*"

I felt humiliated. At the end of the class, I went to see the cleaning schedule posted behind the teacher's desk. I found the team leader responsible for that day. He had just been transferred from a French school. I asked him why he did not clean the classroom. While we were arguing, our male classmates formed a circle around us; the girls stayed away. They started shouting: "Don't be a coward! Come on! Beat him!" The culprit, being a judo black belt, thought that the crowd was cheering him. He pointed his fingers at my face and sputtered: "I don't take orders from any son of a bitch." I immediately grabbed his fingers and pulled them down. He bowed and bent his body to follow the hurting fingers. At that moment, I raised my left knee quickly to hit his face. He was trying to get up, but I pounded his back with my two fists together. Within seconds, he was flat on his face on the ground. The only fistfight in my life was over, and I'd beaten a black belt! Our *surveillant* arrived immediately on the scene. I explained to him the sequence of events and offered to see the principal if there were going to be any disciplinary measures. But my opponent did not want to go. So the dispute was settled *à l'amiable,* or "out of court." From then on, the classroom was always clean.

To widen my horizon, I joined a pen pal club based in Paris and was put in touch with an Algerian girl. We began exchanging letters in French, telling each other about our hobbies, favorite movie stars, recording artists, writers, etc. I also got into stamp collecting. I learned about this from Sichhun, who had joined a philately club in Rimouski, Quebec, Canada.

THE WEDDING

In 1965 my brother Sichhun and our cousin Peou, who had become a teacher, were married in Kampong Cham, at the same house where I lived for a year while attending private school. Peou was a graduate of the teachers' training center at Kampong Kantuot in Kandal province. The United States had built the enormous complex, in the shape of a butterfly. Students or trainees lived on the compound. I was Peou's official escort. She could get out of the center on weekends or during holidays only when I presented myself to accompany her. Her mother, my aunt Chandee, and her family had moved to the provincial capital, where her father had been transferred to the headquarters.

It was a very happy reunion. The families of the bride and the groom were cousins. All of us went from Pochentong to Kampong Cham. Sichhun and a few friends traveled by car from Kampong Trabaek west to Neak Leuang, then north to Prey Veng, to Svay Antor and Tonle Bet on the east bank. They took the ferry to cross the Mekong toward Kampong Cham. In the middle of the river, the ferry stalled and began to float downstream. It floated for hours. At the bride's house, everybody became nervous and worried. No one could come up with any alternative plan to deal with the situation if Sichhun did not arrive. One possibility was for him to be married in absentia; another was to have me stand in. I was scared to death. Fortunately, the ferry engines were repaired. My brother came back up the river and arrived in time for the ceremony.

A traditional wedding in Cambodia can last for days. The whole community joins in to help in the celebration. It starts with a groom's parade, *hae kown kamlos*. The ceremony consists of having the groom walk to the bride's house, preceded by people carrying trays of presents—food, fruits, silk, silver—for the future in-laws. The next ceremony is *tiaul rung* ("enter the hall"). The spokesman of the groom's family asks the permission of the bride's family to set up a temporary shelter on the grounds of the bride's house. Then comes the *ptim* (pairing the bride and groom), followed by *bangvel popil* (passing candles around the new couple) and *kat sak* (a symbolic haircut, as the scissors never touch the hair of the bride and groom; a ceremony to get rid of evil and start everything new and clean). The final ceremony is *chawng dai*, or tying the knots. The hair-cutting and knot-tying ceremonies are performed by senior members of both families, including grandparents, aunts, uncles, elder siblings, and close family friends.

During the course of the wedding ceremony, the bride and groom have to change clothes many times. Each time, two or three people help them get dressed in colorful ceremonial outfits. The final event is the banquet, usually followed by dancing to live bands. All the women put on their beautiful, colorful dresses, with glittering jewelry. Sichhun and Peou managed to smile warmly throughout the whole ceremony. As my brother was well established in Kampong Trabaek and in the province of Prey Veng, he had to have another banquet there for all his friends and colleagues the following week. Both our families joined the newlyweds to have a second celebration.

THE TRAVELS

The Northwest

In the early 1960s my brother-in-law San Chhuon was sent to Siem Reap. My sister Sarin and her children went along but stayed in the city while her husband went to various command assignments in remote areas of the province. Their eldest daughter, Samnang, with whom Sarin was pregnant when our father died, had been living with us since she was a toddler. She called my mother *Mae* (as all of Mother's grandchildren did) and had become part of our family. Sichhun told me of a close call when he brought Samnang from Sisophon. They were traveling second class on the express train *autorail* when Samnang became very thirsty. He told her to wait until the train stopped at the next station or until the steward arrived. The steward never showed up, and Samnang started to cry. The second-class car had no access to the first-class car, where the food service was located. Sichhun had to move on the narrow outside platform. As he was sticking his head out before stepping on it, he saw the frame of a bridge rushing toward him. He was quick enough to retreat before the train went through the bridge.

During summer vacations, I went to stay with Sarin for weeks. I was happy to be back in Siem Reap so soon after my first visit in 1959. I had a fresh memory of our picnic at the *barays* (reservoirs). We went to Banteay Srei, built in 967 during the reign of Rajendravarman II (944–968). The Hindu temple remains the most exquisite of all, with very detailed carvings and sculptures. Afterward we went to Phnom Kulen, where Jayavarman II founded the Angkor civilization in 802.

In the middle 1960s, San Chhuon was transferred from the military district of Siem Reap to attend a course for battalion commander at the Royal Military Academy in Phnom Penh and brought his whole family along. I was in my late teens and helped him with some of his homework, especially his research on the first atomic explosion at Alamogordo in New Mexico. He was very pleased to get the top grade, and he let me use his car more often. Officially, Cambodians had to be eighteen years old before they could obtain a driver's license. But if your parents were somebody powerful, you could get one at any age, or you could drive without a license.

After the military academy, Chhuon was assigned to the Garde Royale at Chamkarmon to provide protection and security for the head of state, Prince Sihanouk. He traveled all over the kingdom with the prince, who was presented with fruits, vegetables, and flowers, most of which ended up at Chhuon's house. He started bringing beautiful orchids home and established quite a collection.

The Northeast

San Chhuon was later sent to remote areas of the country where it was difficult to take dependents because the regions were still wild. I accompanied Sarin to visit her husband, usually with one or two of her youngest children.

The trip to Ratanakiri ("Mountain of Diamonds") in the northeast, at the border area between Cambodia, Laos, and Vietnam, was a most memorable one. We took the boat that traveled all night up the Mekong to the provincial capital of Kratie, north of Kampong Cham. The following morning, we took a bus, continuing north. We stopped for a late lunch and turned eastward. The unpaved road traversed an area of rich volcanic soil, very good for rubber plantations. The province had been inhabited by Khmer Leu, Cambodian highlanders, many still living there in primitive conditions. After a long and bumpy ride, we stopped briefly, near a volcanic lake. Then we moved to Lumphat, Ratanakiri's capital, on a bank of the Srae Pok River, one of the Mekong's tributaries. We stayed at the officers' quarters, from where I walked to swim every day in the Srae Pok. In Lumphat, I was introduced to the most exotic dishes of Cambodia: deer, boar, snakes, and *ansawng*—a kind of lizard measuring up to two feet long. This was the best trip I had ever made with Sarin in Cambodia.

The Southeast

After a few years in Kampong Trabaek, my brother Sichhun was appointed district chief of Preah Sadach, at the Vietnamese border. Most of Prey Veng was flooded for about six months of the year. The province has some remains of pre-Angkorean civilization, dating from the beginning of the seventh century, when King Isanavarman I built a capital to pay homage to his ancestors.

My cousin Panha, whose marriage was arranged by my mother, had become an army veterinarian at Kampong Trabaek. I usually stayed with his family for one night before taking a cargo boat. I had no idea that it was fully loaded with smuggled goods for Vietnam. We went down the river to Peam Montia, a floating village near the border. Many of the Vietnamese fishermen living there were sympathizers of the Vietcong with weapons hidden in their boats. No wonder they looked at my unfamiliar face with such apprehension.

I got off the boat quietly and walked for a few hours to reach Preah Sadach by late afternoon. There, I spent my days resting, reading, or listening to French records and those of Trini Lopez singing "Besame Mucho," "Cuando Calienta el Sol," "Guantanamera," "Perfidia," and "Quizas, Quizas, Quizas."

Sometimes, I traveled with Sichhun during his tours of the district. He went around on a big horse named Phok, accompanied by some members of his staff. We got up early and, after a big breakfast, set out on horseback, bicycles, or motorcycles. I was on horseback. But Cambodian horses, except for some like my brother's, are generally small. Mine was so small that my feet touched the ground. Sichhun had a custom-made saddle, but the rest of us rode bareback with just a blanket. Having been influenced by western movies, I was very excited to be on a horse and, like a cowboy, tried to make it run at full speed.

But mine was not well trained. When he saw a stream which people had dug to let water flow from one field to another, he suddenly stopped. And there I was, taking off from the horse and landing in the field a few yards away. Everyone laughed at my muddy face. So did the horse, I bet.

Preah Sadach was well known for delicious freshwater lobsters and fish. I always had a great time spending vacations with my sister and brother.

THE VISITORS

During the 1960s, Cambodia was host to many state visits and international events. Primary school children and secondary school students were asked to participate in welcoming the visitors. We were told to wear our school uniforms. Sisowath, like other high schools in the country, had a uniform consisting of khaki pants and white shirts for boys and navy blue skirts and white blouses for girls. For special occasions like state visits, the uniform was upgraded to all white with red ties for boys and white blouses and red silk *sampots* (skirts) for girls. We were placed next to students from an elite girls' school, Norodom, with their green silk *sampots* and white blouses. We were there to welcome royalty, prime ministers, presidents, capitalists and communists, democrats and dictators. They were all friends of Cambodia and admirers of Angkor.

On August 30, 1966, General Charles de Gaulle, who had been reelected president of France two years earlier, came. This was the first time that Cambodia had welcomed the incumbent leader of its former colonizer. De Gaulle was accompanied by his wife and the foreign minister, Maurice Couve de Murville. Cambodia's reception was grand. The queen mother and Prince Sihanouk went to greet the general and his wife at Pochentong, now a modern international airport which had been accommodating Air France Boeing 707s since the early 1960s.

During their stay in Phnom Penh, a special Water Festival was organized in their honor; usually, this festival occurred a few months later in the year. They were treated to a gala dinner, a performance by the Royal Ballet, and various folk dances. De Gaulle delivered his "Discours de Phnom Penh" speech at a rally of some 100,000 people at the newly built Olympic stadium. He asked for the withdrawal of American forces from South Vietnam, without mentioning what the North Vietnamese communists and the Vietcong had done to the South Vietnamese. *Paris Match* reported, "At the frontiers of war, de Gaulle speaks of peace." He was made an honorary general of the Royal Khmer Armed Forces (FARK). Two avenues were named after him—one in Phnom Penh and one in Siem Reap. At Angkor Wat, he was treated to a sound-and-light re-creation of the coronation of an Angkor king. Prince Sihanouk toasted him, referring to Cambodia's ideals: "You alone in the West have recognized and supported them in the name of France."

Three months after de Gaulle's visit, Phnom Penh hosted the first Asian Games of the New Emerging Forces. Its official slogan was "Onward! No retreat!" Seventeen mostly developing countries with nearly 1,300 athletes took part. The flame was started at Angkor Wat with two teams of runners circling the great lake of Tonle Sap toward Phnom Penh. At the end of the games, the People's Republic of China had won the most medals, 208, followed by Cambodia and North Korea with 104 each. The games at Phnom Penh coincided with the Asian Games in Bangkok, and some countries had to split their teams to be able to attend both.

I had been made a section chief of the Royal Khmer Socialist Youth (or JSRK, its initials in French). This was the Cambodian version of the Boy Scouts and Girl Scouts, but with a strong political orientation. It was a national youth movement created by Prince Sihanouk as a branch of his Sangkum Reastr Niyum (SRN), which was considered a national rallying of all political parties. We were called upon to provide all kinds of support to these national and international events. We did what the adults wanted us to do. As in my childhood at Pochentong, it was fun to get away from school. But I tried to stay away from politics as well.

As part of our training in JSRK, we went on field trips for a week at a time. On one such trip, we rode our bikes in pairs from Phnom Penh to Kampong Kantuot in Kandal province. At night, we set up our camp by a body of water: a pond, a lake, or a river. We put up our own tents and built a bonfire. Our food was provided by JSRK, but we had to cook it ourselves. We sang, played games, and took care of one another. As a section chief, I had to make sure all assignments were carried out properly, including maintaining discipline and the security of our unit. I had the authority to punish those who did not measure up and reward those who stood out. It was my first lesson in leadership.

One year after France was showered with the ultimate in Khmer hospitality, it was America's turn. And the event took place despite the fact that Cambodia and the United States did not have diplomatic relations, which had been severed by the prince after a series of incidents along the border with South Vietnam.

In August 1967, Jacqueline Kennedy visited Cambodia. *Time* magazine reported in its issue of November 10 that "her reception in Cambodia rivaled any she had received when she was the wife of the President of the United States." After a twelve-hour flight from Rome, she stopped to rest in Bangkok and later flew on a U.S. Air Force C-54 to Phnom Penh. At Pochentong, she was warmly welcomed by Prince Sihanouk, whose youngest daughter, Arunrasmey, presented her with a bouquet of orchids. She called Phnom Penh "one of the nicest cities I have seen and it's the cleanest of all." She later went to Angkor to "fulfill a childhood dream." At a ceremony dedicating an avenue in the resort town of Sihanoukville to her husband, she asked to keep the flags of Cambodia and the United States at the reviewing stand. Prince Sihanouk considered the visit as having relaxed the tension between the two countries and said he would be delighted to resume diplomatic relations after the United States had recognized Cambodia's national sovereignty and territorial integrity within its present borders.

In January 1968, President Lyndon Johnson sent the U.S. ambassador to India, Chester Bowles, as his special envoy to Cambodia. Bowles was accompanied by Philip Habib and four officials. He had a ninety-minute meeting with Prince Sihanouk, who said that the discussions were "friendly in spite of different points of view." Ambassador Bowles had renewed American assurances to respect Cambodian sovereignty, neutrality, and territorial integrity. The Cambodia-U.S. Declaration of January 12 stated that Ambassador Bowles was convinced of Cambodia's good faith and "has emphasized that the United States intend in no way to violate Cambodian territory. He has assured the Royal Khmer Government that the United States will do everything in its power to avoid aggression against Cambodia as well as incidents or accidents which could cause material damage to its inhabitants." The joint declaration was signed by Bowles and Prime Minister Son Sann. It was a positive development, which resulted in the reestablishment of diplomatic relations when Nixon came to the White House.

THE ACCIDENT

After I had passed the first baccalaureate, my mother bought me a Solex—a French-made motorized bicycle. I no longer had to sweat under the ninety-degree sun when I went to Sisowath.

One night, I was hit by a drunk driver right in front of my house. As witnesses later reported, I flew a few feet into the air and landed on the Renault's windshield, which was broken by the impact. I then rolled down and hit the road. The car stopped before it could hit me a second time. I saw a lot of broken glass flying in front of me. I felt warm blood coming down from my head. I heard my mother, my sister, and my nieces crying. I heard my mother screaming for help. I saw familiar faces leaning toward me. They talked to me in very loud, shaky voices, but I did not understand what they were saying. They touched my face and my body but I did not feel any of their loving hands. As their faces came closer to mine, I saw tears in their eyes. Then, their faces began to blur. Their voices began to fade. And everything went blank.

I regained consciousness at Preah Ket Mealea Hospital. My late father's business partner was beside me. He had taken me to the hospital in an ambulance. As a member of parliament, he commanded respect. He told me that I had been operated on immediately on arrival, and he had stayed behind to make sure everything went well. The wound at the back of my head had been sewn up, and I had received a blood transfusion. I was wheeled into a private room. My sister Sarin and a few family friends were waiting outside. The people of Pochentong were always united in time of crisis. However, the person who hit me was also a resident of Pochentong. He was relatively new: he had just returned from his university studies in Long Beach, California. Strangely enough, two decades later, Long Beach would become the Cambodian capital of the free world. And in July 2007, its city council voted to designate a section of Anaheim Street "Cambodia Town USA."

THE LIBRARIES

Kamlaing jawng tae muoy peil, kumnit jawng chea dawrarp.
"Force ties for a time; ideas bind forever."

—Inscription at the National Library of Cambodia

The 1960s were for me a decade of new horizons. Like many high school students of my generation, I spent my free time in libraries. I became a bookworm, an armchair traveler, and a political spectator. My favorite spots were the National Library, the Buddhist Institute, and the USIS library.

The National Library, established on Christmas Eve 1924, is located next to the Hotel Le Royal near Wat Phnom, where the capital was founded in 1432. It also served as the national archives and had an amazing collection of historical documents and old books in Khmer, French, and English. I regularly read the *Journal Officiel du Cambodge*, which contained news on the government's activities.

I became a fan of detective and spy novels. I read many books by Jean Bruce. His main character was a U.S. secret agent with the code name OSS 117. He out-Bonded Ian Fleming's hero in his total commitment to fight evil and save the human race. Agatha Christie was another of my favorites.

The National Library was a place where all were treated as equals. One of the people I saw there regularly was the former prime minister Norodom Kantol, one of Prince Sihanouk's brothers-in-law. He stood in line to check out books like everyone else. Afterward, he left in his BMW; I pedaled my bike back to Pochentong.

The Buddhist Institute, in front of the Royal Palace where the Mekong, Tonle Sap, and Basak rivers met to form the Quatre-Bras, was a learning center for Buddhist studies. It had thousands of books in Pali and Sanskrit, the languages of Theravada and Mahayana Buddhism. It was the publisher of numerous books on the culture and civilization of Cambodia. These included a series on Khmer legends and *Srey Hetopates*, a collection of sayings, ideas, and thoughts. I was quite captivated by Khmer literature. It included stories of people using power to help others or abusing it for their own glory. One story—*Toom Teav*—was a Cambodian version of *Romeo and Juliet*.

The poetry was equally diverse and beautiful. Not only did Cambodian poems rhyme well; they told of romance and valor and gave lessons on ethics, morality, and how to have good karma—actions that could lead to a better life in the future. The famous poet Santhor Mok used his work to attack French colonialism.

One poem—"I Go to the Well"—told the story of a boy who met

a beautiful girl at the village well. He helped steady the water jar on her head and was rewarded with a beautiful smile. He returned to the well the next day but saw only her smile reflected in the water. He went back the following day and the reflection was gone. He was broken-hearted.

The United States Information Service (USIS) library was the most convenient. It stood right behind my lycée, Sisowath, at the corner of Keo Chea and Pasteur streets. I sometimes spent my fifteen-minute breaks between classes in its reading room. I developed an insatiable appetite for knowledge about America. To me, it was a big and powerful land where people seemed to have unlimited freedom and resources to create—everything from the automobile to the airplane, aspirin, lightbulb, and telephone—in order to improve the quality of human life.

I learned more about the United States through the library's Khmer, French, and English materials and its enormous selection of books, magazines, and newspapers. I read Robert Frost, Ernest Hemingway, and Mark Twain—in French. I was excited when Frost was chosen to read one of his poems at President Kennedy's inauguration. American literature was not my only interest. I also studied the geography and history of the United States. I knew by heart the names of all fifty states and their capitals, the largest lakes, the longest rivers, and the highest mountains. I knew that Missouri was the same size as Cambodia, and that the Statue of Liberty was a gift from France. I saw many pictures of the statue, along with the Empire State Building, the Chrysler Building, and other skyscrapers in Manhattan. I could not fathom the fact that New York City had a larger population than Cambodia: "How can eight million people live in one single town?"

America's history seemed much shorter than that of Cambodia. Before I immersed myself in reading at the USIS library, I had heard only of Eisenhower; Kennedy and Nixon (during the 1960 campaign);

and Johnson. Then I was hooked by the eighteenth century and read everything I could find on the founding fathers. I was later able to recite in precise chronological order all the presidents from Washington to Johnson.

I followed the U.S. space programs religiously: Mercury, Gemini, and later Apollo. I knew all the astronauts' names. For example, *Mercury 7*: Scott Carpenter, Gordon Cooper, John Glenn (first in orbit), Virgil Grissom, Walter Schirra, Alan Shepard (first in space), Donald Slayton.

One day, I heard over the radio that President Kennedy had been assassinated. I walked into the USIS library and saw his picture in a black frame with a black ribbon. I sat down, prayed, and signed the condolence book. I was sad then, and even sadder when diplomatic relations between Cambodia and the United States were severed. The USIS library was closed, and I lost a major source of information and knowledge.

My interest in America was, however, very academic. Like many Cambodian teenagers of my generation, I dreamed of being sent to France on scholarship. We all wanted to stay at the Pavillon du Cambodge at the Cité Universitaire in Paris. We all wanted to be able to send home letters with our return address: 27 bis, Boulevard Jourdan. Then, we would be recognized as people who had made it.

The French embassy in Phnom Penh established the Maison de France to compete with the USIS and the British Council libraries. It was a natural venue for the overwhelmingly French-speaking Cambodians to get more updated information about the mother country. My time there was spent reading *Le Figaro, Le Monde, Paris Match,* etc. Among the comics, my favorites were "Asterix," "Tintin," and "Lucky Luke." Luke was an American cowboy whose horse, Jolly Jumper, occasionally outwitted him. I remember that Jolly Jumper once complained, *"Tout le monde est en cheval; et moi, je suis toujours à pied.*—Everyone is on horseback; and me, I am always on foot."

Prince Sihanouk had been publishing a weekly paper, *Neak Chiat Niyum* (*The Nationalist*), which became the voice of his political party. It was in Khmer, with editorials in French, and its purpose was to state "the position of our national feelings regarding the problems of the moment." It was through this paper that I first learned about the 1960 presidential campaign between Kennedy and Nixon.

In 1965 the prince published a monthly illustrated magazine called *Kambuja* in French. It was destined for the international public. It provided excellent reporting on important events in the kingdom. It had regular features on numerous activities and efforts to develop the economy, and special features on lifestyle, culture, and civilization. It was a unique publication devoted to giving the fullest information to anybody interested in Cambodia. Although the French issue was flawless, the English version occasionally left something to be desired. For example, the graduation of the nineteenth class of military cadets was translated in English as the "Passing Out Ceremony of the Nineteenth Promotion of Regular Army Pupil Officers."

In 1966, General Lon Nol became prime minister as a result of the first election in which not all SRN candidates were handpicked by the Prince. *Le Sangkum* published a revealing report by Lon Nol's government, which stated that there were some 60,000 Vietcong and North Vietnamese forces in the eastern part of Cambodia along the border with South Vietnam. These troops were using Cambodian territory as staging areas, logistics supply routes, and rest and recuperation grounds. The FARK numbered only 35,000 troops. They were poorly trained and ill-equipped and could not match such a combat-hardened guerrilla force, should something go wrong. As we later saw, something did go wrong.

I was now eighteen years old. I had regained the paradise that I had lost a decade earlier when my father died. Phnom Penh was full of joie de vivre. Life was really beautiful, and no one paid attention to

Lon Nol's report. And no one, or at least no one in my generation, realized that we were living under a sword.

In August 1968, Richard Nixon was nominated by the Republican National Convention in Miami. At the tumultuous Chicago convention, the Democrats chose former vice president Hubert Humphrey to be their candidate. The following month, Johnson sent his special adviser Eugene Black to Phnom Penh. The envoy, accompanied by his wife and ten colleagues, met with Prime Minister Penn Nouth, who briefly succeeded Lon Nol, and whom he assured of the United States' sincere wish to reestablish diplomatic relations. The delegation was later given a tour of the National Museum and the Royal Palace, and a dinner hosted by the foreign minister.

THE FESTIVAL

Around the same time as Eugene Black's visit, my family got together to plan a major *kathen* festival. During the rainy season from May to October, Buddhist monks stay in the monasteries during a retreat—*Vosar*—that normally lasts for three months. At the end of the third month, Cambodian Buddhists organize the *kathens* to offer new robes, goods, and money to the monks and the *wat* (temple) in order to help them maintain their livelihood and social projects.

It had been my mother's dream to hold a *kathen* at the Tonle Bati temple, near the native village of my father at Hanuman in Takeo province. My mother was a devout Buddhist. After my father died in 1957, she spent a lot of time at Wat Pothisataram, the temple at Pochentong, to organize her thoughts. She was always a major fund-raiser for the *wat*.

The 1968 *kathen* was our joint family effort to achieve merit. Sichhun had been transferred from Preah Sadach to work for the chief of staff of the Royal Police at Tuol Kork. His wife Peou had been teaching at Pochentong Primary School, where Sarin, Sarun, Sichhun, and I had our primary education. My brother-in-law San Chhuon was about to be transferred to FARK headquarters.

We rented a dozen buses to transport Buddhist monks and hundreds of participants to Tonle Bati. We put two bands—*chayam* (long drums and gongs) and *pinpeat* (a classical orchestra)—on two open trucks with loudspeakers. All the celebrators who gathered at Wat Pothisataram were in colorful dress and in a joyful mood. They were given candles, incense, flags, flowers, and balloons to carry in their hands. Some of my family members had left very early to wait for our arrival at Tonle Bati. At around eight AM, after everyone boarded the buses, the convoy was ready. The music began and we rolled.

We were warmly received by our advance team, the people of Tonle Bati, and those from surrounding villages. We paraded around the Preah Vihear (main chapel) three times. My mother carried the new saffron robes on her head, behind the *chayam* band. She was symbolically protected by a big parasol and was followed by my aunts and uncles carrying monks' bowls. Next came Sarin and her husband, Sichhun and his wife, our other relatives, and all the celebrators. After the parade, we entered the main hall to offer the *kathen* to the monks. We raised a lot of money for the Tonle Bati *wat*. After a delightful lunch offered by our hosts, we returned to Pochentong in the late afternoon. We were exhausted, but fully satisfied. To celebrate our successful *bonn*, Sarin, Chhuon, Sichhun, Peou, and I decided to have a special treat. Instead of going to a fancy French eatery in front of the airport, we decided to go to Takamau and had a fantastic Khmer dinner in a floating restaurant. It was a most memorable day and the last time my family was together for such a celebration. We were at the peak of our own joie de vivre.

CHAPTER 6:

THE MOON

U nlike the names of my older siblings—Sarin, Sarun, Sichhun—my name has a meaning: "beautiful moon." As my mother later told me, I was born under a full moon; hence, Sichan.

FLYING FROM THE NEST

One day in 1968, Sichhun came home and reported to me that Royal Air Cambodge (RC), Cambodia's national carrier, would shortly recruit additional flight attendants. The airline, jointly owned by the Royal Government of Cambodia and Air France, was acquiring a new jet, a Caravelle. The purchase of the aircraft was being finalized. The government would own fifty-one percent of the shares and Air France forty-nine percent.

In the 1960s, developing countries wanted to have an airline for the sake of national prestige. Founded shortly after Cambodia became independent, RC started with a few DC-3s. By the 1960s, it had a fleet of one DC-4 and one DC-6.

The ideal candidate for flight attendant should have a high school diploma, good command of French and English, twenty/twenty vision, a "presentable physical appearance," and the ability to swim. Having finished my secondary education, I was now ready to face the world. I found the idea of a career in the sky very appealing. I had grown up with aircraft landing and taking off over my head and always wanted to fly in one. I had been in a plane before. One of our tenants, a mechanic for the air force, got me a seat on a night flight to the northeast in a DC-3 training mission. But an old DC-3 propeller plane was no comparison to a jet. And the new plane was going to be a Caravelle!

The job, I thought, would open and widen horizons for me. It would fulfill my childhood dreams. I would be able to go to all those exotic places I had been reading about as an armchair traveler.

I went to apply personally at the head office of RC on Chan Nak Street. The building had been the chancery of the U.S. embassy. I learned with some satisfaction that there would be no math, which I never liked, in the exam. It consisted of three parts. The written section would have essays in Khmer, French, and English. Only a few candidates, those with the highest scores, would be interviewed in the oral examination. The final part would be a combination of a physical test and a medical exam.

I immediately immersed myself in a crash course I personally designed: geography and history of Southeast Asia, especially Cambodia; the tourism industry; and Angkor. I felt that my Khmer and French were good enough, as I had been speaking both since childhood. That applied to everyone else. I worried about English. So did everyone else. However, I had probably spent more time in the USIS library than anybody else, and that encouraged me. In this kind of contest, an influential and powerful connection would automatically ensure hiring. Unfortunately, I had no such connection inside or outside the company.

My family had built a *chedey* at the village monastery. This is a memorial structure, like a stupa, where people keep the ashes of their relatives. The day before the exam I went to the *wat* to pray. My mother asked the abbot of the monastery to bless me. I had gotten to know him very well. I used to bring food to offer to the monks at Wat Pothisataram. I had done a lot of volunteer work there, from planting trees to building halls and regularly cleaning the courtyards. It was a traditional way of achieving merit in Buddhism. Some people sent their children to live in the monastery as *kameng wat*: temple boys. They believed that the children would not only acquire merit but also learn a new skill, such as carpentry or gardening, and generally become a jack-of-all-trades. I got to know all the temple boys very well. A few were my classmates and one was adopted by my mother.

The abbot chanted some prayers in Pali, the counterpart of Latin of Theravada Buddhism, and poured holy water over me. As I was receiving the blessings, my mind began to wander to Hong Kong, Singapore, Tokyo, and Paris. I had never been overseas before. The only times I had been out of the country were to visit Thailand and Vietnam, just across the Cambodian border. This time, it was going to be big-time. The blessings made me feel good. I presumed that every other candidate must have gone for the same thing.

To my surprise, the contest was not heavily publicized, and only a few hundred candidates went to take the written exam. Still, with fewer than ten jobs available, the competition was quite tough. The written part lasted half a day. I saw a few of my classmates from Sisowath. Some of them were taking the contest for fun. Others, like me, were more serious.

While waiting on pins and needles for the results, I continued to study. I went to RC's head office every day to look for the results on the bulletin board. A few weeks later, I found my name on a short list of two dozen names. Only two men and six women would be chosen.

I went for the interview better dressed than usual: my pants were nicely pressed, and I wore a white long-sleeved shirt, a necktie, and shining shoes. The interview started in French. I was asked to tell a panel of six, including two Frenchmen, about my life and why I wanted to work for RC. They later asked me to say, in English, what I would

advise a tourist to do in Phnom Penh, if he or she had only one day.
We were later asked to take a swimming test at the exclusive Cercle
Sportif (Sports Club). This was my forte, as I had been a regular swim-
mer since my days on the Mekong in Kampong Cham. Most of the
girls did not know how to swim. I assumed the airline management
was satisfied that their beautiful bodies in gorgeous swimsuits could
make up for their lack of aquatic ability. A few days later, a messenger
from RC delivered a letter. I was thrilled when I learned that I was
hired. I was to report to work the following week.

FLYING TO THE MOON

I began training to be an airline steward, a long and competitive process with both security and service components. The trainees alternated between Pochentong and Phnom Penh. At the airport, we took
instructions directly from the cockpit crew in the fleet of all three aircraft: how to use seat belts, oxygen masks, life vests, and airsickness
bags. We participated in a few mock evacuations.

In Phnom Penh, we were taught about French gastronomy at two
of the capital's most famous eateries: Hotel Le Royal and Café de Paris.
Le Royal was established in the 1930s and had remained the grande
dame of hospitality. The Café was probably the best French restaurant
in all of Asia. At both places, we learned how to take orders and to
serve. The owner of the restaurant who trained us was a 250-pound
Corsican. He claimed to eat only an apple for lunch. He told us at the
end of the training that service on the plane would be a little tight.
His parting thought was, "*Le client a toujours raison.*—The customer is
always right."

The third phase of training was a combination of the two: service
in the plane with empty trays and dishes, pushing a cart through a
narrow aisle. During this phase, we were sent to the top tailor in Phnom
Penh to have our uniforms made, from head to toe. The men's uniform

was a navy blue suit, hat, and tie. Our outfit was similar to Air France's. The women wore a light green knee-length skirt, jacket, and hats during boarding and disembarking. They changed to Khmer silk *sampots* during onboard service. Their blouse was white.

The RC fleet consisted of a DC-4, DC-6B, and the new jet. We had been training in all of them. The DC-4 and DC-6B, manufactured by Douglas in the 1930s and 1940s, were both four-propeller planes. The DC-4 carried up to forty-four passengers and cruised at 255 miles per hour with a maximum range of 1,541 miles. The DC-6B, a stretched and pressurized version of the DC-4, accommodated ten more seats. It flew 125 miles per hour faster and had a range about 930 miles longer. The French-built Caravelle, similar to the DC-9, was the first short-haul jetliner to go into service anywhere. Its twin engines were in the rear, midway on the tail fin. Its maximum cruising speed was 513 miles per hour and its range 2,153 miles. It held up to eighty passengers. The airline had only a single class.

On completion of the training, we were told to go to the airport every weekend afternoon to get our schedule for the following week. In January 1969 I became a full-fledged steward for RC. I was one of only a dozen specially trained individuals in a country of nearly 7 million people. I was not sure if my new skills would be marketable in the future, but the future seemed so far away that I simply planned to do my best at what was within my reach.

My first flight was Phnom Penh to Singapore, with a stop in Kuala Lumpur, on the Caravelle. We served breakfast on the way out and lunch on the way back. The airline had three flights a week to Singapore. The ones on Monday and Friday continued on to Denpasar, Bali. It was exciting for me to be in three countries on a single day and be able to end the evening with a movie back in Phnom Penh with friends. I usually brought beautiful things back for my mother, sister, and brother and their families.

The company sent a van to pick the crew up so that we could be aboard the aircraft at least one hour before takeoff. Our job was to go through a complete checklist and make sure that we had enough meals, beverages, and amenities for the passengers. On landing at Pochentong, we transferred the plane over to the ground staff and boarded the company minibus. Since my house was less than a mile from the terminal, I was the last crew member to be picked up and the first to be dropped off. My nieces and nephews would form a welcoming committee. They could tell exactly what time I had arrived by listening to the noise of the landing aircraft. They perfected this to an art form, because they knew that they would always get special treats.

My first stay overseas was at Singapore's Cathay Hotel on Orchard Road. Singapore looked like an enormous shopping center where everything could be found, bargained for, and sold. The next overseas flights were to Hong Kong, Kuala Lumpur, and Denpasar. I remember staying at the Hong Kong's Hotel Miramar, which was one of the best. I could not believe what I could find in the shops on Nathan Road. We also had a weekly flight to Canton. Although I saw mostly airports and hotels, it was a thrill for me to be there and return to tell my family, friends, and neighbors about all those beautiful places.

My favorite flight was, however, the weekend flight to Siem Reap: up to Angkor on Saturday and return to Pochentong Sunday afternoon. We stayed overnight at the famous Grand Hotel d'Angkor. I had twenty-four hours in Siem Reap and would spend most of the time visiting the magnificent temples, with which I had now become quite familiar.

The weekly flight to Canton was the most exotic one. In 1969, only two companies flew there: Pakistan International Airlines and RC. We used the DC-6B to make the four-hour flight. We had a crew of eight: four in the cockpit and four in the cabin. The plane was usually full of Sino-Cambodians. The Chinese, most from the southern provinces speaking Cantonese, *hokien*, and *teowchow* dialects, had been living in Cambodia for centuries. Many had married Cambodians and produced offspring with lighter skin. They went to visit their relatives in China—or that was what they hoped to do. They brought with them everything they could carry, similar to the stuff I used to bring to my relatives in Tonle Bati, including baguettes. The passengers were restless and very noisy. A few minutes after we took off, they were suddenly quiet. They were all airsick. The entire aircraft was filled with the smell of tiger balm, an Asian cure-all. They would then sleep for the entire flight. We flew over Hong Kong before turning west toward Canton.

It was during the Cultural Revolution. What I saw at the airport was beyond my comprehension. The minute we opened the back door of the aircraft, a blast of revolutionary songs came out of dozens of loudspeakers mounted on very tall concrete poles. Dour-faced airport workers in rumpled clothes pushed the stairway toward the plane. The passengers were escorted to an auditorium where they were treated to some revolutionary shows with dancers in peasant and soldier costumes waving flags, pitchforks, and guns, chasing and killing the capitalists and imperialists. On the tables, there were plenty of propaganda materials, from booklets of Mao's thoughts to communist newspapers and magazines in Chinese and English.

After a cup of tea, I walked to the gift shop to pay for my roast duck and basket of fruits. There were always eight sets of these delicious delicacies: one for each of the crew. Sellers at the shop did not want to (or could not) communicate with us directly. If we asked them for the price of some products, they would write it down on a piece of paper. We were required to open an account at the bank of the terminal and deposit our U.S. dollars, which we had earlier changed from Cambodian riels, in exchange for Chinese currency. Whatever was left from our shopping, we had to leave it at the bank before departing. I believe I still have some money left in that bank! I wonder what happened to it.

Before returning to the plane, I looked at the passengers one more time. I did not know where they were going, and they probably did not know either. I saw traces of sadness on their faces. They had realized that they had just walked into the mouth of a tiger, and that the people they were hoping to see might not be there: their friends and relatives were either in a slave labor camp or already dead.

In September 1969, Lon Nol—who had become the prime minister again after Penn Nouth—led a government delegation to participate in the twentieth anniversary of the Chinese communist revolution. We refitted the DC-6B with better seats to accommodate the prime minister status and his delegation. On our arrival at Canton, I was surprised to see that the usually deserted tarmac and terminal were full of people. Hundreds of them were in new, colorful clothes and held balloons, flags, and ribbons. They were dancing, shouting greetings in Chinese, and clapping in unison. After Lon Nol's motorcade left the airport, the greeters melted away without a sound.

One week later, we went back to pick him up. We saw the same scene. The plane, unfortunately, had engine trouble. Lon Nol and his party were escorted back to the VIP lounge. During the few hours it took to fix the problem, the Chinese greeters remained at their assigned spots under the scorching sun. Suddenly, they all stood up, chanting and clapping in unison, and Lon Nol walked slowly toward the plane, smiling and waving.

FLYING INTO THE STORM

In early 1970, RC began flying directly from Hong Kong's Kaitak and Singapore's Paya Lebar to Siem Reap-Angkor. Landing and taking off at Kaitak's runway 13 on the mountainside was always a breathtaking experience. During the approach, planes had to make sharp forty-seven-degree turns (these turns are world-famous) with wingtips almost touching the tops of the high-rise buildings. Now, Hong Kong's ultramodern Chep Lap Kok airport no longer creates the excitement of the good old days.

On March 18, 1970, my flight was Phnom Penh-Singapore-Denpasar-Singapore-Phnom Penh. It had been a long day. We served breakfast in the first segment of the flight, lunch in the second, a snack in the third, and dinner in the fourth and last leg. After the dinner service, I sat down at the back of the Caravelle in the last row, reserved for the crew. I looked out the window and saw the sky all red. It seemed like blood spilled over a white canvas. I wondered whether it was a bad omen. I had seen red skies before but had never compared them to blood.

After we landed, we were told that Prince Sihanouk had been deposed by the national assembly. There had been increasing tension between him and Lon Nol's government. In the end, the prince lost. As I drove through Phnom Penh, I had an eerie feeling. The usually lively city had taken on an air of apprehension and anxiety.

One day in mid-1970, I did the route from Hong Kong to Siem Reap. As we were preparing for the descent, we were told that the flight had to be diverted to Phnom Penh. On the ground, we learned that the Khmer Rouge were closing in at Angkor. These were the radical communist Cambodians, who numbered only a few thousand in the 1960s. They were trained and equipped by the Vietnamese and Chinese communists to fight against Lon Nol's government.

The architect I. M. Pei told me two decades later that he had been waiting to board that RC flight out of Siem Reap. But the plane never came, and he had to take a taxi all the way to the Thai border, where he boarded another taxi to Bangkok. I told him I was sorry for his inconvenience, but it was all destiny. We could have been on that flight together.

I concluded shortly after joining RC that my job as a steward would come to an end sooner or later. The airline wanted its cabin

staff to remain eternally young, beautiful, and handsome. In its thinking, the flight attendants were the face of the company. They must,
therefore, always be *présentable*.

Months later, as Angkor was no longer accessible, tourism began
to decrease. I was laid off. The company said that I was still young and
would certainly find another job. My mother cried. She had not expected this to happen to me. I believe she was more concerned that I
would be heartbroken over having suddenly lost a job which I had so
much enjoyed. *"Never give up hope,"* she told me, as she had always reminded me since my childhood each time I went over a bump in my
life. Shortly after I left, RC added Bangkok, Saigon, and other Southeast Asian cities to its route map. It later dropped the word "Royal"
after Cambodia was proclaimed the Khmer Republic in October 1970.
A year later, the airline asked me to come back. But I was already on
my way to new things.

PART II:

WAR AND PEACE, 1970–1976

*If I cry for having lost the sun, tears will keep
me from seeing the moon.*

—Anonymous

CHAPTER 7:

LIFE UNDER THE SWORD

My first job after high school lasted only two years. This was un-Cambodian, as a job was generally considered a lifetime endeavor. I decided to prepare myself for the next chapter of my life by attending the Royal University of Phnom Penh. I became the first in my family to attend college.

During my high school years, I was a *passable* student: average. That would change once I got into higher education; my brain seemed to work at full capacity and velocity when I was intellectually challenged.

THE STUDENT

My flexible schedule at RC allowed me to be a student at both the Faculté de Droit et des Sciences Économiques (law and economics) and at the Faculté des Lettres et des Sciences Humaines (liberal arts and humanities).

What most Cambodians wanted for their children was to become a *montrey*, an official of the government who had power and commanded both fear and respect, in addition to financial benefits. Many students of my generation went to law school, but not to get a law degree to practice law. The purpose was to enter the prestigious École Nationale d'Administration (ENA), the one and only school of government. Those with a *licence* of law or economics were eligible to apply and later be selected for the two years of training. They would choose between *administration* (civil service), *finance* (treasury), and *diplomatie*. I was aiming for *diplomatie*, which was the most competitive because only a limited number of positions were available. Having traveled overseas quite a bit during my years as a steward, I became more and more interested in international issues and wanted to become a diplomat. In the meantime, I needed something with which I could make, in any small way, important contributions to my society. I passed the entrance examination for the Faculté de Pédagogie, or teachers' college, and would become a teacher of English as a foreign language (TEFL) if I passed all the final exams, which covered numerous topics from educational psychology to class preparation and teaching methodology.

The important teaching practices in a real classroom came toward the end. These were part of a final evaluation and always took place in the presence of our instructors and inspectors. I, like everyone else, was shaking nervously the first time we stood in front of a classroom full of teenagers, not to mention those who were grading us. The students were usually very disciplined and respectful of their teachers. They sat with their hands crossed on the table and listened intently, or at least pretended to do so. They looked at their teachers as role models because the teachers' influence would stay with them for the rest of their lives. The Khmer word *kru*, which is related to "guru" (teacher; *lok kru* for male and *neak kru* for female), is a derivation of *kumru* ("model").

In Cambodia—unlike the United States, where students have the right to interrupt and talk back—students waited until they were allowed to ask questions before raising their hands. They also took the teacher's wisdom as a rule of life.

An old Khmer saying, "At home different mothers, but only one mother in the jungle," placed a lot of importance on the teacher's role in children's upbringing. It means that outside their family circle— that is, in the jungle—children must be considered as belonging to only one family. They come from different families but have only one mother at school—the *kru*, the teacher.

THE TRAINEE

My class went to Singapore for supplemental education in English and teaching English. My mother, afraid that I might miss Khmer food, prepared a big jar of my favorite *kapik ting*, a typical Cambodian snack and side dish made of ground pork, shrimp, and chili pepper, that could be preserved for a long time.

At Pochentong Airport, we were seen off by our large extended families. When we were saying good-bye, my mother started to cry. This was the first time I had left home and the country for a long period of time. I told her not to worry. "I will be very safe in Singapore; there is no war; it is a peaceful country and much more developed than Cambodia."

She held my hand very tightly and whispered, *"No matter what happens, never give up hope!"*

At the Teachers' Training College (TTC) on Patterson Road, we were in a program specifically designed for us. The head of the program was an Englishman, nicely named Ray Tongue. I had classmates from Singapore and Southeast Asia. The principal was Dr. Ruth Wong who once admonished a student for wearing too short a skirt at a graduation rehearsal. This was 1971, when miniskirts were *en vogue*! Singapore, which had been independent for only a few years, was the richest country in Southeast Asia. It wanted to build a clean, proper society with conservative thinking. It had already banned long hair and chewing gum.

On completion of our studies, we were presented with our diplomas in an elaborate ceremony, including a class picture. We said good-bye to our friends and began to pack up for the short flight home. Then Pochentong Airport was shelled by Vietcong rockets and was closed. The Vietnam War had spilled over to Cambodia, and the Vietcong had moved near enough to the Cambodian capital to hit the airport, which they considered a strategic target. I was very worried about my family. I felt relieved after I learned that they were all safe.

We stayed in Singapore for another week before we could return home safely. At Pochentong, the first person I spotted in the cheerful crowd was my sister-in-law Peou. Then, I saw my brother Sichhun and my sister Sarin. My nieces and nephews jumped up and down clapping their hands, anxious to get special treats, as they did during my years as a flight attendant. Finally I saw my mother, in tears, holding the hand of her youngest grandchild. All had big beautiful smiles. Within a short moment we were home. And the distribution of presents began. It was a happy reunion!

THE TEACHER

I graduated at the top of my class at the Faculté de Pédagogie and would be the first to select my assignment. Cambodian teachers were government employees and belonged to the ministry of education. New teachers had to spend their first few years in the provinces before a transfer to the capital was allowed. In a country at war—since 1970, first with the Vietcong and North Vietnamese, then with the Khmer Rouge—it was preferable to stay safe and close to home. My choice would be among the three best locations: Kandal, Battambang, and Kampong Cham. These had lush vegetation, thick forests, green rice fields, and high agricultural production. I had never lived in Battambang but had traveled there often enough to want to live there. Siem Reap would be another good choice. I'd heard that there were two positions in my native province, Kandal. During the assignment selection, we sat in a classroom with a blackboard listing all the provincial openings.

"Siv Sichan?"

"Kandal!"

I answered as soon as my name was called. We took note of our new teaching locations. At the end of the process, we were asked to report immediately to the provincial bureau of secondary education. Mine was in Takamau, the capital of Kandal. I knew it very well in my younger years, having had to buy a lot of baguettes for my relatives at a bus stop there on the way to Tonle Bati.

The provincial director told me that I could go either to Kien Svay, on national route 1 between the Basak and Mekong rivers, about an hour's drive from there; or to Chumpuvorn, on national route 4 (the American Highway). I chose Chumpuvorn. It was a region I knew well, and it was only two and a half miles west of Pochentong. I could still live at home and continue to take classes at the university. Besides, the principal of the high school was a friend of mine. It was a win-win proposition.

I was accepted at the prestigious École Normale Supérieure (ENS), the top teachers' training institution in the French system. I was now required to teach only eight hours a week in order to have time to study for my *licence* and my ENS diploma. On graduation, I could officially list after my name the much coveted ENS alumni title, the crown jewel of the teaching profession in francophone countries:

Siv Sichan
Ancien Élève de l'École Normale Supérieure

After one year at Chumpuvorn, I asked to be transferred to Beng Trabaek secondary school in Chamkarmon, a luxurious neighborhood of Phnom Penh where Prince Sihanouk had his official residence. It was the only school in the country where English, instead of French, was used as the language of instruction in addition to Khmer. It was conveniently located next door to my law school. After teaching, I sometimes slipped through the fence to my law and economics classes.

In 1973 I received a letter from one of my English tutors, Stina Falle, daughter of the British high commissioner in Singapore, Sir Samuel Falle. She wanted me to meet a young Singaporean diplomat, Kishore Mahbubani, who was coming to Phnom Penh to head the embassy. I didn't think much of it at the time.

My brother-in-law San Chhuon had now become a full colonel and the director of national intelligence. It was an ultrasecret body known as SEDOC: Service d'Études et de Documentation (studies and documentation service). Chhuon was sought after by the diplomatic community and the foreign intelligence services. He had asked me to help translate into English some documents captured from the Vietcong and the Khmer Rouge. I had to go to the SEDOC offices to perform this voluntary duty. They were located in an undistinguished building behind a filling station off Monivong Boulevard. The complex used to house the former U.S. military assistance and advisory group in the early 1960s. The employees of SEDOC wore civilian clothes.

Chhuon routinely included me in his functions. At one dinner, I was sitting across the table from a young, bearded diplomat who had just arrived in Phnom Penh. It was his first visit to a Cambodian house.

"I am Kishore Mahbubani. I've just arrived from Singapore. And I am looking for one Siv Sichan."

"You've just found him!" I said smilingly.

Kishore and I became fast friends. We were both twenty-five and eager to find the truth. We ventured everywhere together—to the markets, suburbs, and villages. We traveled incognito: Kishore would leave his chauffeured Mercedes a few blocks away and walk to meet me at the wheel of my jeep.

One day we traveled with the chief British diplomat, David Mac-Killigin, to Chruoy Changwar across the Tonle Sap River, by a ferry (the Japanese-built bridge had been blown up by Vietcong sappers). There, we took a *remauk*, a popular four-seater two-wheel carriage pulled by a motorcycle. We went north to Preaek Lieb, passing the abandoned buildings of the Agricultural Training Center on the right. We came on a military checkpoint denoting the first defense perimeter of Phnom Penh. The soldiers were having their breakfast in a field a few hundred yards from the road. The barrier was up and we went through the checkpoint. Suddenly, we heard some shouting. We looked back and saw a few soldiers running to the roadblock and waving at us. We did not understand what they were saying. So we waved back.

A few minutes later, we asked the *remauk* driver to stop. We jumped off and walked toward the bank of the Mekong River. There were fields of bananas, jackfruits, and papayas. We spotted a few fishing boats through the sun reflecting off the river. We heard nothing but birdsong. It was quiet and tranquil, hardly a war zone. We stood there for a few moments without uttering a word. Then, we walked back across an open field discussing the situation of the day, the week, and the month ahead. There were many uncertainties.

A few heavily armed soldiers were waiting for us at the roadside. Others were surrounding our driver and questioning him. He had turned pale. "What's happening, Sichan? They do not look very happy to see us here." Kishore asked.

"Did we do something wrong?" David joined in.

"We didn't do anything wrong by walking to the river. We didn't do anything wrong by peeing in the banana field," I assured them. "The only thing I can think of is that we didn't stop at the checkpoint. But the barrier was up!" I claimed our innocence. "Let me handle it."

"*Chumrieb suor lok!*" I greeted them with a *sampeah*.

The soldiers looked a bit annoyed.

"*Chumrieb suor lok!*"

The sergeant returned my *sampeah* and mumbled the words of greeting, showing that he was upset. Then, in a firm and angry tone, he continued in Khmer, "Do you know where you've just been to?"

"The Mekong," I responded innocently.

"The Mekong? No! You've just been to a minefield! You've just walked across a minefield! You could have been blown up. Your body parts could have been spread all over this field. And if you got killed, you would have also killed me and my platoon. Did you know that? We were waving at you. We were trying to stop you and warn you not to get off the road. Why didn't you stop?" (I got one right.)

The sergeant's pitch became higher and higher. Kishore and David did not understand what we were saying. But they could tell by the soldiers' faces and the sergeant's tone that they were all very angry.

"*Kanyom som toos. Kanyom awt dueng!*" I spoke to the sergeant in a low, submissive voice, apologizing for our mistake.

I offered him some cigarettes. I did not smoke, but I always carried a pack and a box of matches. It was a good way to strike up an acquaintance.

The sergeant hesitantly took a cigarette. He put it between his lips the minute he saw that I was about to strike a match.

"*Kanyom som toos. Kanyom awt dueng!*—I am sorry. I did not know."

"Please don't do it again. Be careful. *Do not leave the road!*"

The sergeant was now pleading with me. I gave him the whole pack of cigarettes. We exchanged our *sampeah* and I said thank you and good-bye.

"*Soam Awkun. Chumrieb lear!*"

We boarded the *remauk*, turned around, and waved to the soldiers. They waved back at us. This time it was a friendly wave. David and Kishore couldn't wait to ask me, in unison, "What happened, Sichan?" I told them the whole story. The soldiers were doing their job diligently. We discussed the incident and tried to make light of it. What would happen if we got blown apart? "British, Singaporean Diplomats Killed with Cambodian Teacher, Peeing in Banana Field" one headline might read. No, we did not want that.

On the way back, the sergeant's voice stayed with me. "Be careful. Do not leave the road."

Stay on the road! Do not leave the road!

But which road were we on? The road to war or the road to peace?

Offices in Cambodia were open on Saturday morning. Kishore and I belonged to an informal Saturday breakfast club. One of the founding members was the West German ambassador, Walther Baron von Marschall. We would meet every Saturday morning at seven to have a bowl of a famous noodle soup, commonly known as *kuytiev* Phnom Penh. We usually had a big round table that could seat eight or ten. All eating utensils and condiments such as chopsticks, spoon, chili sauce, soy sauce, and sugar were placed at the center of the table. So was a roll of toilet paper, to be used as napkins. The minute we sat down, a waiter would bring us two pots of tea, cups piled on each other in two different stacks, and two glasses of boiling water. We would put the chopsticks and spoons in the hot water to sanitize them. There were only two selections: the regular bowl and the dry one. The latter had the broth served in a separate bowl. Beverages consisted of soft drinks and coffee. Mine was usually a cup of café au lait with condensed milk.

The Saturday breakfast club was our weekly session of food for thought. Besides bonding, it was an opportunity for us to swap gossip, rumors, jokes, and intelligence. Other friends, such as UNICEF's representative Paul Ignatieff and the Israeli diplomat David Matnai, would just join in. They usually put their guests next to me, as I was the only Cambodian at the table.

We occasionally rotated locations, for security and diversity.

Whoever discovered a new restaurant would recommend it to the group for the following Saturday. Our favorite noodle shop was the one at the western end of Kampuchea Krom Boulevard near Pochentong Road. This was one place where we did not have to fight with the flies that tried to dive-bomb our bowls before we could finish the delicious noodles.

One day, Walther brought a British friend. He was seated to my right. He introduced himself as David Cornwell, a British journalist. He was in Cambodia for a few days to find out about the situation on the ground and how the war against the Vietcong, North Vietnamese, and Khmer Rouge was going. I suggested that he should try to get out of Phnom Penh to the field and the provinces, especially those that were still accessible. He said that he was planning to do so.

After the breakfast, Kishore gave me a ride to the school. As I was getting out of his car, he asked if I knew who had been sitting to my right.

"David Cornwell, a British journalist," I responded. Kishore smiled. "That's what he told me," I said.

"No. He wrote *The Spy Who Came In from the Cold!*"

"John Le Carré?"

Years later I read *The Honourable Schoolboy* and saw that our noodle scene made it into the book, if only for one sentence.

THE GRADUATE

I did well with my double life as a teacher and student: teaching full-time and taking university courses. Attending three different schools at the same time was quite a burden, but I managed to have top grades: *bien* (good) or *très bien* (very good).

At the Faculté des Lettres, the *licence* (the equivalent of a bachelor's degree) was conferred on the successful completion of a series of *certificats*. The degree normally took about four years to finish. The first year, known as *Certificat d'Études Littéraires Générales* (CELG), compulsory for everyone. During the next three years, the student had at least one concentration by obtaining a series of *Certificats d'Études Supérieures*. These certificates entitled us to have the degree of our choice. Mine was English studies. With some fluency in English and a good knowledge of America, I thought that this was the right way to go. For the next three years, I studied in great depth the history of Britain and the United States as well as their literature.

All *licence* candidates had to take a certificate of Khmer culture and civilization, with eighty percent of the prescribed readings in French.

I took Japanese and German language courses as well. My Japanese teacher was Motohisa Yamada. He and I became good friends. We occasionally got together to have Japanese food, drink sake, and discuss the issues of the day—or the future. Yamada-san was a great student of Cambodian culture and civilization and once cowrote a book on Angkor.

My Japanese was not good enough for us to have lengthy conversations, so we would end up speaking French. We were regularly joined by Meas Chanleap, who was trained as a pyrotechnical engineer and graduated at the top of his class in Japan. He was the ultimate adman for Japanese values, such as a strict disciplinarian life. The Japanese did this, the Japanese did that. I learned from him and Yamada-san how to bow properly, making sure that both hands descended to the level of my knees. The lower you bowed, the more respectful you were. The other person would try to outdo you by bowing even lower. At one point, one of the greeters would have to stop; otherwise everybody would end up on the ground.

At school, I made friends with everyone, especially the professors and librarians. There were not enough books for everybody. So, librarians were quite important in my studies.

One of my favorite teachers was Roger Jones, who came from

Chelthenham, England. He introduced me to his colleagues at the British Council, who let me use many outstanding audiovisual aids in my class presentations. Another one was Marilyn Lewis, from Auckland, New Zealand. She was so pleased with my performance that she recommended and obtained a New Zealand government scholarship for me. It was for a diploma in TEFL at the University of Wellington. When I went to claim the prize, the ministry of education denied me the scholarship, saying that the Cambodian government should decide who would be the recipient. I later learned that some corrupt officials had decided to secretly auction off the coveted prize.

I graduated with distinction from all my schools, and this made my mother, Sarin, and Sichhun very happy. Despite these academic achievements, I felt that something was still missing.

CHAPTER 8:

CARING AND SHARING

Hate ends not with more hate but with love.
And from that we take hope. Without love
and hope our lives will be empty.
Happiness is something we cannot keep, unless we give it away.

—Mae

THE ATTACKS

In March 1970 large demonstrations by students in Phnom Penh heavily damaged Vietcong and North Vietnamese embassies. These had been preceded by protests in the Parrot's Beak provinces of Svay Rieng and Prey Veng. On March 13, the government of Lon Nol and Sirik Matak issued an ultimatum to the communist Vietcong and North Vietnamese troops to get out of Cambodia within forty-eight hours, by dawn on March 15. On March 18, while I was flying between Singapore and Denpasar, Prince Sihanouk was deposed by both houses of parliament. The coup ended a relative peace in Cambodia.

To protect the sanctuaries which the North Vietnamese had been using in eastern Cambodia, in violation of Cambodian neutrality, Hanoi launched an offensive against the ill-equipped, poorly trained Cambodian army. Fighting broke out in the eastern provinces bordering

South Vietnam where Vietcong and North Vietnamese forces had been concentrating. By mid-April, they were within twenty-five miles of Phnom Penh.

In January 1971, in a four-hour assault, the Vietcong destroyed the entire fleet of the Cambodian Air Force, including Soviet MIG fighters and French Fouga Magister trainers, based on the southeastern side of Pochentong Air Force Base. They also blew up the Chruoy Changwar Bridge over the Tonle Sap River. During these hit-and-run attacks, the Vietnamese communist sappers achieved their objective of instilling fear in the residents of Phnom Penh. They had shown that they could strike us anywhere with minimal cost to themselves: only a few were killed or captured.

The Cambodian and South Vietnamese governments agreed on a forced repatriation of Vietnamese residents in Cambodia. Both governments were concerned that these were sleeper cells of Vietcong agents waiting for the time to attack from inside. Our Vietnamese neighbors, with whom we had enjoyed sharing food and company, were told to return. It was a difficult and painful moment for everyone.

My brother Sichhun, who had inherited our family house, quickly finished some renovation work, including building a bunker in the front yard. It was big enough to accommodate all of us and strong enough to withstand hits from artillery shells.

During the attacks on the airport in the middle of the night, we had our first trial of an emergency evacuation: children and women first. I was the last one to get in. While I was crouching at the entrance of the bunker, there was an enormous explosion. The effect was so strong that the powerful wind suddenly threw me into the bunker. Fortunately, I was not hurt.

We had these alerts over and over. My mother was always the first to wake me. They became so routine that sometimes I just slept through them. Later, as the war between the Vietcong–North Vietnamese and the Cambodians intensified, I learned to go to bed fully dressed.

THE FIRST STATE

In early 1973 my brother Sichhun was selected to go to Huntsville, Alabama, for specialized training at the U.S. Army Ordnance Missile and Munition Center and School at Redstone Arsenal. He took a commercial flight to San Francisco and a military aircraft from Travis Air Force Base to Alabama.

I had my first glimpse of America in postcards my brother sent me from Alabama—the first state, alphabetically. He described the scenery he saw along I-65 during a class trip to Mobile. And he always ended with the memorable words, *"This is a beautiful country!"*

In May, Sichhun returned triumphantly. He was the first in our family to travel outside Asia, the first to travel to the United States. We all went to the airport to welcome him. He brought back loads of gifts: new blue jeans, beautiful shirts, tapes, records, and T-shirts. On his return, Sichhun became a walking ad for the United States: the Americans did this; the Americans did that. His wardrobe overflowed with U.S.-made trousers and shirts. For the first time, through him, our family was directly linked to American culture. I asked if he had visited the state capitol in Montgomery, and his response was, "You mean *Mungumry?*"

"Kanee, do you know where York, Oxford, Geneva, Florence, Athens, and Arab are?" he asked me one day.

"York and Oxford are in England, Geneva in Switzerland, Florence in Italy, Athens in Greece, and there is no such town as Arab," I responded quickly, showing off my skills.

"Yes, there is," retorted my brother with an air of confidence. "Arab, Athens, Florence, Geneva, Oxford, and York are in Alabama." He beamed with his superior knowledge.

My brother-in-law San Chhuon went on several trips in Asia. He brought my sister along. I was happy to see pictures of Sarin smiling broadly at some of the most popular tourist attractions. When they returned to Phnom Penh, everyone went to the airport to greet them and waited anxiously for our special treats. I now enjoyed being a beneficiary of our family tradition of sharing exotic gifts.

THE RELIEF

The Khmer Rouge, numbering only a few thousand at the beginning, took over the fighting in Cambodia from the Vietcong and North Vietnamese in their war against Lon Nol's government, after North and South Vietnam signed an agreement in Paris in January 1973 to end the war and restore peace. The war came closer and closer to home and extracted greater tolls every day. The Khmer Rouge's 122-millimeter rockets rained down regularly and indiscriminately over the capital: on the markets, hospitals, schools, and kindergartens. Like their fellow communists and comrades in arms, the Khmer Rouge killed and maimed innocent civilians, including the poor, destitute, women, and children. Members of my family became more and more terrified. But there was nothing we could do about it, except let fate decide. We had been brought up to believe in fate and destiny.

After seeing so much injury, death, and destruction, I decided to leave my job as a high school teacher to join the U.S. relief organization CARE. Founded in 1945 by about twenty organizations, CARE (Cooperative for American Relief Everywhere) launched the concept of the "CARE package." Good English-speakers with a college education were needed immediately to help manage its multimillion-dollar humanitarian program. I went for an interview and was hired on the spot. I started as a program assistant, the top position for local staff members. The pay was far better than my teacher's salary, and the job gave me the great satisfaction of doing something good in difficult circumstances. My responsibilities included designing program plans; writing budgets; drafting and negotiating contracts; and directing emergency housing, agricultural development projects, and food distributions. I was a principal liaison to the Cambodian government, and I supervised a staff of more than 100.

CARE, along with other nongovernmental organizations (NGOs), provided basic aid to refugees and displaced persons: food, clothing, and shelter. By the end of 1974, the organization was caring for about 500,000 displaced persons pouring into Phnom Penh and other provincial cities. We sent a survey unit as soon as we learned about their arrival. A field team quickly set up emergency shelters and supplied them with necessary tools for self-help and agricultural projects. We regularly distributed rice and other foodstuffs, such as salt, pepper, dried fish, smoked fish, and the classic Cambodian fermented fish paste called *prahok.*

I worked directly with June Magnaldi, whose previous assignment was in Greece. Cambodia was the first Asian country she had set foot in. We traveled around in a four-wheel-drive vehicle to inspect our projects anywhere that was accessible. We went through and to some of the most dangerous places, where we might be ambushed or shot at any time of the day. We discussed ways of finding solutions to crises and problems on constant deadlines, as lives were always at stake. We shared ideas and opinions. We listened to each other's arguments, especially when we disagreed. With June's broader perspective and my indigenous knowledge, we were comfortably complementary. We had quick meals together with our driver at street food stalls and got back on the road right away. At the office, we usually exchanged notes and poetry to maintain our sanity. Her favorite poet was William Carlos Williams; mine was Robert Frost. I occasionally added a few poems that I translated from Khmer or French.

I admired June tremendously for her down-to-earth character, her commitment to help the needy, her humanitarian vocation of caring and sharing, and her austerity (she used every space available on a piece of writing paper). She seemed to be born to provide relief, rehabilitation, and hope to those in need. She was the perfect savior. I had never worked with Americans before, and June gave me a great impression of what the United States and its people stood for.

June and I established such rapport that she did not want me to work for anybody else, except for Bruce Strassburger, our overall boss, who occasionally needed me to accompany him on field trips. Bruce could be intimidating, but his heart was as large as his body. He was overwhelmingly dedicated to relief work and seemed to operate best in emergency situations. He spoke very slowly and clearly and accompanied his sentences with lively body language. He always made sure his gestures supported his verbal communication. One day he and I raced across the runway at Pochentong wearing helmets and flak jackets while cargo planes made their final approaches and rockets were pouring over the airport. We wanted to make sure that the crates of emergency food supplies were being unloaded from the planes and onto the trucks at a reasonable pace. The Mekong River had been the major supply line for the besieged capital. By the spring of 1975, ship convoys were continually being destroyed by Khmer Rouge gunners. With the railroad to Thailand and to the seaport of Kampong Saom cut, provincial highways destroyed, and the Mekong now impassable, an airlift was the only way to bring in about 700 tons of cargo every day.

Neil O'Toole was brought in from India to help speed up the food delivery. Bruce asked June to let me work with him for a few days. Neil was smaller than Bruce, but equally devoted to relief work. He was funny and cheerful. He regretted that he was not related to Peter O'Toole, whose movie *Lord Jim* was filmed in Cambodia in the early 1960s. Neil and I went to our warehouses at Kilometer No. 6 north of Phnom Penh. We brought a few trucks and asked our workers to load them with 110-pound sacks of rice. With a stopwatch, we timed how long it took to fill a truck and how long it would take to empty a single warehouse.

The emergency relief efforts were intense and dangerous. Despite numerous interruptions, we managed to keep the program moving. The staff members, especially those in the field, were extraordinarily dedicated and constantly exposed to life-threatening situations. I counted our blessings: during the final months of the war, we did not lose any of them.

In the meantime, I learned how to keep my head low, survive in hostile environments, and carry out my duties without questioning the morality of the war.

On April 1, 1975, Lon Nol left Phnom Penh and the war in Cambodia. Wealthy and powerful Cambodians followed him in droves. The capital, once a very special place, had become a city of fear and desperation, but many of its residents could not or did not want to leave. Most felt the war would be over soon and expected that its end would bring peace.

The international communities departed, carrying with them bittersweet memories. The American staff of CARE also began leaving for "breathers or vacations." Senior local staff members had been told privately that when the time came, we would be given places in a U.S. evacuation. We did not know if it would be by planes or helicopters.

In the second week of April I found myself running the multimillion-dollar programs. We were determined to carry out the emergency distributions of food and medical supplies. Thousands of people were pouring into the capital. Phnom Penh, the same size as Phoenix in the 1960s, had now swollen to 3 million.

THE EVACUATION

For some months, CARE had been helping 3,175 refugee families in Kampong Speu, about 30 miles southwest of Phnom Penh. I once flew there by helicopter with Paul White of the United States Agency for International Development (USAID), to look at the situation in the camps. We had to make a zigzag approach and land in a soccer field. The crew took off immediately after everyone had jumped to the ground and came back a few hours later to pick us up. It was a hairy flight, and we were lucky not to be shot down.

We used to transport our supplies by trucks, but route 4 had been cut off by Khmer Rouge guerrillas. I asked to see the governor, General Norodom Chantaraingsey. A relative of Prince Sihanouk, he was also commander of the Thirteenth Brigade and the military region that encompassed Kampong Speu and neighboring provinces.

The meeting was scheduled for April 12, 1975, at Trapaing Russey, about an hour's drive southwest of Phnom Penh off the American Highway (route 4).

My mother and I had traveled on this highway to the seaside resort of Sihanoukville. It was a new highway then. I still remember my excitement at seeing the sea for the first time, and at having such a smooth ride. I remember playing with my mother by putting a silver *phatel* (drinking bowl) full of water on my lap. "Look *Mae*, no spill!" I remember her beautiful smile as she showed her affection, admiration, and appreciation for my creativity in applied science.

Since then, the highway had gone for years without proper maintenance. During the early phase of the war, Vietcong troops set up ambushes and laid land mines. Now, route 4 had been completely cut off by the guerrillas.

The international staff of CARE had left the week before, and I felt it was important to keep everything moving as smoothly as possible to avoid creating any impression of a panic. Many staff members realized that we were approaching the end. They were fearful but did not say a word. They did not ask me for my opinion, and I did not volunteer it.

Two days earlier, on April 10, the Voice of America reported President Ford's congressional address in a very somber tone: "The situation

in South Vietnam and Cambodia has reached a critical phase requir-
ing immediate and positive decisions by this government. The options
before us are few, and the time is very short."

At about seven o'clock that morning, I was getting ready to leave
my office when Jeff Millington of USAID showed up. He asked me to
return to my desk and closed the door behind us. He spoke slowly in a
very clear voice, to make sure that I did not miss a word. The U.S.
embassy in Phnom Penh was being evacuated. I was being given a seat
on the helicopter flight out. Only me. And a small bag. And I had to
be at the embassy within an hour. I told him that I was leaving for a
meeting with the governor of Kampong Speu to discuss ways to send
supplies to the stranded displaced people.

"This is it. There is no other way to get out of Phnom Penh." Jeff cut
me off. "Pochentong has been shut down already," he reminded me.

Before he left my office, he turned around and said to me in no
uncertain terms, "Be at the embassy within an hour, if you want to be
airlifted safely out of Cambodia. *One hour!*"

"I'll be there," I said, just to make him feel that he had accomplished his mission. I got into the van with my assistant and said to the
driver, "Let's go!" I began to struggle between heading for the embassy
and heading for Trapaing Russey. As we drove down Avenue de France
toward Wat Phnom, I could not decide what to do. I would surely be
safe going to the embassy.

"But I can't leave without telling *Mae*."

"I can't leave without her."

"I can't leave without Sarin."

"How about Sichhun?"

I asked myself questions that could not be answered. And those
thousands of sick and hungry people in Kampong Speu? Will they be
taken care of?

The driver turned left in front of the cathedral onto Monivong
Boulevard and turned right in front of the railroad station where the

relics of Buddha had been kept since 1957, the year my father died. I prayed silently that the war would be over and peace would return to Cambodia—and that my family and friends would be happy together.

We were now on the airport road heading toward Pochentong and national route 4. I was going to ask the driver to turn around and head for the embassy, but I could not open my mouth. The three of us in the car had been in complete silence since we left the office. And my decision not to decide was taken over by fate.

"Perhaps there will be a good solution," I thought. "Maybe I can make the meeting and get to the embassy in time! And by going to the meeting first, I can save the lives of those people and leave with a clear conscience."

It was not meant to be.

General Chataraingsey and his officers, with sidearms and in green camouflage gear, greeted me warmly in their makeshift command post. We quickly sat down and put our heads together. I told him the amount of rice and medical supplies in our warehouses available for immediate transportation to Kampong Speu. The question was how. Route 4 had seen a lot of ambushes and had become lethally dangerous, and completely inaccessible.

I was sitting facing east toward the sun and noted the shape of some helicopters in the distance. I turned around and saw a Huey 100 yards away. I smiled. I looked at the Huey again. When I turned to him, Chantaraingsey smiled. He could make one helicopter available to me long enough to airlift the emergency supplies to Kampong Speu until the mission was completed. But I had to get the supplies from Kilometer No. 6 to Trapaing Russey. "That should not be a problem."

"*Awkun!*" I thanked him and gave him a *sampeah*. I looked at the Huey one more time before leaving. We were moving east toward the sun and the capital.

As we passed through Pochentong, I noticed some big helicopters taking off in the eastern skies. "What's going on?" I asked. "The U.S. embassy is closing," responded my assistant. I suddenly realized that I was supposed to be at the embassy that morning. "Be at the embassy within an hour, if you want to be airlifted safely out of Cambodia. *One hour!*" Jeff Millington's voice rang in my ear.

I told the driver to speed up, but as we moved closer to Phnom Penh, the traffic became heavily congested. Thousands of people were making their way slowly, in oxcarts and on overloaded bicycles, to seek shelter and safety in the capital.

I finally got to the main compound of the U.S. embassy at the northeast corner of Norodom and Sothearos boulevards. There were a lot of white American sedans with diplomatic license plates parked neatly on the sidewalks. It did not look like an emergency evacuation. I got out of the van and, with some anxiety, walked to the main gate. I gave my name to the security officer, who looked puzzled.

"Siv Sichan!" I said with a shaky voice as my heart began to beat faster.

"Are you supposed to be in the evacuation?"

"*Bart!*" I responded "Yes" with a voice so low that it was barely audible.

"They are gone," responded the officer.

"When are they coming back?" I felt more palpitations of my heart.

"They are not coming back."

"What???"

"They are not coming back. They are gone!"

The guard shouted his answer to emphasize the hard truth. And he added: "It's over. The war is over. We will have peace!"

Speechless, I returned to the van with my head low and an empty heart. As we drove north on Norodom toward the Independence Monument, I asked the driver to turn right at Sihanouk Boulevard toward Sisowath Quay on the riverbank. I wanted to have a clear look at the horizon to see if I could still spot the helicopters. "Maybe they've realized that I was missing. And one of them will come back for me. Maybe!" I was still in denial.

The sky was blue and cloudless. There was nothing on the horizon. Not a black spot anywhere. (Years later, I realized that I had been looking at the wrong horizon. The helicopters flew westward toward the Gulf of Thailand. And I was looking east.)

"They are not coming back. They are gone!"

I was thirty minutes late. My life was going to change forever.

As we drove back to the CARE offices, I kept hearing, "The war is over. We will have peace!"

The following day, April 13, was the Cambodian new year and Mother's sixty-second birthday. We all prayed that our beloved country would return to the stable, peaceful life of the 1960s.

CHAPTER 9:

YEAR OF THE BLOODY PEACE

THE EXODUS

I got up early on April 17, 1975, at my sister Sarin's house. In the past, our homes had always been guesthouses for friends and family. Our relatives from the provinces came to stay with us in Pochentong for months at a time. Now it was Sarin's turn to transform her house into a welcome center.

My parents had a practice of giving a piece of land and a beautiful Khmer-style house to each of their children. My second sister, Sarun, was the first to get married and to receive some family property. In 1955 it was my elder sister, Sarin. Their properties were both behind our family house at 401R Pochentong Road, which Sichhun later inherited. I was the last, and was left without a family property.

Sarin bought a three-story townhouse in Tuek La-ork, after her husband was transferred to Phnom Penh in the late 1960s. Off Kampuchea Krom Boulevard, just east of a primary school named for Santhor Mok (the famous poet), it had plenty of room to accommodate our extended family. We moved there from Pochentong the week before, when we realized that the Khmer Rouge had broken the capital's defense perimeter.

After taking the first of my three daily cold showers, I put on my regular office clothes. There was no field trip scheduled for that day, but I still wore a pair of navy blue pants with a long-sleeved shirt and a pair of dark sneakers. These were standard issue, as my work was usually a combination of desk job, outside meetings, and field trips. I wanted to be able to move quickly without having to change. I kept a suit, a pair of dress shoes, and some ties in the office, just in case I had to put them on for a meeting with a cabinet minister.

I had a bowl of Phnom Penh noodles at a street-side restaurant before beginning another regular workday. I had an eerie feeling while driving my jeep to the office. In my head, I kept hearing the voice of the embassy security officer. "They are not coming back. They are gone. It's over. The war is over. We will have peace."

Well, the war might be over. But would we have peace?

The documents that I had seen at SEDOC seemed to say otherwise. They reported the vow of the Khmer Rouge to use all means to destroy the enemies of the revolution. They exhorted everyone to "pull the grass from the roots." They reminded people that there was nothing to be gained by keeping one of us, and nothing to lose by getting rid of one of us.

Then came the gruesome descriptions of what had taken place: babies thrown into the air and caught with a bayonet, children smashed into trees, villagers having their throats cut with the sharp thorns of palm tree branches, merchants clubbed to death with the back of a hoe. These were all the *satreou* (enemies) of the Khmer Rouge revolution. In one incident at Phnom Baset, west of Phnom Penh, whole families were pushed off the mountain cliffs.

I did not believe what I read: *It wasn't Cambodian. We are Buddhists; we are peaceful people. We would never do that to fellow human beings.*

The reprisals of the Khmer Rouge were so atrocious that one day my brother-in-law San Chhuon asked me to go over some of the translations with his CIA liaison. We went over the last batch of the documents in Khmer. And to my dismay, my English translation stood firm. It gave the same interpretation as previously reported.

It can't be true. I don't believe this shit!

I finally gave my editorial comment after leaving SEDOC. Yet at the back of my mind I had some reservations.

What if it is true? I asked myself. What if there is the slightest possibility? What will happen to my family, friends, and neighbors if the Khmer Rouge carry out their threat to purify society, to exterminate the despised "educated class"?

If it is true, it will be *noruok knong lok,* hell on earth.

"Nothing is permanent," says one Buddhist principle. That's right. "Nothing is permanent, except change."

I gave myself an escape clause: *If it's true, let fate decide.*

"The war is over. We will have peace!" Well, I'd say, "It remains to be seen."

I drove northward on Avenue de France from Wat Phnom. I noticed that the street was empty of traffic but lined with residents of Phnom Penh. A few were still wearing their *kramas* and sarongs. One was brushing his teeth. But all were looking north, waiting for something. Something was going to happen. They looked apprehensive and fearful.

In the distance, I saw people walking in the middle of the avenue. As I turned left to get into the CARE parking lot, the picture became clear: they were Khmer Rouge soldiers, heavily armed with AK-47s, grenade launchers, machine guns, and bazookas. They were dressed in black pajamas, rubber-tire sandals, and Mao hats. Many wore a *krama* around the neck or head. They walked like zombies toward me and the center of the city. I braked to a halt, reversed quickly, turned around, and raced to the Hotel Le Royal. A major institution in Phnom Penh since 1930, the hotel was a blend of Khmer, art deco, and French colonial architecture and the place to see and be seen. It was called Le Phnom between 1970 and 1975. The International Committee of the Red Cross had put up banners all around declaring it a neutral zone.

I parked the car on a side street between the hotel and the National Library, and ran to the front gate. To my disappointment, the gate was closed. My eyes scanned the lucky crowd safely inside. I recognized Murray Carmichael, a physician with the ICRC. I called his name. He gestured for me to go to the east entrance. It was across from the National Library, where I had spent a lot of time in my teenage years dreaming about the outside world.

Murray told me to climb quickly over the locked gate before anybody could see. The moment I landed on my feet, he asked if I could be the interpreter. I said yes. He immediately took me to one of the bungalows, which the ICRC had turned into an emergency operating room. I rushed in and almost stepped on a severely injured patient. There was fresh blood all over the floor. I ran from one operating table to another interpreting in both French and English. The medical staff came mostly from Europe: half of them spoke French, the other half English. Sometimes, I spoke French to the English-speakers, and sometimes the other way around. And sometimes, I spoke Khmer to all of them. Somehow, we managed to get through our communications challenges.

A girl who lay on a corner table had been hit by shrapnel that morning in front of her house while watching the approaching conquering army. Her mother was pleading with the doctor, through me, to save her daughter's life. I thought of Sarin and one of her daughters who was the same age as the wounded girl.

I spent all day in the temporary emergency room doing what I could to help. I came out briefly to get some fresh air and ran to the Monivong Boulevard side to see the Khmer Rouge being welcomed by Phnom Penh's residents. People seemed genuinely happy that the war had ended. They all said, "The war is over. We will have peace!"

I was agonizing over the contrast between the euphoria expressed by the people and the atrocities described in the SEDOC papers. I still did not want to believe what I had read.

The previous night I had gone to see San Chhuon at his office. I saw a pair of gold stars on his desk. He was going to be promoted to brigadier general. He had worked hard nonstop since he took the job. I was happy for him. I thought it was a well-deserved promotion. But I had come to get his opinion on what was really going to happen. Before I opened my mouth, he passed me a manila envelope and said, "Give this to your sister. Tell her not to worry about me. I will disappear for a while." He answered my question with that sentence. Now, having seen the expressionless faces of the Khmer Rouge troops, I began to tilt toward SEDOC's findings.

"We are all Cambodians and will work together to rebuild the country," said one jubilant person. It remains to be seen, I told myself.

I was looking for Sichhun. I had reminded him the previous night to be at the hotel to seek protection. "Where is he? He should be here by now. He may be here already." To avoid the anguish of not finding my brother, I went back to the temporary operating room.

In late afternoon, we were told to get out. The Khmer Rouge announced over a loudspeaker that we were to leave the city as soon as possible. Otherwise, they could not be responsible for our lives. The United States was going to bomb, they said.

I didn't believe it, but there was no time to find out.

Shortly after that, the Khmer Rouge rammed a military truck through the front gate and broke it open. The euphoria disappeared.

I looked for Sichhun everywhere. I went into Le Cyrène, the elegant French restaurant north of the swimming pool. He was not there. I went to the front garden on the south. He was not there. I went into the lobby and stood against the wall to avoid being crushed by the tidal wave of people trying to get out.

"Kanee! Kanee!" A very familiar voice called me by my nickname. I turned around—it was Sichhun, waving at me from the other side of the lobby. A thick crowd of people rushing to get to the front gate separated us. I signaled to my brother for him to meet me at the eastern gate.

I struggled to get out of the lobby in a different direction from the human wave and bumped into one of the nurses.

"*Où allez-vous?*—Where are you going?" I asked her frantically.

"*Aucune idée.*—No idea," she answered, equally frantically.

"*Bonne chance!*" We wished each other good luck. I turned away and headed toward the eastern gate.

"French embassy!" shouted somebody. He pointed his hand to the northwest to make sure I knew where it was. I moved my lips silently to say, "Thank you!"

Sichhun was waiting for me with a friend. We jumped over the wall and into my car. We arrived a few minutes later at the enormous French embassy at the north end of Monivong Boulevard. We rushed to the main gate, but were refused entrance. Only *baraing* (foreigners) were allowed in. We could have jumped over the wall, but we decided to return to the car. This was a fateful development. The French had saved my life. A few days later, the Khmer Rouge demanded that all Cambodians at the French embassy be turned over. Among them was Prince Sirik Matak. He was immediately killed, along with his family.

I quickly took off my white undershirt and tied it to the car antenna. Everyone had a white flag or something white. It was the sign of peace (read submission, surrender) and it would protect us. That was what we were made to believe.

We went through various barricades down Monivong, and near the central market we dropped off Sichhun's friend, who immediately disappeared after we exchanged *sampeahs*. We turned right at Kampuchea Krom and sped toward our sister Sarin's house.

There, everyone had just finished packing. Khmer Rouge soldiers, known in Khmer as *yothia*, had gone from house to house telling the residents to get out and to bring enough belongings for just a few days.

There were sixteen of us: our mother, Sarin, Sichhun, Peou, and their children.

We departed that evening of April 17, 1975, the first day of peace. It was to become the darkest night of our lives. We left in two cars overloaded with our meager possessions and food supplies. The youngest members of the family and the older women rode in the cars. The strongest ones pushed them. We were among the first of some 3 million people who tried to leave at the same time. At Pochentong, we found that our house was occupied by a few families. We went to Wat Pothisataram, our village temple. The monks were already gone, and there were bodies lying around. Mother was sobbing. The women and girls were choking. The boys and men were all silent.

We arrived at Chumpuvorn, where I used to teach in the evening, exhausted, and decided to camp there. It had taken us nearly five hours to travel the eight-mile distance. I was lying between Mother and Sarin. "I don't know what is going to happen to us," said my sister softly, tears coming down her cheeks.

"Kanee, what do you think we should be doing?" asked Sichhun.

Mother said, "This is our bad karma. We must have done something very bad in our previous lives to have to go through this kind of suffering." I tried to comfort everyone, reassuring Mother first that it could not be our bad karma, because the entire country was going through the same suffering. It would be best for us to hear nothing, see nothing, and speak of nothing, and *let fate decide*.

The following morning, we saw a few teenage *yothia* coming by. They were still learning how to ride motorcycles. They crashed into anything they saw on the road. Sometimes they crashed into each other while riding in pairs. My nephew and I went to help them get up. We asked them to tell us where we were supposed to go.

"Go to your native village!"

We were all born in Phnom Penh. My nephew was brave enough to follow up with another question.

"Go to the native village of your parents, grandparents!"

So we decided that Hanuman in *srok* Tonle Bati, my father's native village, would be our final destination.

THE HELL

After Chumpuvorn, my family moved south across the dry rice fields to reach national route 3, which led to Takeo and Kampot. We witnessed more depressing scenes. Charred cars and trucks were everywhere. More and more people died along the roads that seemed to lead nowhere. They died of hardship, exhaustion, and summary executions by the Khmer Rouge. We saw decomposing bodies with arms tied behind their backs. One had the throat slit open. One had a big black mark at the back of the neck. A woman had her baby still at her breast.

The SEDOC documents were haunting me, and they were now winning the debate on the atrocities of the Khmer Rouge. Nothing could be worse than killing our own people. Cambodia was slowly turning into a land of blood and tears. It was becoming *noruork knong lok*, a hell on earth.

During the entire exodus, we were terrified each time we saw *yothia* coming in their black pajamas and rubber-tire sandals. We avoided catching their eyes.

It took us ten days to reach the temple where our family had held a *kathen* festival seven years earlier, in 1968. We went to the main *sala*, a Khmer-style building without walls used by the monks as a dining hall. We found an empty corner and planned to spend the night. It was April 27.

I lay down on a mat and began to shiver. My temperature skyrocketed. Mother kept piling blankets over me and tried to hold me to keep me from shaking. Sarin came, put her hand briefly on my forehead, sighed deeply, and left. Half an hour later, she returned with some *sdao*, a bitter plant tasting of quinine. She extracted green liquid until she could fill a silver *phatel* and made me drink the whole bowl of awful-looking, bitter-tasting medicine. I dropped my head to the pillow and went into a deep sleep.

I woke up a few hours later and found that I was surrounded by my loved ones. Mother was still holding my right hand and Sarin the left one. I had no blanket over me, just a big *krama*. The fever had disappeared. Sichhun and Peou were sitting near their daughter. They were quietly discussing the latest news heard over the Voice of America broadcast from Washington. Queen Kossomak, Prince Sihanouk's mother, had died that day in Peking (now Beijing).

The following morning, one of our relatives at Hanuman came to see us. He said that Angka ("The Organization")—the omnipresent, all-powerful, mysterious "National United Front of Kampuchea," led by the Khmer Rouge—was waiting to "welcome" us at the village.

We packed up for the last time. Hanuman and Tonle Bati came under the control of the Khmer Rouge in the early years of the war, during which our relatives had been able to visit us in Phnom Penh.

We arrived at the village in mid-morning on April 28. Our relatives had not changed much and appeared to be happy to see us, at least until the arrival of the Khmer Rouge cadres. They came to record everything that we had brought with us, and our biographies. We were split into three groups: Sarin and her five children; Sichhun, Peou, and their three-year-old daughter; Mother, my three orphaned nieces, two members of our extended families, and me. Each group was sent to live with a "base" family, who had been with the Khmer Rouge from the beginning. We had an eerie feeling that something was going very wrong. Why did they split us up?

Who are these people?

We have never seen them before.

They are not from here.

Have we made a fatal mistake by returning to our ancestral village?

Everyone knows our backgrounds: the police, the military, the government.

Have we walked into the mouth of the lion?

The following day, while I was still recovering from my fever, we were immediately put to toil in slave labor camps. While Mother, Sarin, Peou, and the youngest ones stayed behind to work in the village, the rest of us were sent as "delegates" to Sampoch. We got up before dawn and walked for one hour to join the huge forced-labor site. There were at least 5,000 people, all dressed in black. It was one of the Khmer Rouge dam construction projects. The sound of a drum started the working day even before the first ray of sunlight hit us. We were given only hoes and baskets. We formed antlike rows and passed the baskets of soil from one person to another.

Each village had built small huts for its slave laborers to take a short break at lunchtime. We worked nonstop under the blazing sun in the afternoon and walked back to the village before dark.

It was painful for our family not to be able to communicate verbally. Through our eyes, we shared with each other our sadness and grief, as well as our enormous love and affection.

I was hungry for news and put a transistor radio to my ear at the lowest volume in order to listen to Voice of America. I was risking death, but I was eager to hear the truth. One night, one of the base people, having heard the crackling sound of a broadcast, confiscated the radio and warned me that I would *but kluan*, if I was not careful. "Disappear"—*but kluan*—became the most terrifying two words in the Khmer Rouge vocabulary.

To eliminate the travel time between the village and the forced-labor site, Angka decided that we should live in the makeshift shacks. Some thirty of us slept in a small thatched hut. The roof was quickly damaged in the first rainstorms and we became completely soaked. In the evenings, we sat on the wet, muddy ground listening to communist propaganda about the "new society" and the "new revolutionary person."

You must clean yourselves of everything that has belonged to the old society and work hard to build a brand-new life. You must stop thinking of the evil life of the city. You must serve only the just policies of Angka.

On May 11, my family was told to return to Hanuman. Sichhun, Peou, and other people who had worked in the previous regime were informed that they would be sent to a *prachum* (meeting) on May 14.

At Sampoch labor camp, we had heard about Angka's purification program. We suspected that everyone attending the meeting would be killed. We discreetly asked a relative who was a village elder about our suspicions. He assured us that no such thing would happen. He turned away quickly before we could detect any insincerity in his look.

I was not to be sent to the meeting. Angka did not know that I was a teacher, and therefore, from their point of view, part of the intellectual class. It did not know that I once worked for an airline. In colloquial Khmer, the word *kapal hos* (aircraft) can be understood as airline or air force. Sooner or later, the Khmer Rouge would find out that I had worked for a U.S. agency. So my background posed a great danger to everyone in the family. I was college-educated. I was a teacher. I had worked for the capitalists and imperialists. I had all the qualifications to be immediately eliminated. Thus I felt very insecure; my presence could jeopardize everyone else.

In the dark of the night, I went to Mother and asked for her blessing. It was a heart-wrenching moment.

"You should have left with the Americans," she reminded me of my thirty-minute tardiness. She knew that I could not decide to leave without her. Before I could say anything, she added, "You should not worry about me. I am old. I can die any time. You are young and you have a full life in front of you. Remember what I have been telling you since you were a child: No matter what happens, never give up hope."

"*Bart, Mae*—Yes, Mother," I whispered back to her. I held her hand very tightly. I felt a tear on my hand. Next to me on my right side, Sarin sobbed silently. She reached for my right hand and put some money in it.

"May all the merits I have acquired in my life protect you," *Mae* continued. Then she gave me her wedding ring and a gold necklace that had belonged to her father, Sok Chea, the governor.

I was to begin a desperate bid for freedom. Vietnam, I learned through Voice of America, had fallen to the communists on April 30. My only hope was Thailand, but it was so far away. And I had to leave the village soon, before Angka found out about my real background.

My cousin Panha, who controlled the fraternity purse when I was in a private school in Kampong Cham, had been separated from his family during the exodus, and showed up. I said I would help him find his family. We went to the village chief, who gave us a three-day pass. We did not ask and did not want to know the consequences if we did not return.

The day of the departure, I strapped a yellow bag of rice and some dry fish to the rack of my bicycle behind me. I wrapped Mother's red-and-white checkered *krama* around my neck. I said good-bye to Mother, Sarin, Sichhun, Peou, my nieces, and my nephew without saying a word. Our eyes said it all.

I "saw" *Mae* saying, "May you be protected by the merits I have earned in my life." She added, "Never give up hope" without moving her lips. I knew that Sarin was weeping, but there were no tears. I felt she was saying to me, "I have always loved you. I always will." I "told" her, "I know. So do I." Sichhun and Peou transmitted these words, "Be strong, be well, and be successful," without producing a sound.

It was the most heartbreaking moment.

I turned around quickly before anybody could shed a tear.

We had learned that emotions were totally forbidden in the Khmer Rouge society. And expressing them could mean *but kluan*. I pedaled away in anguished grief, fearful that I would never see *Mae* or the rest of my family again.

At first, Panha and I went to every village along the Bassac (or Basak) River. At Koh Thom, we entered an empty Buddhist temple and found notes for lost loved ones. They were posted everywhere, on abandoned cars in the courtyard, in the main *sala*, at the feet of Buddha images.

One was from a mother telling her daughter that she had moved on southward. One was from a new bride who was separated from her husband because he was on duty in a hospital. She was telling him to go to "that place where you and I were in March and we decided to spend the rest of our lives together." All these loving words tore me apart. It was painful to see families separated by the end of the war.

We looked for notes and names from Panha's family. Nothing. We decided to cross the river to the eastern side. We gave a hand to a teen-age *yothia*. He was struggling to walk his bicycle while carrying a big heavy basket full of green mangoes down the steep bank. We helped him steady it on the human ferry. If he spilled the mangoes into the river, he would be gone. On the other side, we helped him bring his cargo up the riverbank. He did not thank us for our help. We did not thank him for the two mangoes that had disappeared from his basket into our pockets.

It was May 14. We arrived at Leuk Daek and found Panha's family on a register of "new people" who had just arrived to join Angka. We looked for them from house to house of "base families." There was no clue of their living in the area. We concluded that they had just registered their names and proceeded to Kampong Trabaek, where they used to live.

Loudspeakers blasted the news that the Khmer Rouge had captured a capitalist, imperialist ship in the bay of Kampong Som two days earlier. Angka later decided to release the vessel in the spirit of international understanding. It was the *Mayaguez*.

I thought to myself that my poor Cambodia was now being dragged to pure hell by the Khmer Rouge, a bunch of stupid, idiotic, ignorant killers. They became so arrogant after their so-called victory over the Lon Non regime that they thought they could take up a fight with the United States.

The *Mayaguez*, an American merchant ship, was carrying a cargo of food and other merchandise from Hong Kong to the Thai port of Sattahip when it was seized in international waters by Khmer Rouge gunboats. After the humiliating retreat from Cambodia and South Vietnam the previous month, President Ford was determined not to have America's resolve tested. Diplomacy was tried first. The problem was that nobody knew who was running Cambodia and the Chinese refused to be the go-between. The president also ordered measured responses by sending the aircraft carrier USS *Coral Sea* and other ships to the Gulf of Thailand, as well as ordering limited bombing of Khmer Rouge positions, and landing the Marines on Koh Tang. Realizing that they were going to be annihilated, the Khmer Rouge decided to release the crew and the ship. After sixty-five hours, one of the major crises in the Ford administration was over. The cost was high—forty-one Americans were killed during the operations, including some in a helicopter crash.

Freedom is not free.

My cousin and I found many fish in the area. I had been thinking of my family every minute of the day. I was thinking particularly of

Sichhun and Peou. It was the day they were supposed to go to that "meeting." I wanted to bring some fish to *Mae* and Sarin. But I was not sure if they would be there when I arrived. And my return would probably put them in greater danger.

One evening, we prepared our supper and got set to spend the night before dark when I overheard a nearby family mention New Zealand. The whole story came out from a sobbing woman. Her husband was studying in New Zealand for a TEFL diploma. I said to her that if there was a way to get through to her husband, she should tell him not to come back. The Khmer Rouge were undertaking a massive purification program. And those who went overseas to study would be among the first to be killed.

Along the road northward, the sight of decomposed corpses still shocked me, even though they had become familiar since our flight out of Phnom Penh the month before. We reached national route 1 and followed it eastward toward the ferry crossing point of Neak Leuang, on the bank of the Mekong River. The once bustling town had been completely destroyed. The Khmer Rouge set up a welcome center between two walls that were still standing. A voice announced over a loudspeaker that trucks and vans on the eastern bank would transport "newly liberated people" to new homes so that they could take part in "our productive activities outlined by Angka's just and clear-sighted policies." The voice warned us to comply with its moral codes, to become good citizens, and to be ready to fight against all enemies. "We must destroy them."

As I sat down to open my lunch box, I heard some Chinese Cambodians crying in the *yothia* area. Angka had caught one of their sons pumping gas from an abandoned vehicle. The family was begging for his return. "You must disperse right now and do nothing to cause disorder," said an angry voice over the loudspeaker. "Your son will be all right. We sent him to Angka Leu ("Higher Organization," that is, the executioner) to be reeducated (killed). Don't make Angka angry; otherwise you will be very sorry!" A few minutes after the group dispersed, I heard a gun-shot.

The next day, my cousin and I reached Kampong Trabaek. There was no human being, only rubble and a few stray dogs. We moved on to Kansaom Awk and found everybody, including Panha's father.

I am now on my own. I cannot go to Vietnam. I am not going to jump from a communist frying pan into a communist fire. My hope is Thailand. But it is about 500 miles away. I will have to travel from the Parrot's Beak in the southeastern part of Cambodia all the way to the northwest. There will be hundreds of checkpoints. The prospect of my getting there unnoticed looks grim.

Then I heard Mae's voice: *"No matter what happens, never give up hope!"*

The following day, I left. I was the loneliest person on earth. Not knowing what had happened to *Mae*, my sister, and my brother was torturing me. But I had to move onward.

I had developed a strategy, if I wanted to stay alive and make it to freedom. I would learn the names of a few villages in the direction I was traveling. That way, if I was stopped by Khmer Rouge soldiers, I would tell them I was going to the next village.

I pedaled my bike north toward the Mekong River. I reached the village of Svay Antor and went west through Cheehae in Kampong Cham where my aunt used to live. There I bartered some rice for tobacco and palm sugar. These were my trading currencies. The riel had been banned from circulation. Cambodia was now a country without currency.

At the riverbank, I got a ride on a boat crossing to the other side. I moved west but came on the river again. I realized that I was on an is-land, which was totally deserted. I was frightened at the thought that I was going to spend the rest of my life there. I was sitting on the bank, praying and hoping that I would be rescued. Every day since I left my family, before I had my meals I always put a few grains of rice on a tree leaf as an offering to supernatural powers, seeking their protection. Cambodians believe that there are protective spirits who live in the trees and forest. They are known as *rukhak tevoda*.

By late afternoon, two fishermen rowed their boats by. I proposed giving them some rice, if they took me to the west bank. One agreed to do so the next morning. He told me I could spend the night on his boat.

"What did you do in the old regime?" the fisherman asked.

"I was a taxi and bus driver," I responded without thinking.

"Where?"

"Kampong Cham!"

"Where are you going?"

"Kampong Thom!"

"What are you going to do there?"

"Join my family, who have been with Angka since the beginning of the revolution!"

As I looked at the bright skies, I felt that *Mae* was looking at the same stars. At one point, I saw the shape of her face. Her voice called out to me: "Never give up hope."

Before I went to sleep that night, I realized that I must have a new identity. Although my vision was not good, I had thrown away my glasses since the exodus from Phnom Penh, knowing that they were a sign of an educated person.

I could not be an educated person.

The first time I filled out the *pravatarup* (the Khmer Rouge word for biography), I put myself down as having a primary education. I found out that this was still high. So I reduced it to third grade. I ran through my new bio in my head:

What's your level of education?

I can read a little bit.

What did you do in the old regime?

I was a taxi and bus driver. If they ask me to drive one, I can do it.

What is your name?

My name is Sok Chan.

I had to cut my first name in half. "Sichan" sounded upper-class and would give away my true identity. I used the name of my great-grandfather as a family name.

Where are you from?

Kampong Cham.

That is less dangerous than being from Phnom Penh. Besides, if they wanted to test my knowledge of the city, I would pass.

The Khmer Rouge had smashed Cambodia into two groups of submissive beings: the workers, or *kamakaw*; and the peasants, or *kaksekaw*—or *neak srae* in colloquial Khmer. I could be both, but I decided to make myself a *kamakaw*, hoping that if they asked me to drive, I would have no problem.

I woke up with the fisherman before dawn. He floated the boat down the river and started to throw his net into the Mekong. He caught a lot of fish and I helped him empty his net. A few hours later, he let me off the boat at Piamcheekawng. I gave him some rice and he offered me some fish. I gave him a *sampeah* and said *Awkun!*

As I was steadying my bike on the bank, the fisherman came to me and whispered, "I hope you will find your family." He knew that I had lied to him about my background. I was not supposed to salute him and thank him. There was to be no courtesy in the new, pure society. But he added slowly, "Be very careful! *Stay on the road!*"

"*Bart!*"

I left the fishing village that morning counting my blessings. I reached national route 6 north of Skoon and headed for Santuk and Kampong Thom. I realized that I was now exactly at the center of Cambodia.

I have made some progress, inching slowly toward Thailand. I have only halfway to go.

The road became more deserted. Most of the time, I found myself

alone. And the Khmer Rouge checkpoints were getting more frequent. The people at the checkpoints asked me the same questions:
"Where are you coming from? Where are you going? Do you have a
pass?"

My answer was always the same: "I am coming from serving
Angka. I am going back to———. Yes, I do have a pass." I filled in the
blank with the name of the next village.

I felt that I had to outsmart the Khmer Rouge in order to survive.
I always gave them the name of the next village to assure them that I
was not going far; they could catch me there if they wanted to. My
travel pass had expired. I had changed the number of days twice already. First, by drawing a rising tail on the Khmer number three, I got
a seven. Then I added a one before the seven and it became seventeen.
Soon, I would need a new pass.

But how do I get a pass?

I hurried on, stopping briefly for quick meals. At night I found a
big tree far from the road. I laid my bike on the ground and prayed
before I went into a fitful sleep.

On May 24, 1975, at Staung a *yothia* caught me off guard by not
asking the usual questions. I told him anyway that I was coming from
digging irrigation canals in Kampong Thom; I was going to Kampong
Kdei; I had a pass.

He did not listen to me and asked me to follow him. Actually, he
walked behind me. He carried an AK-47, which was as tall as he was.
He must have been twelve or thirteen. He brought me to a *wat* where I
joined some 300 people. That evening in a large *sala*, the chief of the
commune committee instructed us to tell Angka our true identity so
that we could be properly reeducated as "new revolutionary citizens."
He said, "The traitor Lon Nol has let you down; he has fled for his own
life. Angka will never abandon you." We were assigned to live in different villages to start our new, productive lives.

As the night was getting darker, I walked clockwise around the *preah vihear* (main chapel) pretending to look for some firewood. I looked at the skies, trying to find *Mae*'s face. And I prayed.

The next morning, it was quite chaotic. The "new" people were trying to find the "old" people who represented the villages of their new lives.

In the confusion, I jumped on my bike and rode away. A few minutes later, I heard long, sustained machine-gun shots. I pedaled very fast for at least a few hours before I slowed down. I was thankful that I had just escaped, even barely, being machine-gunned and buried in a mass grave. I was fast enough to flee as the guns were about to open up.

Near Kampong Kdei, which is known for a twelfth-century bridge, I learned that the Khmer Rouge were arresting anybody on national route 6, which I was still following. I hid for two days and then set out at nightfall.

In the heart of darkness as I approached Kampong Kdei, I heard a shout:

"Hey, *Mit*, where are you going?"

"To the other side of the bridge!" I shouted back. I heard footsteps running toward me, but I did not stop. I was holding my breath for the sound of an AK-47. None. Taking me for a local villager, the soldiers decided not to pursue me or shoot me.

Rain began to fall very heavily and forced me to take refuge under an enormous banyan tree not too far from the road. There I fell asleep for a few hours. I was awakened by the sound of voices and approaching footsteps. I was crouching now and pulled my legs closer to my body. I wrapped them tight with my arms. It was a small unit of Khmer Rouge soldiers who were patrolling the area. They stopped. And I saw a flashlight beam hitting the banyan tree. I was on the other side.

"Are you sure he was a local villager?" asked an authoritative voice

"Yes. He did not have anything on his bike," answered one boyish-sounding voice. "He was probably coming from serving Angka and hurrying home," said another.

The flashlight hit the tree a few more times. But the Khmer Rouge did not leave the road to walk toward the banyan tree.

"We will check it out one more time in the morning," said the first voice.

The footsteps faded away. And the night became completely silent. I did not go back to sleep. I waited until the starry skies became clear to look for Mother's face. The first crow of the rooster indicated that the sun would rise shortly.

I got up and fell down. I attempted to get up again but could not. My legs were locked in a tight crouching position. I massaged my limbs for a long time before I managed to get up slowly.

At the pre-Angkor capital of Roluos, I knew I could not get through Siem Reap safely and detoured north through rice paddies and a forest. I emerged behind one of the major temples of Angkor and came on at least 200 Khmer Rouge soldiers resting by the roadside. A few of them surrounded me. They asked where I was coming from, where I was going, and if I had a pass.

"I came from digging an irrigation canal at Preah Dak. I am going to Krabei Real. Yes, I have a pass!"

I went back to my standard answers, which had not worked at Staung. But this time I changed the story a little bit. I told them that the chief of my unit would be coming along shortly. He also had a pass for our entire group. I gave the soldiers some tobacco; they let me go.

I rode my bike along the southern moat of Angkor Wat. I remembered my first visit with *Mae*, and the subsequent ones. I remembered that aborted HKG-REP flight in 1970, shortly before Angkor came under the control of the Khmer Rouge.

I became quite emotional when I saw the banyan tree under which *Mae* and I, along with my uncle and his family, had a picnic the first day we arrived for our pilgrimage in 1959.

I noticed three Khmer Rouge soldiers relaxing under the tree. One slept in a hammock; one slept on a split-bamboo bed; the third was crouching against the tree. Each had an AK-47 with a tiny red ribbon tied to the barrel. It must have been the insignia of their unit. Hearing the sound of my bike, they all stood up but did not touch their guns. I approached them slowly and gave them my standard answers before hearing their questions. I shared with them some dessert of black beans and palm sugar, which I had prepared that morning. After the dessert, I asked them if I could go inside to have a quick look. The *yothia* responded negatively. They said that Angkor Wat was a prohibited zone because *mitneary* (female soldiers) were staying there. They allowed me to go down to the moat to replenish my water supply.

I knelt down, drank a lot of water from the moat, and filled my bottle with it. As I admired the beauty of Angkor Wat for what could be the last time, I prayed that *Mae*'s merits and all the supernatural powers would guide me safely out of Cambodia.

I left Angkor Wat in the afternoon and rode westward toward the airport. I stopped a few times to look back at the magnificent monument behind me. At the airport, I turned left and soon was back on national route 6. That night as I was looking for a place to sleep, I heard laughter coming out of a little wooden house.

"*Mit!* Comrades! May I come in?" I shouted.

Out of the sudden quietness, a voice asked, "Who is there?"

"I came from serving Angka in some productive works near Angkor Wat."

Out of the door, I saw a kerosene lamp first, then a right hand, and then a kid with a gun over his left shoulder. The house turned out to be a Khmer Rouge command post. It was manned by seven soldiers. They must have been between fourteen and sixteen years old.

As a Cambodian saying goes, "If you are in the mouth of a tiger, play with its teeth!" The teenage *yothia* led me inside and shared his supper of freshly cooked rice and dry fish. After we had gone to sleep on the floor, five more soldiers arrived. They asked about my presence and the reply was, "Don't make any noise. Our *bong* (older brother or sister) is resting. He is just back from serving our Angka."

I never knew that word had so much power.

The next day, as I was approaching Puak and the border between Siem Reap and Battambang, I heard that the control was extremely strict. I would not get through without a pass. I was slowed down by a bent wheel and a few broken spokes. Although Angka prohibited trading, I approached a villager and proposed exchanging some rice and a sarong given to me by my sister Sarin for a wheel of her abandoned bike. She was unmoved by the merchandise, even though people were eager to get new clothing.

I must have that wheel. The difference between walking and riding a bike is day and night. I must get to the border as quickly as possible.

I told her that Angka would appreciate her helping me out. I had come from carrying out some revolutionary work. She still did not budge. The goddamned Angka, so powerful last night, had lost its luster.

"Do you have any *thanam?*" she said, finally opening her mouth.

"*Bart!*" I answered positively and added a pile of tobacco in front of her.

"No, *thanam!*" she corrected me.

This is a confusing word—it means both tobacco and medicine. She must be looking for the latter. I reached out for my little leather "Alabama" pouch that Sichhun gave me. I found some tablets and gave her a few aspirins. I told her how to use them and when: only in absolute necessity. She removed the wheel from the bike and handed it over to me.

The following day, I stopped at another peasant's house. I asked a little naked boy playing near a big water jar if he had any paper for me to roll a cigarette. He ran inside the mud house and returned with a torn page from a schoolbook. I asked him if he had anything pointed, like a pencil or a pen, for me to remove something from my feet. He ran in and came back with a red Bic pen. I gave him a piece of palm sugar. He happily grabbed it.

A moment later, I stopped to have lunch under a big banyan tree, which Cambodians considered sacred. As always, I put some rice on a leaf and offered it to the spirits and supernatural powers. I prayed for a safe journey to freedom. I took out the piece of paper and wrote my own pass with some familiar words: "National United Front . . . blah, blah, blah . . . The Chief of Puak village allows Comrade Chan to travel to Sisophon in the province of Battambang to look for his family for seven days, from May 30 to June 5, 1975."

At the first barricade I encountered, the soldier looked at the pass upside down and exclaimed, "Who was the comrade who used a red pen to write a dirty pass like this?" I told him that my village chief was working in the rice paddy and could not get a proper piece of paper. I added in a firm tone that I had served Angka for a long time; otherwise, I would not be able to get a seven-day leave. Acknowledging my seniority, he let me pass.

The teenager with a machine gun at the next checkpoint could not read and called out for his commander. He came to grab the paper from the soldier. He looked at it on both sides, back and forth, upside down and downside up, and gave it back to me.

I had gone for miles without seeing a mile marker. The markers must have been removed. The very few that were still there had the numbers painted over. I had no idea where I was, except that I was still on national route 6. The road had now become completely deserted.

Somewhere between Kralanh and Preah Netr Preah, I came upon a convoy of trucks, vans, and cars chained to each other. They were towed by an International Harvester truck. The Khmer Rouge were collecting all abandoned vehicles on the roadside and bringing them back to Sisophon. I went to meet their chief, a tall man who spoke with a heavy northwestern accent. We went through the usual introductions.

"What's your name?"

"Chan!"

"Where are you coming from?"

"Puak."

"Were you born there?"

"No. Kampong Cham!"

"Where are you going?"

"Svay!" I gave him the popular name for Sisophon.

"Svay?"

"*Bart*, Svay!"

"Do you know anybody there?"

"*Bart!* My family used to live there!"

"Do you have a travel authorization?"

"*Bart!*"

"Does it have a provincial seal?"

"*Bart!*"

I managed to remain calm on the surface although my heart was pounding faster and faster as I answered the chief's questions and I felt a lump in my throat: the last one could have given me away. To my great relief, he did not ask to see the pass, which did not have a provincial seal. I asked him for a ride. He told me to put my bike on the last truck. As I turned around to lift my precious transportation, he shouted:

"*Mit!*"

"*Bart?*"

"Can you steer a wheel?"

"*Bart!* I was a truck driver!"

"Good. You take that one."

We stopped at a *wat* to add two more trucks. I helped chain them together and went back to mine. As I was cleaning my new vehicle, the chief sent for me to join the convoy party for lunch. For the first time since I left Phnom Penh, I had more than one dish. And it was not dry salty fish, but freshly prepared dishes with chicken and vegetables. I ate like a pig.

During our frequent stops to check the towing chains, I noticed more and more soldiers. Before dusk, we made it to Sisophon, a very important strategic town, where routes 5 and 6 merged toward Thailand.

At Sisophon, we parked all the vehicles inside an empty school. The ground was strewn with all kinds of books. The town had been emptied. Only Angka was there. It was everywhere.

I went to thank the chief quietly for the lift and told him that I did not know where my family was. Until I was able to join them, "I will do anything for Angka." The following morning, the chief told me that I could work in his unit as a mechanic. I knew nothing about car engines and had to learn the Khmer version of broken French used by the mechanics. The first few weeks I got many cuts and bruises, but I continued to work very hard to earn the trust of the Khmer Rouge. One night, the chief of our work gang came to me for a chat. This was quite unusual. I suspected he was trying to get more information about my background.

"Do you still have your travel authorization with the provincial seal?"

"*Bart!*"

"Can you show it to me?"

"*Bart!*" I said my prayers when pretending to look for it.

"Keep it there safely!" The senior Khmer Rouge official instructed me, stood up, and left, as he was being called away.

That was a close call. I lay down on my folded bamboo bed and looked at the skies. It was June 4, 1975. I was searching for *Mae*'s face. I was thinking of Sarin. I had come to Sisophon many times to visit her when I was a young boy. I remembered that she took me across the Thai border to Aranyaprathet. I faded and fell asleep.

I was wakened by two Khmer Rouge cadres and two soldiers carrying AK-47s. They wore black pajamas, tire sandals, checkered *kramas*, and Mao caps. They instructed me to drive them to Preah Netr Preah ("Buddha's Eyes") immediately. I went to the garage and looked for a car with the newest license number and an ignition key. I found a Peugeot 404 station wagon. I turned the key and it started. At Preah Netr

Preah, I waited for my passengers in the courtyard of a school after they went into a meeting. When they came out, the car would not start; its tank was empty. We pushed it to the side and got another one from a nearby garage. This time I made sure that there was gas in the tank. I was praying all the way back to Sisophon. When the Khmer Rouge got out of the car, the most senior cadre (with three pens in his breast pocket—the more pens, the higher the person) gave me a pack of cigarettes. I was so thankful—instead of being punished I was rewarded—that I forgot the rules and gave him a *sampeah*. "Don't ever do that!" He warned me and disappeared into the night.

The following day, our group was sent to Tamaw Puak. We were going to retrieve some more abandoned vehicles and bring them back to Sisophon. In mid-afternoon, I asked my chief for permission to look for my family. After walking west for a few hours, I arrived at Kauk Romiat. This was the last village before the border. It was dark, and I asked a villager for shelter. He invited me to join his family for supper and let me sleep on the verandah.

The next morning, five men came to take me to see the village chief. To the inevitable question about a pass, I told him I was traveling with a vehicular unit in Tamaw Puak and that the chief had the pass. The village leader asked his men to search my bag. They found some rice and a few clothes. Concluding that I was trying to cross the border, they "asked" to tie my arms behind my back above the elbows.

Two of them escorted me back to Tamaw Puak. One walked in front. The other followed me with a machete. He kept on slashing plants, vines, and trees along the way. I was frightened that he might miss them and hit me. Or he could simply hit me.

I prayed to Lord Buddha, to *Mae*'s merits, to the *rukhak tevodas* (forest spirits), to everything.

I was taken to the commune chief of Tamaw Puak. He asked his people to untie me. He gave me a delicious meal of chicken and beef and invited me to spend the night there before continuing the search for my family.

My unit chief, sensing that I would be executed if I stayed overnight, insisted that I be returned to his team. He needed me to steer
one of the trucks back: "Angka needs *mit* Chan at Sisophon." The
commune chief relented after having realized that he was outranked
by the mysterious Angka at the district level.

Chim Chun was a real *neak srae*, a peasant, from Battambang. He had
been a truck driver all his adult life, and the northwest was his territory. I did not think he was a Khmer Rouge. But the Khmer Rouge needed
him. They made him the chief of the Sisophon motor vehicle unit. Besides being a *kamakaw*, Chun knew the region like the palm of his hand.
In the old society, he had driven everywhere in the northwest: Kampong
Thom, Preah Vihear, Siem Reap, Odaw Meanchey, Battambang, and
Posat. Route 69 between Sisophon and Samraong was his playground. He
had relatives in Tabaen, Treas, Slaw Kram, and Tamaw Puak. His mother
was still living in the Svay Chek area. On the way back to Sisophon, we
stopped there to inspect the towing chain and take a little break.

The previous week, the chief had let me ride in his convoy through
one of the heavily controlled cordons into Sisophon. And he got me a
job in Angka. Now, he had just saved my life from it. And he was angry. He walked to the back of the convoy to warn me to stay with the
unit, "Be careful. *Don't leave the road.*" I had a feeling that he knew I
was not what I said—that I was somebody else. But he did not say a
word. He never inquired further about my background to find out more
than I had already said. It was a classic "live and let live" situation.

THE MONK

A few days later our unit was moved to the Wat Svay Chas, Sisophon's
main Buddhist temple. I managed to smuggle with me to the *wat* some
geography books, which I had found on the school grounds. I tore a

few pages out to show that I had been using them to roll cigarettes. I had learned to smoke, because the Khmer Rouge distributed tobacco as part of our ration and allowed smoke breaks during the slaves' workday, and cigarettes could be used to barter. I choked a few times and blamed the incidents on the different flavor of the tobacco. A fellow *kamakaw* knew I did not know how to smoke but kept his mouth shut. It was an unstated code, which we, the "new" people, had come to learn and live with.

Hungry, sick, and exhausted, I had managed to drag myself this far across my burning homeland. I was so close, yet so far. And I was approaching the end of me. I was physically weak, but my spiritual and moral strength now received a boost from the Buddhist temple.

None of my coworkers wanted to live at the *wat*. The workers had moved into some of the best houses nearby. I had the whole empty monastery to myself. I found a small, beautiful wooden *kod* (monk's house) on the bank of the Sisophon River. There was a mosquito net over a simple wooden bed. A small statue of Buddha and incense sticks in a can of fine sand were placed on a tiny altar, above a small window that opened up to a nice view of the river. It was perfect for me. I found a straw broom and began to clean the *kod* and its surroundings.

One afternoon I came back from the garage and was stunned to see a Buddhist monk getting off a boat.

How can it be?

Am I hallucinating?

Angka had been disrobing monks and killing them, calling them, Buddhism, and other religions the bloodsuckers of our society.

Is this real? I asked myself again and again.

The monk told me that he used to live at the *wat*, in that little wooden *kod*. He had been a monk since he was a boy. He was now living by himself in a makeshift monastery about an hour downstream. He asked if the statue of Buddha was still there. I said yes and invited him inside. He thanked me for keeping his little *kod* and the ground so neat. I picked up the image of Buddha with both hands to present it to the monk, but he stopped me.

"No. You should keep it."

"I have plenty of Buddha statues in the *preah vihear*," I assured him.

"I know, but I want you to keep mine. This way I can communicate with you. Lord Buddha will protect you. He will lead you out of this hell. He will lead you to Thailand. Your mother's merits will also protect you. And if your mother's milk is dear (*tuck dos mae thalay*), you will make it to freedom. And you will make it anywhere. The little stand on which the Buddha sits is hollow. There we can leave messages for each other. I'll be back! I'll be back! At least one more time!"

I knelt down in front of the monk, put my two hands in front of my forehead, and brought them down three times to the wooden floor while the monk whispered some blessings. He left, boarded the raggedy palm-tree boat, and disappeared into the mist and the sunset.

Early in the morning, I went to the *preah vihear* and collected candles, incense, and matches. I wrapped them properly with rubber bands and hid them under my pillow. I put a bundle of dry firewood on the bed and dropped the mosquito net over it. I left a short note for the monk under the statue of Buddha.

As a member of a mobile *kamakaw* gang of some thirty slave workers, I was sent from one place to another. We did all kinds of forced labor for eighteen to twenty hours a day. We demolished, reassembled, and rebuilt houses. We made the dikes around the rice paddies straight. Angka wanted it that way, because the old curved dikes were from the exploiting colonialist and capitalist classes and thus did not conform to the *padevort* (revolution). Never mind that Cambodians had been cultivating rice for a few thousand years and that the curved dikes had been built that way to contain water in the fields.

We rebuilt roads and dug irrigation canals. We plowed land. We planted, harvested, and husked rice. My boyhood experience in rice cultivation with my relatives in Tonle Bati came in handy. We sometimes worked in water up to our chests and we were bitten incessantly by mosquitoes, other insects, and leeches.

We returned to Sisophon for a few days to fix some vehicles. I rushed to my little monk's house. I lifted the mosquito net and my pillow: everything was gone. I gently lifted the statue of Buddha and found the following message:

"Thank you very much for the candles, incense, and matches which I need so badly. I will also make good use of the firewood. Lord Buddha will protect you. Your mother's merits and milk will help you make it anywhere. May you always be blessed by the triple gem. Follow the sun and the moon. Memorize these words!"

I was thrilled to be able to communicate with the mysterious, wise monk. Before my unit departed for another deathly slave camp, I managed to leave the same things for him.

Our group lived in abandoned houses or shelters that we put up ourselves. A small *sethakej* (economy) team of two people would be responsible for finding food and preparing meals. We were entitled to a mere tin of rice per day. Those who got sick had their ration cut in half. In the summer, we were bitten by mosquitoes. When it got cold, we had no blankets. And we were not allowed to burn firewood to keep ourselves warm.

I had completely changed my identity. My mantra was, "I see nothing; I hear nothing; I know nothing." I had learned not to open my mouth, fearing that French words would come out. The greater danger for me, however, was my height. And I could not do anything about it, except crouch when I was in company of other people. At six feet, I was very tall for a Cambodian. That could create some suspicion among the Khmer Rouge. I must have been well fed in the past. I must have belonged to the despised bourgeois class—a class that must be destroyed.

E ach night, after eighteen hours of hard labor, we continued to be lectured on the revolution. I managed to find water—in rice paddies, ponds, creeks, rivers—and took a bath every night before I went to sleep. I decided that if I were going to die that night, I would die clean, just like my father, who was bathed before being put into a coffin in 1957. I looked at the skies searching for *Mae*'s presence and praying, before I closed my eyes, that I would live to see freedom. Dark clouds began to block the moon from my view. Suddenly, a giant helicopter appeared, with soldiers sliding down the ropes. Two of them strapped a harness around my torso and hooked it to a cable from the helicopter. A teenage Khmer Rouge soldier, hidden behind a tree, started shooting at the chopper. A bullet hit me.

I woke up and realized that I was still alive, and still in Cambodia. I would tell myself that I would make it to Thailand. I used ashes as toothpaste and my index finger as toothbrush. And then I would try to survive another day of tyrannical slave labor.

On September 8, we learned that Prince Sihanouk had returned to Cambodia from his exile in China. A Khmer Rouge soldier listening to the radio with us exclaimed, "He is still the enemy of our revolution."

We were never certain who was ruling Cambodia. One thing was sure: teenage soldiers had the power of life and death over ordinary citizens. As time went by, the rules became more and more strict. We were urged to make more sacrifices for Angka. We were instructed to continue to enlarge and strengthen our revolutionary position. Our political education became an open threat: if we could not follow the pace of the revolution, we would be crushed by the wheel of history. I listened to the communist propaganda with revulsion. These thugs had been completely brainwashed. They were ruling Cambodia with mindless horror and terror. And I felt that there was a deafening silence from the outside world.

Death could come in many ways. Besides exhaustion, starvation, and sickness, making mistakes could mean the end. *But kluan*—you would just disappear.

I n mid-September 1975 our work gang was sent to rebuild a section of route 69 between Makak and Treas. We set up our base camp at Kalaeng Poar. That was where we brought our trucks to get soil from bulldozers and earthmoving equipment. One rainy night, I was driving a heavy truck fully loaded. I slowly backed up to unload the soil, but the back wheels slid and the truck flipped on its side. I crawled out of the truck on broken glass and cut my hands, knees, and nose. My immediate reaction was to escape the hell right away: destruction of state property incurred a death sentence. But it was the height of the rainy season and there was water everywhere. I would not make it very far. So I ran quickly to get help to put the truck upright. We got the truck back on the road the minute the supervising Khmer Rouge soldiers arrived. The commander asked about the damages.

Chim Chun, ever the guardian angel, saved my life for the second time. "It takes only a few moments to fix it." He asked, and received the permission, for me to drive the truck back to Sisophon. He feared I might be executed that night.

On arrival, I rushed to the monastery. At the monk's house, my heart sank. The statue of Buddha, the mosquito net, the pillow, and the straw mat had all disappeared.

For three days, I sat by the little window looking out for the monk to return. That night I saw the monk in a dream. I saw him through my *kod's* window. He was standing on the water, in the misty river. He told me not to worry about him.

"I will disappear for a while. But you must take good care of yourself. Remember the words I left for you in the message under the Buddha. Follow the sun and the moon and you will be all right!"

As his image disappeared, I woke up and ran outside. I looked all around. He was nowhere to be found. I saw the reflection of the moon in the river. I looked up and saw the incredible beauty of the full moon.

It took us three days to fix a bent hydraulic pump. I returned to our base camp and was assigned to the kitchen for the day. The regular cook was sick and every *kamakaw* had done his tour.

Our unit had gotten smaller and now had equal numbers of workers and soldiers—six and six. I had to cook for the whole gang. The only supplies provided by Angka were rice and salt. The cook was responsible for getting the meals together. We had been eating all kinds of things: insects, lizards, rats, snakes.

I set out immediately to search for food. I found some green papayas and made them into pickles. That was not enough for twelve people, especially for the six soldiers. I must find something else quickly. Suddenly, bang! A brief sound of a dying animal followed, and total silence. I ran to the road and saw a black van speeding away. It was obviously a Khmer Rouge vehicle. Nobody else had cars in Cambodia. After the dust settled, I saw a dead dog. I looked at the dog for a moment to make sure it was really dead. I dragged it to the kitchen and worked on it. Although dogs are a delicacy in some Asian countries, especially China, Korea, and Vietnam, I had never cooked one before. It was the first time for me. And also the last time. The Khmer Rouge were delighted to have meat and complimented me on my cooking skills.

We were supposed to train the *yothia* to use the heavy equipment. Once they learned how to operate it, the trainers would be sent back to their villages or to their regular prisoner-slave gangs. My job as a truck driver was still safe. The Khmer Rouge thought they could learn how to drive a truck anytime. They were more interested in learning how to operate the heavier equipment: bulldozers, graders, levelers, and loaders.

I continued to build more trust with the *yothias*. One day, I found an AK-47 left behind under a tree by the dusty road. One of the Khmer Rouge soldiers, excited about getting a ride on a leveler to the base camp, had forgotten his weapon. For a brief moment, I thought that I could use it to kill all six of them. But I would not escape their pursuit. They were everywhere. I was close to the border but not close enough to make it in a single run.

I brought the gun back to the base camp. The Khmer Rouge were having their lunch. Their chief exclaimed, "*Mit* Chan is a true member of the revolution. He could have sprayed us all with bullets, but he did not." The soldier who forgot the gun could have been punished severely for losing his weapon. But the Khmer Rouge had different standards of correction.

In October, I developed a high fever and a bad case of diarrhea. The soldiers took me to a small hospital in a nearby *wat*. There was nothing for the teenage medical assistants to treat me with. I was thinking of Sarin. If she were with me, she would have given me some *sdao*.

Having seen me brought in by *yothia*, the nurses assumed that I was also a soldier. They sent for an ambulance to transport me to a large revolutionary hospital in Sisophon, where I was placed in a ward reserved for *yothia*. Medicine was also scarce there. Young and inexperienced medical staff members came in and asked if I had an injection. They gave me one every day. I did not know what the injection was. They did not bother to find out what kind of illness I was suffering from. But they gave an injection, one every day. That should be enough. As good revolutionaries, we were expected to cope with pain.

The hospital in Sisophon also served as a medical school. The first lesson for the new trainees was to bury corpses—up to a dozen a day.

They would dig a hole big enough for two or three bodies and bury them all together. No patient dared to complain about anything, much less the depressing scene of the burial site. Life was indescribably cheap under the Khmer Rouge and Pol Pot. He and his top comrades (fewer than ten people) had joined the French leftist movement in the 1950s while studying in Paris on government scholarships. They were all related by marriage and through radical communist ideology. On returning to Cambodia, they were outcasts from a peaceful society. They joined the maquis and began to spread their "revolutionary" culture. The Vietcong and North Vietnamese nurtured them. And the Khmer Rouge unexpectedly defeated the Lon Nol regime in April 1975.

Our food ration consisted of porridge, soup containing tiny pieces of vegetables, salt, and soy sauce. After fifteen days, I had regained enough strength to leave the medical school-cum-hospital-cum-burial ground.

In November, Angka was looking for a crane operator. I raised my hand, saying that I had been one in the previous regime. I had never been in a crane before in my life, but I knew the job would take me even closer to the border. The Khmer Rouge were going to use the crane to pick up some teak near the famous twelfth-century temple of Banteay Chamar. They needed the wood to build new warehouses. I was transferred to a sawmill unit and was now living on its compound.

How am I going to operate the crane?

I found an instructional manual! At night, I burned a small candle, pulling a blanket over me, even though I was aware that this could give me away. I studied the manual and felt comfortable enough to climb onto the crane. I was horrified when I saw my new equipment. It was a raggedy old machine converted from an ancient GMC truck, with a single cable and two long pieces of wood used to support the hook. The first few times, it was a challenging trial. I assured the Khmer Rouge that it was a different machine and I would get used to it soon enough. I remember an old saying, "In the kingdom of the blind, the one-eyed man is king."

We made trips to the frontier area two or three times a week. Each trip allowed me to study the terrain. I found out that the shortest distance to Thailand was somewhere between the timber pickup point at Banteay Chamar and the nearest town of Tamaw Puak. I seized every opportunity when I was out of earshot of the Khmer Rouge to ask peasants, villagers, and people familiar with the area about the region. They told me it took them less than a day to reach the border by foot from either place.

I also learned that the border between route 69 and Thailand was strictly patrolled. It was heavily mined, and the jungle could be very thick. I told myself that I had a fifty-fifty chance of making it.

The geography books I found in the schoolyard at Sisophon were helpful. If I walked due west, I could not get anywhere but Thailand.

THE LEAP

It had been a long, exhausting day. I stared numbly at the hauling chain as it lifted one heavy tree trunk after the next. I had spent the entire work shift trying to analyze my chances for survival, if I took the leap that afternoon.

I knew that I was terribly weak, after months of existing on the one bowl of rancid vegetable soup provided each day by the surly gangsters who ran the slave labor system for Angka. Already weighing less than 130 pounds—at six feet tall—and battling chronic dysentery along with many tormenting skin infections, I understood that I was rapidly running out of strength, and time.

My nervous system was also near collapse.

Working eighteen hours a day at gunpoint, enduring incessant threats, watching while other struggling wretches went to their knees and then fell face-first into the mud—how long would it be before I began to shriek and babble like so many other demented souls in this murderous hell?

Shoveling mud out of a ditch, or clawing with blistered fingers at another rain-soaked log, I had spent endless hours fighting back waves of devastating grief as I summoned up memories of the world I had lost—the world of tiny Pochentong. And my brother and sister. And my nephew and nieces skipping rope in the deep, sweet grass of the green fields. And my beloved *Mae*, slowly stirring her pot of fragrant vegetable soup, the savory *samlaw kawko* which had been my favorite mealtime treat.

Those things were gone. Forever.

But I couldn't cry. There were no tears left. Not even when I remembered how my mother held me in her arms, long ago in the innocence of my vanished childhood, and had sung old Khmer songs to me until finally she would smile with gentle love, and remind me once again of how she had chosen the birth name for her youngest son: "You were born under the full moon, dear son; you will always be my Sichan, my 'beautiful moon.'"

Gone.

I was twenty-seven years old now, with childhood far behind me. I was also a prisoner of the most vicious and homicidal slave labor system of its time. And if I somehow did manage to escape from these insane tormentors (not very likely, given my weakened physical condition), would I ever be able to find my sixty-three-year-old mother and my brother and sister again? Were they even alive? Would I ever again walk the streets of my drowsy, tranquil Pochentong, or watch the tropical sunset flash bright gold in the lapping waters of the Tonle Sap?

Probably not.

The Cambodia that I had known and loved had gone up in smoke, before my eyes.

Although I had not read a single newspaper during the past ten months in the labor camps, I had witnessed enough horrors to guess the awful truth. My country was being destroyed, day by day and hour by hour. And its people were being slaughtered like helpless sheep.

Less than one year after the victorious Khmer Rouge had come swaggering into Phnom Penh (April 17, 1975), the countryside lay in ruins. The mass extermination of nearly 2 million Cambodians was well under way. With a population of only 8 million, and an area the size of Missouri, this country had been flung into one of the twentieth century's grimmest nightmares. The insane youth squads directed by Pol Pot and his Khmer Rouge henchmen did their best to "cleanse" the landscape of the educated middle class, and to replace it with a uto-pian, agrarian society that would be free of "western imperialism and corruption."

After enduring almost five years of the brutal violence that had accompanied the war between the Cambodians and the Vietcong and North Vietnamese, the communist Khmer Rouge had finally prevailed—and had obviously been driven insane by the relentless pounding they had taken from all sides.

M y country was on fire, and there was nobody who could put the fire out. During an eternity of agony seeing people starve, die, and disappear and watching children writhe in disease, I had been forced to admit the ghastly truth: I couldn't save Cambodia.

But could I save the tiny part of Cambodia that was me?

Dear Lord Buddha . . .

Trembling with fatigue and malnutrition, I watched a brief rain shower spatter the glistening teak logs. I weighed my chances for sur-viving a leap into the abyss.

But there was not much time left for such speculation; the work shift at this timber-loading site was rapidly coming to an end.

In a few moments, our unit would be climbing back on the rusty GMC log-hauler for the two-hour ride back to the district town of

Sisophon, its headquarters. Quickly, I ticked off the few precious assets that I knew I could count on during a desperate attempt at flight. These included my strong U.S. Army ranger boots and my black-dyed fatigue jacket. I also had a bayonet-knife from an American-made M-16 rifle that had been given to me months before, after I returned an AK-47 to the Khmer Rouge unit that controlled my work gang.

I also had a bottle of fresh water that I carried everywhere. Accustomed to watching me take swigs from this precious vessel in recent weeks, the guards at the labor camp no longer found it suspicious, or worried that it might be part of an escape attempt.

So far, so good.

The best weapon I had was a lucky break that had taken place earlier in the day. That morning, as we had loaded the truck at Sisophon, I had made a startling discovery: Angka was running one soldier short on that day! Instead of the two scowling teenage *yothia* with the nasty-looking AK-47s slung over their shoulders, a single gun-toting thug would be ordering us about during the shift.

"*Mit!* Comrades . . . back on the truck!"

Blinking slowly, almost unable to believe my eyes, I saw how fortune was continuing to smile on me. The armed guard, still alone, was climbing into the cab of the logger. Already, the engine was chugging, and the Khmer Rouge soldier was settling onto the front seat beside the driver, being careful to place the butt end of the automatic rifle between his feet.

Like the cunning Khmer hawk that sits atop the roof of the ancestral temple, watching and waiting, I studied the layout with microscopic intensity. The driver of the logging truck, another prisoner, would be no threat. And since the truck mechanic who also usually joined us on these runs was off visiting a relative in nearby Tamaw Puak, I knew that the only real danger would come from the young man with the AK-47. There was no question that he would shoot to kill, if he saw me fleeing.

He would also be quick to sound the alarm, by screaming and sounding the horn. And if I was unlucky, that might alert some of the nearby labor crews and their heavily armed Angka masters to join the pursuit—so that I would be hunted down quickly, and then executed without mercy. (Angka's penalty for "desertion" was always death.)

We were rolling now.

Pulling out of the timber camp, the mud smeared-logger rattled onto route 69.

Somewhere off to the west—somewhere in the direction of the golden, sinking sun—lay the border of Thailand, and the road that might eventually take me to freedom.

Did I really have a choice?

Dear Lord Buddha, let my mother's prayer and merits help me now!

Perched alone atop the teak logs, I watched the rifle-carrying guard turn in his seat, then glare back at me. I held my breath, then got a violent shock, as I saw him bending to the floor to retrieve something—his still wet *krama*!

I watched, amazed, as he lifted the dripping, bright red-and-white checked scarf and began to hang it over the truck's rearview mirror.

Yes, the guards at the timber-works had gotten a chance to take one of their rare baths, earlier in the day, and our gun-carrying guard had gone into the water wearing only his *krama*, which was still soaked. And now, with the bulky truck able to clatter along at no more than fifteen miles an hour (so that the garment wouldn't blow away), he was hanging his laundry out to dry, and using the mirror as his clothes-line!

The reflecting glass was covered now. It was a gift. The guard would be able to see me only by twisting awkwardly in his seat to look through the back window. And I was alone at the back of the truck.

Unsteadily, I crawled to my knees on the topmost teak log.

I felt a wave of icy dread roll over me, as the truck swung through a long curve, then leveled off on what looked like a mile-long straight-away.

The moment had arrived.

Crouching as low as possible, I began to slither along the stack of logs.

Inch by inch, I crept along the slippery teak. My heart was hammering inside my ribs, and I kept gasping for air. A few more feet, and I would reach the back end of the stack.

Am I really doing this?

Am I really about to put my life on the line for a dream of freedom?

Close to panic now, I took one last look back over one shoulder: The shotgun rider was still chatting aimlessly away with the driver.

The logging truck was put-putting along the flat road, throwing up clouds of orange dust, dust that would help to camouflage my next move, if only I could find the courage to make it.

Clutching my water bottle, I patted my belt: the bayonet-knife was still anchored securely.

I paused for one last instant. And I knew it was a moment I would never forget. On both sides of the dirt road, the teak forest stretched away to the horizon—a vast sea of rolling green, broken here and there by jagged-looking sawgrass stands, wind-bent thorn trees, and snakelike vines that clung to the tree trunks as if intent on strangling them.

My Cambodia.

I tensed my body for the leap—and heard my mother's voice somewhere deep in my soul. She was calling out to me with the same loving words that she had used so many times before, during the first agonizing days of the "revolution": "Kanee, whatever you do—never give up hope!"

I jumped. It was about twelve feet, from the top of the teak logs to the dirt road—and as I tumbled through space, eyes closed, I could feel my legs already beginning their mad scramble into the jungle cover that I hoped would shield me from the deadly snout of the AK-47.

I tumbled and tumbled—and suddenly was grabbed in midair! I was stunned. I felt some huge powerful force take hold of my heavy fatigue jacket.

And then, a moment later, I was being dragged along behind the truck. In a flash, I understood the worst: the jacket had gotten hung up in a row of "crocodile teeth." These were heavy metal clamps, like two grinning jaws, that were used to keep the logs from sliding out of position on the truck.

Unable to raise my arms because of the ferocious pull of gravity, and unable to keep my feet on the ground because of the truck's speed, I floundered desperately, with my shoulders slamming into the back end of the teak logs again and again.

Ten seconds, twenty seconds. With my vision blurring and shooting pains through my chest, I knew that my chances were growing slimmer by the moment. I needed another miracle—and fast.

Was it my mother's prayer and merits with Lord Buddha that caused the truck to hit a jumbo-sized pothole? A moment later, freeing the jacket from the vicious-looking sawtoothed clamps and flinging myself high into the air, I plunged to earth butt-first, and rolled like a sack all the way to the edge of route 69.

Clambering to my feet, I shuddered with relief, as I saw the logging truck continuing to rumble placidly down the road, throwing up a boiling cloud of orange dust behind it.

So far, it seemed, no one had noticed my departure.

And I had no intention of sticking around until someone did notice. Within a few seconds, I reached the edge of the tree line, and dived headfirst into the deep gloom of the jungle canopy.

A moment after that, I was tearing along in a panic. Ignoring the thorns and vines that lashed me at every step, I groaned with terror as I heard the dry leaves crackle beneath my feet. It sounded as if a giant were stomping his way through this noisy foliage!

I ran on and on, thorns ripping at my hands. More than once, I stumbled into jarring headfirst collisions with tree trunks, producing numbing blows that knocked the wind from me and left me sprawled and panting in the deep undergrowth. At last, having covered at least 500 to 600 yards, I paused to gather what was left of my wits. With my right hand, I patted a wet spot on my cheek and felt the blood that had been raised by the whipping thorns. I could hear my breath whistling in and out of my mouth: I sounded like an overworked horse struggling to remain on his exhausted legs.

But I was still alive.

I had a chance to achieve the unthinkable: to escape from the hellish firestorm of the Angka genocide. Once again, my mother's milk and merits had plucked me from the flames!

Quickly now, I took stock of my situation. Bayonet-knife: OK. Water bottle: OK. No broken bones. I could feel my strength returning little by little.

Frowning with effort, and breathing a bit easier now, I tried to remember my geography. According to the maps I had studied earlier, the Thai border lay almost directly to the west. It was late afternoon—which made my direction clear: I must walk directly toward the sun.

When darkness fell, of course, I would be able to orient myself by looking at the moon—so that I could continue moving throughout most of the night. And then in the morning, if I survived until morning, I must "put the sun behind me," at least until noon, if I wanted to remain accurately on course.

I was ready now.

I was going to try to walk out of Cambodia—through numerous border patrols and Khmer Rouge encampments, and past hundreds of lethal land mines that had been placed all along the border, precisely in order to stop runaways like me.

I took a single step. Then another. Soon, full of determination, I was following the dim shafts of sunlight that filtered through the jungle canopy.

And with every step, I could feel the guiding, loving presence of Mae, my mother: *Kanee, Sichan, my beautiful moon. . . . No matter what happens, never give up hope!*

CHAPTER 10:

FRIDAY THE THIRTEENTH

THE SUN AND THE MOON

It was Friday, February 13, 1976. It was to be my liberation from slavery, from horror, from terror, from eternal threats of execution. I felt as if I had been untied, unchained, unshackled, and unblindfolded. I felt that a heavy burden had been taken off my shoulders, a thick veil of darkness removed from my eyes.

I have been liberated! I am free!

I may be alone, but I am no longer the loneliest person on earth. I have the wilderness as my company.

The mysterious monk at Sisophon told me to follow the sun and the moon.

I will always have the sun, the moon, and the stars with me.

I felt rejuvenated for having made a break for freedom. Even if I were going to die in the jungle, I would die free.

Thailand is west of Cambodia; Thailand is where the sun sets. The monk's words were a constant reminder during my preparation for the final escape. I must make sure that the sun was behind me in the morning and in front of me in the afternoon. How about at night? The moon should be behind me in the evening and in front of me after midnight and in the early morning. No compass, no problem. The sun and the moon were going to be my guiding lights. And according to the villagers, I should be less than a day's walk from Thailand.

The *preah vihear* and statues of Buddha in a *wat* always face east. This could be a helpful sign, although I doubted very much that I would encounter any Buddhist monastery on the escape route.

I followed the last beam of the setting sun and tried not to deviate from my course. "Be careful; do not leave the road"—the voices of the sergeant, the fisherman, and Chim Chun resounded in my ears.

When the jungle became completely dark, I rested until the moon came up. It should be behind me for a few hours. I stopped when it hovered above my head, as I could not tell which direction it was moving in. At about three o'clock in the morning, I saw a bright light projected on the top of the trees. It came from a few hundred yards away. It must be a forest fire. I could not see very clearly without my glasses, so I kept on crawling inch by inch toward the source. I got close enough to find two soldiers with guns sitting at a campfire, while two others were deeply asleep on the ground.

I quickly crawled back into the darkness. Never play with fire. About thirty minutes later, I could no longer see the light on the tall trees. I lay down on my back and fell asleep. I woke up when I felt something heavy moving over my stomach. I opened my eyes little by little and saw the scales of something big reflecting the moonlight. The scales were moving very slowly to the right. I held my breath until the shape of a tail appeared at the corner of my eyes. It got smaller and disappeared. It had to be a big snake. It could have been a boa constrictor. I waited for a few minutes to make sure that the snake had moved far enough away. I jumped up and ran in a different direction.

The next morning, the sun rose behind me.

I am still on course, I thought to myself.

I have been walking for one night. Where is Thailand? And how will I know I have arrived?

I moved on slowly but steadily. I avoided the jungle paths. Those were where the land mines were laid. Staying on the road meant I should stay on course, not necessarily on the well-trodden path. Cutting across the forest was slower, but certainly much safer.

Although the jungle was thick, the day still got hot very quickly. It was also humid. I sweated a lot. I stopped for a few hours when I could not tell where the sun was going, probably between eleven AM and one PM. Occasionally, I put a short stick on the ground and tried to determine the direction by following its shadow. The books I found at the schoolyard in Sisophon told me that I could tell the direction by touching the trunks of trees. The warm side is usually the side of the sun. But the forest in northwest Cambodia was a dense tropical jungle where the sunlight could hardly reach the tree trunk.

I ran out of water by mid-afternoon, although I had consumed it moderately. As the sun was setting, I came upon a pond in the middle of an open field. I crawled toward it. I put my face down to the level of the water. On the other side, my eyes caught the sight of two bloated bodies being devoured by ugly-looking vultures and giant flies. I crawled back without being able to quench my thirst.

It has been twenty-four hours now: one night and one day. And Thailand is nowhere to be seen. I cannot go on without water for three days.

Either I would get to Thailand within the next twenty-four hours or I would die of exhaustion, if not be killed by land mines or Khmer Rouge patrols.

I pondered what to do next. The moon rose behind me. It was a full moon. It was so pretty. "Kanee, Sichan, my beautiful moon! Never give up hope, no matter what happens!" I searched for *Mae's* face on the moon.

I kept on fighting my way through tall, sharp sawgrass. Through the brush, I saw the moon reflected in a body of water. It looked like a narrow river, or it might be a creek. I took off my clothes, wrapped them in Mother's *krama*, and put the bundle over my head. I swam across it to the other side. I found myself walking across a wide muddy field before I reached the jungle again. The moon was now right above me. I had to stop and wait until it was descending into the horizon in front of me.

I was thirsty and hungry. I could not drink the water in the jungle and dared not eat any leaves for fear of poisoning. All along, I heard explosions. I had no idea if animals or human beings had stepped on land mines.

Suddenly, I heard a voice. It seemed to be carried by the wind from a distant loudspeaker. It came and went quickly. I stopped to listen carefully. I caught a few words. They sounded like Khmer. I heard the word *miakabojia*. It is a Buddhist festival that happens during the full moon in the third month of the Buddhist calendar. It usually falls in the second half of February.

Yes, it's the full moon and it's February.

I must be delirious.

The Khmer Rouge had not allowed any religion since they came to power.

The voice must be from Thailand. But if it is from Thailand, why is it in Khmer? I am crazy. Aren't I?

I kept on following the moon and battled my way through the thick jungle. My puzzlement was suddenly interrupted when I fell into a deep hole. I felt excruciating pain in my legs. I bit my lips so hard to prevent myself from crying that they started to bleed. I was so terrified that I used the remaining strength of my body to pull myself out of the dreaded booby trap. I managed to climb out of the hellhole. I clinched my teeth to control my pain and to prevent a cry from bursting out. I limped away from the pit and dropped to the ground. I had thought of land mines and heavy patrols as lethal obstacles in the escape. But I had not thought of a booby trap or *pungi* sticks. These sticks were made out of sharp bamboo to trap and kill animals or human beings.

The voice came back, on and off. It was still in Khmer and each word became clearer: "Please . . . temple . . . us . . . *miaka* . . . break . . . monks . . . tradition . . . Buddhism . . ."

The moon was now at the horizon. Its soft glow was replaced by the first ray of sunlight. The voice came back one more time in clear Khmer:

"Please come to the temple to join us in celebrating *miakabojia*. We will begin by offering breakfast to the monks. It is an important tradition to maintain our practice of Buddhism."

I sat near some thick bamboo trees. The dry field in front of me became clearer under the rising sun. I noticed that its dikes were still curved.

I saw my poor limbs. My trousers had been torn apart. My legs and knees had suffered severe injuries. I had dry blood all over me. But I was lucky.

I am tall for a Cambodian.

When I fell into the trap, the sharp *pungi* sticks hit my legs instead of my heart or my stomach.

I am wounded, but I am still alive.

The voice came back. Again, I got every word, loud and clear.

"Please come to earn merit at the temple on the occasion of *miakabojia*. We will make our breakfast offerings to the monks shortly. This is one of our most important Buddhist celebrations."

I still think I am hallucinating.

I must be crazy. Am I?

People are being invited to a Buddhist celebration?

Has Cambodia changed that much in thirty-six hours?

It may be a ploy by the Khmer Rouge to lure me back. They must have realized by now that I have escaped their hell. They want me back for the most severe punishment, to serve as an example for those who think of fleeing their bloody regime.

No, I am not going back. I am gone!

I have not left the road; Thailand must be in front of me.

Then, the other voice came back again in Khmer, loud and clear. This time, however, it was followed by a long monologue in Thai. I managed to catch a few words, but could not make anything out of the whole thing.

I must be in Thailand. But why was the voice in Khmer?

I rested for a few hours. After I recovered some strength, I got up slowly and moved one step at a time.

I hear some engine noise. It sounds like a motorcycle.

I see a banana field. There are no bananas. They must have just been harvested.

I see some fruit cans with Thai labels.

But Thai products can be easily found inside Cambodia, especially near the border.

I crawled out of the banana field and came on a footpath.

I see sneaker prints. Sneakers do not exist under the Khmer Rouge. There are only rubber-tire sandals.

I stumbled into a bush and decided to hide behind it until I found out exactly where I was. A raised country road appeared 100 yards ahead of me. I was looking for any foot or vehicular traffic. I was still afraid that a wrong conclusion now would mean the end of me.

I see a motorcycle with a man and a woman.

I see a trailer full of men and women wearing colorful clothes and carrying umbrellas. Maybe they are going to the monastery.

This is Thailand! Mixed couples are not allowed to ride together in the new Cambodia, nor does anybody there wear anything but black pajamas.

I stood up and found myself face-to-face with a young farmer dressed in bright clothing. He was terrified to see a skeleton wrapped in black garb. He dropped the haystack on his feet.

"*Sawaddee!*" I greeted him in Thai.

"*Bart?*" He answered in Khmer. I almost dropped dead.

I am still in Cambodia. It has been a hallucination: the Thai voice and the colorful people. But I must not give up hope.

"What is the name of the village?" I asked the young man in Khmer.

"Sagnae!"

I had memorized this name of a Thai village, just across the border from Cambodia, in the geography book.

"If it's Sagnae, I must be in Thailand?"

"Yes. You are in Thailand!"

"If we are in Thailand, why did you speak Khmer to me?"

"I was born in Cambodia. I have been living here for seven years. There are a lot of people in this area who speak Khmer," the young peasant reassured me.

"I've just escaped from the Khmer Rouge. What should I do?"

"Let me go and get my father!"

A few minutes later, the young man returned with his father, who asked me if I had seen any Khmer Rouge at the border. I told him that I did not know where the border was. He pointed to the bamboo trees where I had been sitting, resting, and listening to the voice. Our conversation revealed that several days before, Khmer Rouge forces and Thai soldiers had clashed near that very area. The farmer asked me to wait with his son while he went to inform the local authorities. About fifteen minutes later, six heavily armed border patrol guards arrived. They quickly searched my body and confiscated the knife and a nonworking watch. They escorted me to their chief, who greeted me very warmly in perfect Khmer. He had been born in Battambang. He offered me a huge meal, which I could barely eat. My mouth had become extremely sore.

Learning about my arrival, many Cambodians living in the area came to ask about conditions on the other side of the border. The chief invited me to walk in the parade going to the wat for the *miakabojia* celebration. There the abbot blessed me with some prayers and holy water. He asked an attendant to bring me a washcloth to clean the dried blood off my legs, and to give me some medicine. Through the border patrol chief who acted as an interpreter, he asked me about life in Cambodia, and especially about Buddhism, if it was still being practiced. Our conversation was broadcast over the loudspeakers. While I was telling him the story of hell under the rule of the Khmer Rouge, my eyes wandered among the two dozen saffron-robed monks listening intently in the *sala*. I was looking for my own monk from Sisophon. He was not there.

By the end of the afternoon, I could no longer walk and had to be helped to the police station at Tapraya, where I was placed in a cell with four other men. They had escaped from Cambodia during the previous weeks.

I was interrogated and searched again. One of the police officers was especially interested in the gold necklace and ring Mother had given me. Several times he demanded that I give them to him. He also wanted my sturdy U.S. Army jacket, which I had dyed black and which had protected my upper body during my escape. I agreed to give him the jacket if he would bring me some Thai desserts, which I was now craving. In minutes he brought the cakes, and I shared them with my cell mates.

The young officer continued to demand the two gold items even after I had handed him the jacket. He was getting angry when I refused. He kicked and banged our cage. My cell mates pleaded with me. I repeatedly explained that they were my family's heritage. The policeman threatened to send me to the border area to look for land mines. I still said no. He grabbed my shirt collar, pulled me against the bars, spit on me, and beat me with a broom. Before leaving, he said I had better change my mind by the time he returned or I would be sorry.

At suppertime, each of us was given rice with stir-fried chicken and vegetables in a metal plate. I cleaned it up. There was not a grain of rice left. I licked the plate so clean that it looked as though it had been washed many times. Since then, I have never left anything on my plate.

As the sound of music from the festival filled the air, I fell asleep.

THE PRISON AND THE CAMP

The following morning, my cell mates and I were transported in a charcoal truck to Kabinburi. We were unloaded at the prison. A guard stared at me and repeatedly shouted *"Khamen Daeng!"* (Khmer Rouge in Thai.) Immediately, others came running to kick, punch, and slap me. They were angry about recent border clashes with the Khmer Rouge, during which a few Thais were killed.

At the central courtyard of the Kabinburi jail, I was lined up with other new prisoners. We were ordered to take off our clothes. We stood naked while the other prisoners looked at us and made fun of us. Thirty minutes later the guards returned with our clothes and threw them at our faces. I touched my torn trousers at the waistband and felt that my family heirloom was gone. Since May 1975, when I left Hanuman, I managed to hide my grandfather's necklace and Mother's wedding ring in that secret safe, and about sixty dollars my sister Sarin had given me. The Thai prison guards succeeded in finding them. They also took my U.S. Army boots, which were instrumental in helping me get through the jungle.

Not all was gone. Mother's red-and-white checkered *krama* and a tiny yellow cotton bag I had been using to store my meager food supply were still with me.

And of course, my heart full of hope was going to be always with me.

Old inmates of the prison decided on work assignments for newcomers. They had the authority to punish those who disobeyed their orders. I was assigned to an opium addict who had six more months of his sentence to serve. He sent me to pull grass and to collect and burn garbage. My third assignment was to remove bamboo and rattan from the trucks. Finally, I had to load baskets made by the prisoners onto the trucks.

The degree of an inmate's crime could be told by the size and weight of the metal chain that shackled his ankles. The heavier the chain, the more severe the crime. Some of the chains were so heavy that the prisoners had to tie a rope to the center and pull the rope up from the ground in order to be able to walk.

One prisoner with a very big, heavy chain called me over to clean up his area. He was polishing a bamboo trunk. When I finished, he asked me to stay around with him to keep his area neat. We heard a whistle. It had been the command for our action throughout the day. It now signaled our lunch break. We stood in line, walked to the dining area, received our meal, and sat down on the ground, all at the blow of a whistle. The next sound allowed us to eat quickly. I put a few grains on the side, said a little prayer, and ate with my hands. My new boss took pity on me and handed me a spoon. The next whistle ordered us to finish eating and return to our work.

The opium addict came to claim me, saying he needed me to load some more baskets. The heavily chained inmate refused to let me go. He won by mere size of the metal shackles. I worked with him in the shade. And he began to tell me his story in Khmer. There were many Khmer-speakers in northeastern Thailand, known as Isarn. It was a region that had once belonged to the Khmer empire. After a few hundred years, people still spoke Khmer at home.

At supper, some of the inmates did not eat. They turned their plates upside down and made quite a mess of the dining floor. Toilets or outhouses in the prison compound had no doors, no windows, and no walls. I had a hard time making nature calls. Shower areas were also in the open. The most seniors inmates had theirs first. Everyone seemed to enjoy showing off tattoos all over his body, especially the most private parts.

We were counted one by one and searched thoroughly for drugs or weapons, before being admitted into the sleeping area.

I was among some 100 inmates locked up in one open hall. Those with chains slept in smaller cells and sometimes individually. A prisoner with seniority found out that I could speak English and demanded that I conduct a class. I started with some basic greetings. We all had a big laugh trying to pronounce the English words correctly. Suddenly, there was total silence. Everybody was looking stone-faced toward the hallway behind me. I felt a piece of metal at my head. I slowly turned around and saw a barrel of a gun pointed at me by one of the guards. My heart was pumping at lightning speed. After having survived the killing fields, I was about to be executed in a Thai prison. "Bang!" I was startled. I touched my body for the wound and blood. Roaring laughter followed. After scaring the hell out of me, the guard pulled the gun away, and said, "Nyce mitting you. Sankyou." All the inmates laughed even harder, bowed their heads to the floor, and said to him in unison, "Sankyou, Mista." I hated the crazy prankster but laughed with everyone else.

At eight PM we stood up at the sound of a gong. We recited some Buddhist prayers and sang the Thai national anthem. Many of the inmates had their relatives bring them food boxes during the day. No wonder they did not eat the prison food. They invited me to join them for a second, tastier supper. They gave me some slacks, a shirt, and a pair of plastic sandals. I took off my black uniform and changed quickly. At nine PM we went to bed. For the first time in a year, I felt safe and free. Ironically, it was in a Thai prison.

Two mornings later, I was brought to the court with eleven other prisoners. We were handcuffed in pairs. A clerk translated the sentence to me. I was charged with illegal entry and ordered to pay 800 bahts (forty dollars). Otherwise I had to serve a two-week sentence in jail. I told the court that I had sixty dollars in my pants when I arrived at the prison and the guards took it. Before the translation was completed, the gavel came down. The Khmer-speaking clerk asked me if I knew anybody who could bail me out. I asked him to mail a letter to my Japanese teacher Yamada-san, who had been transferred to Bangkok and whose address I had memorized.

A few days later, one of the inmates came to have his final English practice: "You go I sink you. I sank you for Inglis. I pray you hepi. OK?" I took his hand and spoke to him slowly: "Yes, I know. I will also think of you. I thank you for being kind to me. And I will also pray for you to be happy. OK?"

It was February 24, 1976. I was transferred to a dark ten-by-twelve-foot cell at the nearby police station. It was a transit point for people who had committed no crime. We were removed from the overcrowded jail before we could be finally released back into society.

At the time, there were fifteen people in the cell. Some of us had to sleep sitting up. There were a lot of scribbles in Khmer on the wall. I remember one that said, "I should be free and be home before long. Please wait for me . . ."

Our principal activity of the day was to carry a water jug used as a toilet bowl and dump all the excrement into the river. Two of the newest arrivals were designated as the duty officers. We were handcuffed by a long chain and escorted to the river and back by a police officer with a shotgun.

My Japanese teacher Yamada-san and his wife came to bail me out. One morning, I was ordered to leave the cell and to bring with me all my possessions. They now consisted of Mother's *krama* and yellow cotton bag. It took me a few minutes to adapt to the bright sunlight. I stumbled down the stairs, as I could not open my eyes. I was handcuffed by a police officer, who ordered me to follow him. I told him there was no need to handcuff me, because I had no place to go but to be with him. He did not understand me, and it was probably a standard order for him to escort a prisoner handcuffed.

We got on a *remauk* and rode it to the Kabinburi bus station, where we were surrounded by people who asked what had happened. After we climbed onto the next bus, the officer used his rifle to move a passenger away and gave me the seat. I asked him where we were going, but he could not explain to me in English. Although Thai branched off from Khmer some 500 years earlier, the two languages are not mutually understandable except for words that have roots in Pali and Sanskrit—the languages of Buddhism. Pali is to Buddhism what Latin is to Catholicism. Regular words are pronounced differently in Khmer and Thai and can mean totally different things. During the years when I went to visit my sister Sarin at Sisophon, I had learned to count in Thai and had learned some basic greetings, but not enough to carry on a meaningful conversation.

I saw the sign ARANYAPRATHET and was frightened that I was being returned to Cambodia. We got off the bus and boarded a man-powered *remauk* to the district headquarters. The police officer took off my handcuffs and handed me over to a local official, who signed a piece of paper acknowledging custody of me. A few minutes later, we hopped onto his motorcycle and he drove me to a makeshift camp in front of one of the Buddhist monasteries in the southern part of Aranyaprathet

Wat Koh refugee camp was to be my home for the next few months. It was the size of a soccer field and surrounded by barbed wire. There were some 3,500 refugees, crowded into temporary shacks. I was received warmly by fellow refugees who were eager to get news from our burning homeland. They said that only one out of ten people who attempted to cross the border to Thailand made it. Most of these refugees came from northwestern Cambodia.

The camp administration gave me a mat, a mosquito net, a blanket, and a bottle of *tuek trey* (fish sauce), also known in Thai as *nam pla*. Each day, tanker trucks brought us drinking water. We were allowed to go to a nearby river for bathing. Food supplies were distributed twice a day. I gave my ration to a family who took care of me and had my meals with them. Church organizations and the Red Cross provided medical care. At first we had to get passes to go to the market at Aranyaprathet, but so many people wanted passes that the administration stopped bothering to require them. Some refugees arranged to work for Thais in the area, but if they were caught, they were severely punished.

I noticed that many refugees were suffering severe mental depression. They sat around all day feeling sorry about the past and worrying about the future. I thought the best way to help them was to keep them busy. Many were going to be resettled in English-speaking countries: Australia, New Zealand, Britain, Canada, and the United States. But none spoke the English language. I launched my own English cultural revolution with classes where the language of Shakespeare was taught and used in real-life situations.

My first class had only thirty-two students. But the word spread very quickly in the camp, and within a few days the register contained some 200 students. I had to divide my classes into smaller ones and asked some of my best students to help out as teaching assistants. The basic rule was that no one was allowed to speak anything but English with me and in the class environment. The offenders would be fined five Thai bahts, to be spent on our social activities. We had a lot of fun going to the market or having picnics, speaking to each other in English and using it in contests and games. Not only did the students overcome their shyness by speaking English regularly; they also learned to sing a few songs, including "Mary Had a Little Lamb" and "Qué Sera, Sera."

We were always anxious to get news during mail call. On March 18, I was delighted to get a letter from my colleague at CARE, June Magnaldi, from Colombo, Sri Lanka. She was overjoyed to have news that I had reached Thailand. She had gotten word from a former colleague who had worked for the Catholic Relief Service in Phnom Penh and was now attached to the Khmer Refugee Section at the U.S. embassy in Bangkok, headed by Lionel Rosenblatt.

As soon as I arrived at the refugee camp, I wrote a letter to Rosenblatt, telling him about my plight, especially the missed evacuation from Phnom Penh. I asked for the embassy's help. Unbeknownst to me, June had earlier written to the refugee office asking them to be on the lookout for me. By pure coincidence, I arrived in Thailand two weeks after the embassy had received her letter.

June thought the same way about my main activity in the camp: "I'm delighted you are giving English lessons. It's important to fill your time doing something useful, as you are doing, rather than remaining idle, with painful thoughts about the past and questions about the future. I will do everything I can to get you out of Thailand."

Teaching five hours a day without any materials could be very tiring. Besides, I wanted to keep the program going after I left. I decided to select some of my best students and train them to be teachers. Soon enough, I got a letter from June suggesting the same thing: "To ensure that the English program (as well as the Khmer cultural program) continues, you need to train your teaching staff so that they can fully take over once you leave. This is the highest mark of the teacher, made for you especially difficult, since you have little or nothing in the way of teaching materials. But I am sure your inventive mind will find a solution, somehow."

She also told me that during April 1975, she went to the French embassy in Bangkok several times and asked the staff to transmit several radio messages to their embassy in Phnom Penh. In one message, she mentioned my name and hoped that I would be given priority, if there had been another special air flight out of Phnom Penh. None of the messages ever reached me.

With June in Colombo and Bruce Strassburger in Jakarta, I became reconnected with the outside world. They were overwhelmingly happy that I had made it to Thailand. Together, they devised a strategy to get me to America. Both asked for my patience.

One day I fell very sick. My students and fellow refugees brought me on a *tuk-tuk* (a motorized Thai rickshaw) to the local hospital. A nurse came with a routine questionnaire. It was quite confusing because some Thai and Khmer words which sounded similar had totally different meanings. She asked me what my name was and I told her that I might have malaria. When she asked if I spoke Thai, I told her that I was not lying. We both agreed to give up trying to communicate in two different languages.

After a few days the hospital asked me to leave. It needed the bed for other Thai patients. My fellow refugees decided to bring me to the *sala* at Wat Koh, the temple near the camp known in Thai as Wat Chana Chai Si. The monastery was more peaceful and quiet, an ideal place for sick people to recover. The abbot not only let me sleep there but asked a novice to bring me some medicine. I was thinking of Sarin and Mae, and tears were coming down my cheeks. Soon, I recovered enough strength to go back to teach.

After an afternoon class, I was having a break when it began to rain. One of my students came to tell me that there was somebody from the American embassy in Bangkok who was looking for me.

"Please tell him that I am waiting here." The student looked a little puzzled and did not move. "Go ahead. Tell him I am right here."

He hesitated a moment, then ran away. Shortly, he came back.

"Is he coming?" I asked anxiously.

"No. I did not tell him that you are here," answered the student sheepishly.

"Why not?"

"I cannot tell an American to come to see you. We should go to see him."

"All right. Please tell him this: I cannot walk under the rain to go and meet him. I am recovering from malaria. Getting soaked in the rain will result in a relapse. You tell him that and he will understand. If he is an American diplomat, he will come."

A moment later, I saw a tall American with a mustache running from one hut to another and finally to me.

"You are Siv Sichan?"

"Yes, sir."

"I am Lionel Rosenblatt. I run the refugee program at the embassy. We were expecting you. Welcome to Thailand. We will try our best to get you out of here as soon as possible. Take good care of yourself and stay busy."

After Lionel left, my clout in the refugee camp was at its strongest. Everyone talked about *Lok Kru* Sichan making an American come to pay his respects. Many journalists descended on the camp and asked for me. My name was called over the public system on a daily basis. I became very popular in the camp. The Bangkok-based foreign correspondents were hungry for firsthand news and were delighted to find someone who could speak both French and English. One of them was the Australian journalist extraordinaire Anthony Paul, who was an editor of *Reader's Digest* in Hong Kong. He told me he was researching a book about what really happened in Cambodia. Nobody seemed to believe that genocide had taken place under the Khmer Rouge. He and I spent several hours together. In 1977 Tony and John Barron published a dramatic account of the atrocities of the Khmer Rouge, *Murder of a Gentle Land: The Untold Story of Communist Genocide in Cambodia*. The title said it all and summed up their findings.

I received a few copies of the Asian edition of *Time* for April 26, 1976. The cover carried the picture of many refugees at Wat Koh camp with the headline. "Cambodia: The Secret Terror." The four-page article was accompanied by illustrations of atrocities. A few months later

I went to the Hartford Public Library to locate the U.S. edition of that issue. The story was only a quarter of a page.

In the meantime, I had been interviewed by representatives of the UN High Commissioner for Refugees (UNHCR), and the French, Australian, and Canadian embassies. They all offered encouraging words, with the same parting thoughts: "Take care of yourself and stay busy."

THE MONASTERY

Most males in a Buddhist society spend a period of time in a monastery learning precepts and scriptures. This period can last from a few days to a few years, unlike the priesthood or a rabbinate which is quite permanent. It is a rite of passage to complete manhood. By becoming monks, we believe that we earn merits and do deeds which we dedicate to loved ones. Since my painful separation from Mother, Sarin, and Sichhun, I had prayed daily that if I managed to escape to Thailand, I would become a monk. I would dedicate all the merit to them and to the rest of my family.

I had waited to keep my vow and now, April, would be the perfect timing. Mother was born on April 13 when Cambodians, Thais, and other Theravada Buddhists celebrate the new year. I went to call on Phra Kru Rattana Panyathorn, the abbot of Wat Chana Chai Si, and asked him to ordain me. He was extremely happy. By ordaining me, Phra Kru would also earn merits. Once I was ordained, I would have to move from a refugee camp to a monastery.

I immersed myself in another crash course, similar to the one I took while preparing for my exam for Royal Air Cambodge eight years earlier. I had been brought up as a Buddhist by a devout Buddhist mother. I had been quite well versed in Buddhist prayers and scriptures as well as in the vocabulary used by the Buddhist clergy.

In the Khmer language, there are at least five kinds of vocabulary for different levels of society: animals, peasants, urbanites, royalty, Buddhist monks. For example "to eat" is:

> *See* for animals.
> *Nyam* for urban families and in affectionate address, especially
>   to younger persons and children.
> *Pisa* for older people.
> *Saoy* for royalty.
> *Chhan* for Buddhist monks.
> *Haup* for peasants. The Khmer Rouge used this word for
>   everyone.

We also have *totual tian* for regular polite conversation and *jras jrom* as a demeaning word.

The use of the wrong word for a particular group of people can be a disastrous cultural mistake.

Between you and me, we would probably use *nyam*. "Eat" is usually followed by the word "rice." When a Cambodian greets a visitor, he or she usually asks, "Have you eaten rice?"

Despite my familiarity with Buddhist vocabulary, I now had to learn the ordination procedures. A few days later, I was ready. The abbot shaved my head and eyebrows and I was dressed in white, similar to the outfit I was in when I was the official mourner at my father's funeral. Thai and Cambodian monks at Wat Chana Chai Si attended the ceremony, which took place in *preah vihear*, the main chapel. As the highest-ranking monk, Phra Kru Rattana Panyathorn sat closest to the statues of Buddha. He was followed by others, in descending order of seniority. Other Cambodian refugees and some local Thai villagers packed the chapel. We were all sitting on the floor.

At the center of the cavernous hall, I paid respects to the Buddha by putting both hands in front of my forehead and bowing until my head touched the ground. I did this three times. I then lit two candles and three incense sticks. I turned to Phra Kru and paid my respects the same way. I recited some Pali passages requesting ordination.

The change from a white outfit to a saffron robe was the major transition from being a layman to monkhood. I sat facing the monks with my hands in front of my chest receiving their final blessings including Buddhist chants and holy water. In one hour, the ordination was over. I paid my respects to the monks and the Buddha again, and got up to enter a new world. The abbot asked me to stay in his *kod*, or monk's house, and I was going to study under his direct supervision.

Buddhists in Thailand, Cambodia, Burma (Myanmar), Bangladesh, Laos, Nepal, India, and Sri Lanka belong to the Theravada sect, which is more conservative than the Mahayana sect of Vietnam, Bhutan, Tibet, China, Korea, and Japan. Monks live in monasteries and must fast between noon and sunrise. Material possessions beyond basic necessities are prohibited. The monks cannot touch a woman or anything that belongs to her, to avoid temptation. They go well beyond the basic five precepts for a Buddhist:

1. *Refrain from taking lives.*
2. *Refrain from taking what is not given.*
3. *Refrain from sexual misconduct.*
4. *Refrain from false, harsh, frivolous, slanderous speeches.*
5. *Refrain from using intoxicants.*

They also include additional restrains: not eating at the wrong time of day; abstaining from dancing, singing, and entertainment, from wearing jewelry, and from sleeping on a high bed.

My daily schedule began around four-thirty AM when we went to the *preah vihear* for the first recitals of Buddhist scriptures. These are all in Pali. We later spent about thirty minutes in deep meditation. During the meditation all lights were turned off except one tiny bulb inside a glass Buddha. We were supposed to concentrate our brain to the point when we could not see anything in our mind's eye. It was an incredible way to clear the head and organize and discipline thoughts.

Around six-thirty AM, I followed a few senior monks to the village and market. We walked barefoot to ask for alms. As the newest monk, I was the last in our single file. Aranyaprathet's residents were waiting for us, to make the offerings and earn merit. The minute we stopped in front of them, they put a few spoonfuls of rice and other food in our bowls. We blessed them silently and moved on. Once our bowls were full, we returned to the *wat*.

After a quick breakfast, we spent the morning studying Buddhist scriptures. There are some 84,000 topics of *dharma*, which constitutes the Buddhist doctrine that fits into *sila*, Pali for morality; *samiti* (concentration); and *panya* (wisdom). We also did various chores on the monastery grounds. We had to finish our lunch before noon, when we began our daily fast: nothing except liquids was consumed between noon and sunrise. The afternoon was spent the same way. And the evening was dedicated solely to our studies. We turned the light off at about ten PM. And another day began at the first crow of the roosters.

It was a totally different life. It was completely peaceful, serene, and fulfilling. I wanted to stay longer, but could not. I had to go back to teaching English to my fellow refugees. With a high level of concentration and intense study, a few weeks should be enough for me to remain in the monkhood. In a brief ceremony presided by the abbot, I took off my saffron robe and returned to a layperson's life.

In mid-April, my students, fellow refugees, and I organized a Cambodian new year festival. We dedicated all the merits earned under Buddhist principles to our parents and relatives who were still suffering in Cambodia and to the memory of the many who had died. I prayed for my mother on her birthday.

Friends and former colleagues became more aware of my being in the refugee camp. They sent me a lot of comforting letters. Bruce Strassburger came to see me one day and took me to a big lunch in downtown Aranyaprathet. He brought me books, stationery, and clothing. We spent the whole day together catching up. At the end, he said that they all were trying to get me out of there as quickly as they could. I stood and looked at his car until he disappeared from view.

I came to know two amazing French priests, Father Vernier and Father Venet. The former had been living in Bangkok for a long time and seemed to know everyone at the French embassy. The latter used to live in Kampong Thom and spoke Khmer fluently. Both spent their time helping people finding a home in France.

The French were the first to give me a visa. I was happy to have it, but it also put me in a bind. I was not sure whether I should go to France, where I had friends but where life was very tough for refugees, or wait till I secured a U.S. visa. This might never come. Although I had worked for a U.S. organization in a management position, I belonged to a low-priority group as far as a visa was concerned. The United States might run out of visa numbers before reaching my category. And I knew no one in America. So I risked losing the French visa and ending up not having the U.S. one. Staying in a refugee camp forever was not an option.

I was so afraid that I might miss a chance to get resettled in a third country that I sent a telegram to June. She told me to try to hold on to the French visa for as long as I could. Three days later, I was approved for resettlement by the United States. I was overjoyed. On May 12 I was interviewed by an immigration officer and given a parole number. I spent my final weeks in Thailand helping various organizations at the U.S. embassy in Bangkok as an interpreter and translator.

June told me in one of her letters that I would need a suit for my job interviews in the United States. She suggested that I get some money from one of her friends and have one made in Bangkok. She also introduced me to Sam Oglesby, who worked for the UN Development

Program. Sam in turn put me in touch with a Cambodian prince who worked at the United Nations Economic and Social Commission in Bangkok. He was very happy to meet a survivor and to be able to get up-to-date information on the tragic situation of Cambodia. He gave me a lot of clothing, which I shared with my fellow refugees.

O n the evening of June 4, I was at Don Muang airport getting ready to embark on the last leg of my journey to freedom. Before boarding the plane, I was handed a plastic bag. "This is going to be the most important plastic bag you will ever carry in your life," I was told. "It has all key information about your travel, where you are headed, and whom you are going to live with. It contains your official travel documents that allow you to resettle in America as a refugee. The papers also have key information about your sponsors, Mr. and Mrs. Robert Charles of Wallingford, Connecticut. Keep it safe. Have a good trip. And good luck."

Shortly before midnight, I boarded a Belgian Sabena Boeing 747 for Brussels via Bombay and Athens. That was the largest plane I'd ever flown in—a giant aircraft that had almost five times the capacity of a Caravelle, with two aisles, more than ten seats abreast, and seemingly endless rows. It looked more like a ship. I was awestruck by its size.

I sat next to a Hungarian woman who was on her way home from Manila. Flight attendants came around to serve drinks and dinner. It reminded me of my experience at Royal Air Cambodge doing exactly the same thing. I told them in French that I had been also a flight attendant. They asked me what kind of aircraft I was flying in. When I told them it was a Caravelle, they responded that they had heard of it but had never been in one. I stayed awake long enough to watch the movie *Diamonds* starring Robert Shaw and Richard Roundtree.

I pondered briefly what was lying ahead. I would probably never know what had happened to my family. Ironically, I was separated from them by the end of a war, by peace. The world's most brutal tyranny under Pol Pot and his Khmer Rouge goons had enslaved an entire populace and violated every standard of human dignity: slave labor was the only means of production, backward agrarian output was the only support of the economy, and death the only correctional remedy for mistakes.

I had survived a brutal year of starvation, exhaustion, fear, horror, and terror. But my future was full of promise and innumerable opportunities for a successful life. I looked forward to the challenges of a great society, which guaranteed freedom and peace to all people of goodwill. As I dreamed of a beautiful future ahead, I dozed off and fell asleep. It was the first night I went to sleep without bathing.

Second Episode:
AMERICA

PART III:

FREEDOM AND SURVIVAL

Give me your tired, your poor,
Your huddled masses yearning to breathe free,
The wretched refuse of your teeming shore,
Send these, the homeless, tempest-tossed, to me:
I lift my lamp beside the golden door.

—Emma Lazarus, *inscription for the Statue of Liberty*

CHAPTER 11:

NEW ENGLAND

The Sabena Boeing 747 banked slightly to make its final approach for John F. Kennedy International Airport, displaying through its left windows the amazing sight of the Manhattan skyline. The twin towers of the World Trade Center, the East River bridges, the Empire State Building, the Chrysler Building, and Rockefeller Center paraded quickly before my eyes. I kept turning my head to the point of straining my neck, following the breathtaking view from one window to the next until we landed.

At the immigration counter, I took my I-94 form out of The Bag and showed it to the inspector. He looked at it thoroughly, looked at me, and said "Welcome to America!" Outside the customs area, there were a lot of smiling and anxious-looking people of all ages waiting for their families and friends. I inched through the crowd toward a man holding a sign with my name. I identified myself. He shook my hand, asked me if I had a good trip, and exclaimed, "Welcome to America!"

This gentleman, who had a Greek-sounding name, told me that he was working for the U.S. Catholic Conference. His job was to help me and my traveling companions make our connecting flights. The two dozen Laotians who began the journey with me the day before were headed for Tennessee. I was going to New Haven. We said good-bye and wished each other good luck in our new lives. We kept on looking at each other as we walked away until a group of travelers blocked the view.

I boarded a small Pilgrim Airlines propeller plane in the middle of the afternoon of June 4. I remember Sichhun had told me that he gained a day when he was flying to San Francisco in February 1973 on his way to Huntsville, Alabama. My mind was too foggy to try to understand why I arrived in New York on the same day I left Bangkok, after some thirty hours of travel, including a long layover in Brussels, where I was helped by a ground agent who took me from one gate to another.

I was now on the final leg of my journey to freedom. I had heard of New Haven during my days at the USIS library, where I learned the names of several prestigious U.S. universities and their locations: Columbia in New York, Harvard in Massachusetts, Princeton in New Jersey, Stanford in California, and Yale in New Haven, Connecticut. Besides, the first Khmer-language study books I had seen were published by Yale University Press. During my interview in Bangkok, I was excited to know that my sponsoring family lived not too far from New Haven. I thought that I would certainly have a chance to visit the Yale campus, which I had seen only in pictures.

Nancy Charles had written to me while I was in the refugee camp, telling me that she; her husband, Bob; and their children, Julia and Peter, looked forward to welcoming me to their home. In the late 1960s and early 1970s they had lived in Thailand, where Bob was the regional director of the Peace Corps at Khon Kaen in the northeast, called *I-sarn*. Yes, they had been to Cambodia. Nancy's older sister, Anne Farnam, an art historian, went to visit them in 1969 and took them to Angkor with Julia, who was then a baby.

Nancy had been a classmate of my CARE colleague June Magnaldi at Bennington College in Vermont. She was the one who encouraged June to take the assignment in Cambodia. It was June who called her from Colombo and asked her and Bob to sponsor me. Nancy readily said yes.

In the 1970s, refugees who wanted to resettle in the United States were required to have a sponsor: a relative, friend, church, or organization. I did not know anyone. Bob and Nancy, out of the goodness of their hearts, brought me in from the cold. I was excited to realize that within one hour I would meet a family which would become mine.

"In *one hour*, I will begin my new life as a free man!"

On the JFK-HVN flight, I looked out the window and saw an incredible land. No burned-out buildings. No abandoned towns and villages. No people in black pajamas working under teenage guards. Everything was simply beautiful: the houses, the lawns, and the swimming pools. I saw green hills and attractive rivers. I saw vehicles moving in an organized fashion in lanes marked by painted white lines. I saw sailboats and yachts in the blue sea. June 4, 1976, must be the most perfect day in America. I took a deep breath and murmured, *"This is a beautiful country."*

"Ladies and gentleman! We are beginning our descent to New Haven–Tweed Airport . . ."

I became a little nervous after we landed. As the aircraft turned on the tarmac to park near the terminal, I peered through the window and looked for a family of four with two little children jumping up and down. None. In the terminal, I called the Charleses. There was no answer. The airport became completely deserted. I waited and began to worry, but my heart was full of hope.

A heavyset man wearing a short-sleeved shirt outside his pants showed up at the back door and asked me if I needed a taxi. I told him I wanted to go to the Wallingford bus station.

"Buses to Wallingford stop running at five o'clock."

"How do I get to Wallingford?"

"The only way for you to get there is to take my taxi."

"How much?"

"Thirteen dollars," said the cab driver. He also showed me a chart to ensure that he was telling me the truth. I said OK after finding fifteen dollars in my pocket. I grabbed my only piece of luggage. The driver led me to a big yellow car and opened the back door for me. I was not sure if I was supposed to sit in the back by myself, but I climbed in. The passenger area was very spacious, with two jump seats.

WALLINGFORD APPLES

As we left the airport, I observed every detail. The driver took Fort Hale Road for a few minutes, and stopped at the first traffic light before turning right at Townsend Road. Elegant houses with well-tended lawns and oak trees lined the road. A sign said SPEED LIMIT 30. I assumed it meant thirty *miles* per hour.

We followed the sign 95 SOUTH NEW HAVEN. I thought that Wallingford was in the north and wondered why we were going south toward New Haven. As we were getting on the highway, the driver accelerated rapidly to catch up with the other vehicles in the southbound traffic. Three big green panels appeared over the highway: 95 SOUTH NEW YORK CITY, 34 WEST DOWNTOWN NEW HAVEN, 91 NORTH HARTFORD EXIT 48.

The driver chose the lane for exit 48, and we were now on 91 on the way to Wallingford. I caught sight of EXIT 3 YALE UNIVERSITY, looked to the left, and saw some spires jutting into the sky above treetops. I pressed my face against the glass window, looking for Yale University, when an enormous tire rolled by. I retreated immediately from the window. Two more; and two more. They were followed by a big shining container and four more tires. So, nine tires all together on one side: the giant truck had eighteen tires. That was big. What was it carrying? Where was it going? Why was it going so fast? In 1973 Sichhun wrote to me about what he saw on I-65 in Alabama: "There are so many cars, vans, trucks, and enormous eighteen-wheelers on the highway. I don't know where they are going so late at night. But they all seem to be in a hurry."

On Interstate 91, everything seemed to be so big, so fast, and so beautiful! Both sides were lined with green trees. I had a fantasy of being the driver of an eighteen-wheeler, and having a house with a yard, a lawn, and trees, but came back to reality when I saw:

EXIT 13
5
WALLINGFORD
NORTH HAVEN
1 MILE
LEFT EXIT

I turned my head around and saw a few cars taking that left exit. I was curious why we did not get off the highway. I hoped the driver knew where he was taking me. I leaned forward in the enormous passenger cabin to ask him when another sign appeared on the right: EXITS 13–15 WALLINGFORD TOWN LINE, followed by

EXIT 14
150
WOODHOUSE AVE
WALLINGFORD
1 MILE

The same sign reappeared in less than a minute, ending with ½ MILE.

The cabbie moved the car to the extreme right lane and slowed down near the exit. At the end of the ramp, he turned left following WALLINGFORD DOWNTOWN. We went under Interstate 91 down a hill, crossed a traffic light, and went up another hill. I saw a sign GOLF CARTS XING but did not understand what XING meant. I had never heard of this word. WALLINGFORD COUNTRY CLUB showed up on the right. I kept looking for WHIRLWIND HILL ROAD.

More beautiful houses in all kinds of colors, including white, light blue, beige, green, red, and yellow; a gas station; and another traffic light. We took a left, went up and down a few more hills on Center Street, and came to a crossroad at what might be the highest point in town. There stood a big post office and a brown church on the left. When the light turned green, the driver turned right and stopped 100 yards from the corner. He turned to me, smiling:

"Here you are in Wallingford."

"But I want to go to Whirlwind Hill Road, number 1290, please!"

"I don't know where it is. I work only in New Haven. This is my first trip to Wallingford."

"Please don't leave me here. I don't know anybody here. I don't know a single human being in America. I don't even know the people with whom I am going to live. Please take me to 1290 Whirlwind Hill Road."

"Wait a minute, let me ask."

The cabbie noticed a few firemen chatting in front of the Wallingford Fire Station. After hearing the driver's question, I saw one of them pointing his right hand to the direction we had just come from.

"I've got it. I think I know exactly where it is. It's four miles from here on the other side of I-91 in the rural area of Wallingford," the driver told me as he slid behind the wheel. We got back on Center Street, which turned into East Center. We crossed Interstate 91 once more, this time above it. INTERSTATE 91 NORTH HARTFORD was painted on a solid-green background. *It's the capital of Connecticut; one day I am going to visit that city,* I thought to myself.

We crossed a railroad track and continued on winding East Center Street for about three-fourths of a mile. A park on the right and a body of water after a sharp curve—it looked like a lake to me. A sign read MACKENZIE RESERVOIR PUBLIC WATER SUPPLY. And FISHING BY PER-

MIT ONLY. *Why does one need a permit just to fish?* We came to a complete halt at a stop sign. And there it was.

Whirlwind Hill Road was a causeway that cut across Mackenzie Reservoir in the middle. A few fishermen were trying their luck on both sides. *They must have permits,* I thought.

We turned right onto Whirlwind Hill and climbed two steep hills. A red barn, a silo, and a white farmhouse on the right. Eureka!— 1290 on a red mailbox. We turned left on a gravel driveway. A farmer in the middle of a cornfield on the right looked up and stared at us. The driver stopped the big yellow cab in front of a red house, turned to me, and said smilingly, "Finally you are at home in Wallingford, Connecticut."

"Thank you very much for taking me to my final destination. This is all I have." I reached for the fifteen dollars in my pocket and gave them to the driver. He gave me back two dollars.

"Keep this. You may need it more than I do. Welcome to America! And good luck!"

He helped me with my luggage, got into the cab, and drove away. I looked at him until he disappeared down Whirlwind Hill. He seemed to be a happy man. *One day, I will be like him. A happy taxi driver!*

I knocked on the door of the red wooden house. There was no answer. I peered through the windows of what seemed to be the living room and noted some children's drawings on a coffee table. The furniture seemed quite old.

There was a blue station wagon parked in the driveway. I was feeling a little scared. I sat down on the stone steps, and then the farmer waved at me. I waved back and walked toward him. He shouted: "You must be from Cambodia?"

"Yes. How do you know?"

"Everybody knows about you. But we didn't know you were coming so soon."

"Where are the Charleses?"

"They must have gone out briefly."

"Their car is here."

"They have two cars. If they went away on vacation, they would have told me. Come on over to my house."

The farmer took me through the back door into his kitchen and gave me a glass of water. I gulped it down in a single shot.

"Let me call Nancy; I think she is here," he said after giving me some more water.

"If Nancy is here, why didn't she answer the door?"

"No. This is Nancy's mother, whose name is also Nancy. She's just across the street." He made a quick phone call.

"She's coming over right now; you can wait at the Charleses'," he told me after hanging up the phone. I thanked him and walked back across the cornfield.

"Welcome to America, Sichan!" Nancy Farnam greeted me warmly with a beautiful smile. We were exchanging courtesies when a car pulled up the driveway. It was Bob and Nancy and the two children: Julia, six; and Peter, four. They were all excited to see me. Unfortunately, they had not been notified about my arrival. Otherwise, they would have been at the New Haven airport.

Peter showed me upstairs to his bedroom, which he had relinquished for me. I was wordless to see the view from the window: endless rolling hills, tall green trees, and a tranquil pond. It was already early evening and there was still light.

Are days longer in America?

Shortly after I got to Wallingford, I received my first letter. It was from June Magnaldi.

> . . . I hope that you will approach your "new life" with the same adaptability, resourcefulness, and fearlessness of hard work that

have marked the other endeavors I have seen you undertake. With these qualities you will succeed . . . anywhere.

My thoughts are with you as well as my confidence in your ability to be resourceful, flexible, hardworking, and patient. All will not happen overnight, but with hard work, all will come.

June's words became the foundation of my adaptability in America. They were the beacons for my navigation through the challenges of survival and success in my new life as a free man.

Within a short time, I had been exposed to two extremes of modern civilization: the killing fields of Cambodia; and the world's most advanced society, the United States. My mantra became: "Forget the painful past and focus on the brighter future. Adapt and be adopted." The curse and sorrow of losing my country, of not knowing what had happened to *Mae*, Sarin, Sichhun and my family, remained a burning grief inside me. But, as I had told my fellow refugees in Aranyaprathet, there was no use to continue feeling sorry about the past and worrying about the future. The best means to cope with this would be to keep busy. So I did.

The first few days of my adjustment period in America were quite a culture shock. I woke up in the middle of the night feeling very thirsty but could not find any bottled water. Nancy told me later that I could drink from the tap. There was no need to boil the water as in Cambodia.

I was still weak and I got tired very easily. I would throw up in the car. I thought I could never drive again. All this was part of my slow recovery from malaria. I struggled to keep my spirits up. While Bob went to work in Hartford, Nancy sweetly spent a lot of time with me. She took me to New Haven to get my Connecticut driver's license. Fortunately, I passed the test without throwing up on the examiner. She also helped me open an account at the Dime Savings Bank of Wallingford and get a local public library card.

I wanted to be on my own feet and started my new life literally at the bottom of the ladder. When I learned that Young Orchards in Wallingford needed apple pickers, I went to see the supervisor, William Carr, and was hired immediately. I had to use a wooden ladder to climb the apple trees. My coworkers were half a dozen Jamaicans who had arrived from Miami after riding a Greyhound bus all day and all night. They called me the China Man. I told them that I was Cambodian, not Chinese. "Cambodian, Chinese, Japanese, you all look the same!" they said. We were paid by the bushel, and we could eat and take as many apples as we wanted. I ate apples every day, enough to last a lifetime. And I brought apples home for Nancy to make all kinds of things.

The first U.S. city I visited was Boston, Massachusetts. Bob had a meeting there and asked me to go for a ride with him. We took I-91 north to Hartford, where we changed to I-84 east until we reached the Massachusetts Turnpike (the Pike, I-90). We stayed on the Pike going east till we arrived in Boston. Along the way, we stopped to pay tolls. I asked Bob why we had to do this. He explained that the money collected would be used to maintain the roads. I had thought the government was using tax money to do it. Besides, there was no toll system in the old Cambodia.

The Charleses' saltbox house had been built in Branford, Connecticut, in 1742. It was then known as the Jonathan Towner Half Way Tavern, as it was a travelers' stop halfway between New York and Boston on the Boston Post Road, now route 1. The Charleses had it brought to Wallingford in 1975 and reconstructed it.

My initial transition to life in America was made easier for me thanks to the Charleses' warmth and kindness and their knowledge of Asian culture. Both Bob and Nancy loved cooking, and their kitchen produced some of the most delicious Asian food, especially Thai dishes. The idyllic surroundings on their property were most soothing and rejuvenating.

JEFFERSONVILLE BICENTENNIAL

The Charleses spent part of their summer vacation with Nancy's grandparents, James and Margaret Forgan, in Vermont. James Forgan had been the head of the First National Bank of Chicago for many years before retiring. He and his wife had an enormous spread in Cambridge; and Nancy's parents, the Farnams, had a house in Underhill. Both had incredible views of the mountains.

I was as excited about the trip as Peter and Julia. They had been telling me about their previous visits and how much fun they had playing all the time. For me, it would be my first Fourth of July, which happened to be the bicentennial of the United States—the 200th anniversary of the signing of the Declaration of Independence.

We started the trip in the early morning after a huge breakfast. Bob was always the driver. From Wallingford, we went north on I-91 through Hartford and the western Massachusetts towns of Springfield, Holyoke, and Northampton before reaching Vermont. We stayed on I-91 until White River Junction, where we changed to I-89 north.

To keep Julia and Peter from asking, "Aren't we there yet?" Bob and Nancy came up with a series of games. I did not understand any but came to enjoy them as we all tried to compete with each other. We began with spotting something unusual on the highway, such as a trailer carrying a mobile home. How about a boat, a camper, a canoe, bicycles, motorcycles? Then we identified out-of-state license plates. We started with New Jersey, New York, and the states of New England and kept on moving farther away to end up with Alaska and Hawaii. We moved to the capitals of various states and countries. My brain, which I'd forced to become blank under the Khmer Rouge, was struggling to bring back memories from my days at the USIS library. We really had endless choices and the games did keep Peter from crying. The question became, "Aren't we having fun yet?"

While sitting in the back with Peter and Julia and playing all those road games, I enjoyed the scenery along the highway: a panorama of lush green hills and mountains; peaceful ponds, streams, and rivers; and beautiful New England houses. I was particularly taken with the church spires jutting into the sky above treetops. They reminded me of my first train trip to visit my sister Sarin at Sisophon, when I noticed the shining roofs of Buddhist temples in the distance.

I was happy to be alive, yet sad to be away from *Mae*, Sarin, and Sichhun. I wanted to cry, but couldn't. "Men are not supposed to shed tears. Not in public. That's what we have been all brought up to think." So the grief of not knowing continued to burn inside me.

Somewhere between Montpelier and Burlington, we left I-89. We drove north on attractive country roads through Stowe, the home of the Von Trapp Family of *The Sound of Music* (they were refugees too), Smuggler's Notch, and Jeffersonville. Thirty minutes later we arrived at our summer vacation home.

I could not believe the beauty of the 360-degree view. No wonder the French called the state "Green Mountain." I still felt nostalgic for the French language. The first few weeks after I arrived in the United States, I mentally translated everything back and forth between French and English. If somebody spoke to me, I quickly translated the phrases into French in my mind, thought of the answer in French, and translated it back into English before responding. It was a slow multistep process, but I couldn't omit it. Over time, I became more comfortable in English and got rid of my internal interpretation system.

July 4, 1976, was exactly one month after my arrival in America. The bicentennial was the first major celebration of freedom and democracy by a major power that I was privileged to witness. We drove to Jeffersonville for my first Fourth of July parade. As I stood next to a lamppost, I watched the joyful marchers passing in front of me one by one: local elected officials, church choirs, farmers. They wore colorful clothes. They were on horses, flatbed trucks, tractors, and all kinds of

agricultural equipment. They were followed by a fire engine and a patrol car. They turned their sirens on and off. I was scared at first, but
got used to it after hearing the children screaming in excitement. I
became excited and screamed along with the children.

The people in the parade pointed to the people in the crowd who
pointed back and clapped their hands nonstop. They called each other
by their first names. The spectators were even more excited when the
high school bands arrived. Everybody seemed to have a daughter or a
son marching. Veterans of World Wars I and II in their old uniforms
with medals and decorations saluted the adoring crowd and received
sustained applause. I did not know anybody in the parade but clapped
along.

It was a celebration of freedom and patriotism that rang true in my
spirit and soul. I was probably the only Asian and certainly the only
Cambodian at the festivities. Yet I felt very much a part of them already, after just one month. I hoped they felt the same way, that I was
one of them. At the happiest event I had attended, I was rejuvenated.
My initial cultural shock was over on the Fourth of July. The image of
a little girl dressed as the Statue of Liberty in a red wagon pulled by a
golden retriever stuck with me. I said to myself, *"This is a beautiful
country,"* just as Sichhun had written to me in his postcards from Alabama in 1973.

It was now my country!

George Bronson Farnam, Nancy's father and patriarch of the fam-
ily, was happy to practice with me the French he had learned in
World War II: *Je parle français comme une vache espagnole*—"I speak
French like a Spanish cow"—was his favorite sentence. I drove him to
Essex to get some things for his yacht, *Sans Terre*, and we often watched
the news together.

I followed with great curiosity the Democratic and Republican national conventions of 1976. I found it quite amusing to see people wearing funny hats applauding, shouting, screaming, whistling, and jumping on their chairs. Bronson explained that it was a political convention, that these people were delegates, that they were selecting their party's nominee after a long primary campaign.

"And at the end, we will have two to choose from: one Democrat, one Republican."

"So, you are not really electing the candidate of your choice from the beginning?"

"That's right. That's why we have this elaborate process."

"It is very complicated."

"We have had this for 200 years. And we go through it every four."

"I don't understand this process."

"If you want to understand it, you have to get involved."

I thought to myself, "Yes, I will get involved. I don't know how, when, and where, but I will definitely get involved as soon as I can."

The Farnams began their High Meadow farm in 1940. It was famous for the herd of Brown Swiss cows and was once part of a large dairy farming community. One of their ancestors donated a house to be used as the official residence of the president of Yale University, where there is also a Farnam Hall. When Bronson and Nancy Forgan were married in Vermont in the summer of 1938, it was a notable society wedding. The Asian scholar and veteran diplomat Fred Brown, a cousin of theirs, was nine years old and recalled passing champagne to the guests.

In August, we joined the Farnams on the *Sans Terre* off Martha's Vineyard. Nancy Charles gave me my first sailing lesson in a dinghy. I later took it out by myself, was swept out to the open sea, managed not to capsize, and returned an hour later to the scared looks of both Nancys. On the way back to the coast, we encountered very rough seas. I was seasick and flat on my back, but Bronson, at the command of his beloved boat, was having a great time cutting through the big waves.

MIDDLETOWN ICE CREAM

After spending a few months picking apples and eating enough of them to last a lifetime, I spotted an ad in the *Hartford Courant, New Haven Register,* and *Meriden Record-Journal.* Friendly Ice Cream was looking for store managers. The ideal candidates should have stability, leadership quality, an interest in people, and the ability to work hard to accomplish career goals and objectives. I did not understand what all this meant, but I went for an interview and was hired.

The new recruits were invited to meet with the district manager. He gave us a pep talk about hard work, commitment to good service, and dedication to the customers. He asked all of us to introduce ourselves. Most of the trainees came from New England. Sitting in the back, I was the last person to speak. I stood up and said in a low voice, "Sichan Siv!"

Following Nancy's suggestion, I had reversed the order of my names to avoid confusion between my given name and my family name.

"I didn't catch it. Can you repeat your name?"

"Sichan Siv!"

"And where are you from, C.C.?" The district manager couldn't pronounce my name and decided to give me a new one.

"Wallingford, Connecticut."

"I know exactly where it is. It's a beautiful place." He displayed his knowledge of the region and wanted to get more out of me.

"And where are you from . . . *originally*, C.C.?"

"Cambodia!"

"Well, C.C., when you and everyone in this room finish the training, you will have your own store. You will have people working for you. You will establish good relationships with your customers. They are our business and our most valuable assets. They are the reason you are getting paid. Treat them well like your house guests and they will return."

My memory flashed back quickly to the owner of Café de Paris in Phnom Penh: The customer is always right.

"They will become your regular visitors. When they keep on coming, coming, and coming, you will increase your sales. And one day [he paused], one day [he paused again], C.C. [he paused for a few more seconds] . . . and you, and you, and you [he pointed to everyone in the room] will become a district manager . . . like me [he pointed to himself]. You will be responsible for many stores. And all you have to do—are you ready?—all you have to do is drive around, listen to your favorite tunes and radio stations, joke and laugh on your CB radio with the eighteen-wheeler drivers you've never met, and visit your stores, where you are always treated like a king. Is it a great life or what?"

He stopped short of stepping on my feet, fixed his eyes on me for a few seconds, and then glanced quickly at everyone in the last row left to right and the next row right to left. He put seven fingers up and asked, "How many fingers do I have?"

"You have three left," shouted a big fellow in the back. A few laughs.

"Wise guy!" shot back the manager.

"You have five left fingers and two right fingers up and three right fingers down. I'd say seven!" chimed a woman in a red dress in the front row.

"That's right. Seven. You only have to do seven things to have this great life: smile, sell, show, serve, sell, collect, and clean. Wear a smile all the time, sell the products, show the order to the grill person, serve the food, sell more products with follow-up suggestions, collect the money, and clean the counter." The district manager finally broke the spell. "Your store could end up bringing $500,000 a year and your annual paycheck could balloon to $50,000. What a great life!" He exuded such enthusiasm that I left the meeting feeling optimistic that I would soon become a manager. "Fifty thousand dollars! That's a lot of money! Wow! What a speech! One day I will be like him. And that woman in red was really smart. I could never come up with that kind of an answer. I am sure she will be the first to become a district manager."

Each trainee was sent to work in a store under the supervision of the manager. Mine was in Middletown, about thirty minutes north of Wallingford and the home of Wesleyan University. My regular company uniform consisted of navy blue trousers, a short-sleeved shirt with "C.C." on a name tag, and a white hat.

A few days after I started as a management trainee, a man walked in to see me. I was cleaning the counter.

"May I help you?" I asked with a hesitant smile.

"I'm Clayton Hewitt. I've heard that you are looking for a place to live. I have a house on Hunting Hill Avenue with a room to spare. Come on over to have a look if you are interested."

I took down the address and thanked him for the offer. After I finished my shift, I walked over to the nice one-story blue house. Both Clayton and Mary Jo Hewitt were at home. They showed me the room, which had a separate entrance and was adjacent to their garage. They warned me that I would hear the noise of the automatic garage door each time they took the cars in or out. Automatic garage door? The Charles family did not have a garage. I had no idea how such a door worked.

The room, with a private bath and a baby refrigerator, was linked to the main house through a screened patio. The Hewitts' rental fee was below a quarter of my net income (spending no more than a fourth of your income for housing was considered a magic formula for not incurring debt). Mary Jo helped me make the decision.

"We understand you are from Cambodia. We have baguettes at home all the time. And I know how to make a *bûche de Noel*."

"When can I move in?"

I now had my own place. I quickly saved enough money to buy a secondhand car. But my home was still 1290 Whirlwind Hill Road, Wallingford, and my heart was with the Charleses. They were the only family I had. I always looked forward to going to Wallingford on my days off.

I kept on writing letters to June Magnaldi in Sri Lanka, Bruce Strassburger in Indonesia, and other friends living outside Cambodia, whose addresses I had learned by heart, to give them updates on my new life.

It reminded me of my days in Kampong Cham, when I had looked forward to spending weekends with my cousins in Cheehae and had spent time writing letters to *Mae*, Sarin, and Sichhun. Every night before I went to bed, I continued to pray that they were safe.

The Friendly training was becoming a big challenge. As part of the program, I had to learn about all the operations of the store. I had no problem washing dishes, cleaning counters, and sweeping floors. But the rest was more difficult to master. I perspired quite a bit at the grill, not so much because it was hot as because it was confusing. I had never seen a hamburger in my life, and suddenly I was hearing "Rare!" "Medium rare!" "Well done!" By the time I got to the "rare," the "well done" had been burned. Then, I heard "Hold the lettuce!" "Hold the tomato!" I was holding the lettuce when a coworker shouted, "*Hold* the lettuce, C.C.!" I did not understand why he was telling me to hold the lettuce when I was already holding it. He told me later that this meant the customer did not want the lettuce on his hamburger.

I had known only three ice cream flavors: vanilla, coffee, and chocolate. At Friendly's, I had to memorize two dozen flavors, plus a few more flavors of the month. The last straw was the cash register. I had to remember that a quarter was worth twenty-five cents, a dime ten cents, and a nickel five cents. I could not figure out why the dime was smaller than the nickel but worth more. There was no change in the old Cambodia and no currency in the new Cambodia.

All the stores were open every day except Thanksgiving and Christmas. My shifts were very irregular. I worked the last shift, which ended at midnight before Thanksgiving and on the first shift at five AM the day after. "This is not the way I want to spend the rest of my life. I am leaving. I am not coming back. I'm gone!"

CHAPTER 12:

NEW YORK

Animals do not run into the mouth of a sleeping lion.

—Cambodian proverb

After my first Christmas in America in 1976, I told Bob and Nancy and the Hewitts that I was moving on. I did not know what I was going to do, but New York City would be my destination.

On a cold day in January 1977, I got my first job as an assistant cashier at a Brew Burger restaurant near Madison Square Garden. It was like jumping from the frying pan of one burger store to the fire of another. But I needed money to get started. And making a living by counting money was not a bad way to do it. I had been very confused by the small change, and now I was doing the same thing, except that this time I was only changing money—nothing else. The head cashier was patient with me. During the rush hour at lunchtime, she watched me handle the bills. One customer shouted, "Look, honey, if you want him to be the cashier of the year, why don't you train him when it's not this busy!" She did not flinch and stuck with me till mid-afternoon when the pace was slower. At the end of the week, the manager showed me a spread sheet: a dollar off here and there, "But it's OK, you still have the job." I thanked him and my trainer profusely for their compassion.

TAXI DRIVER

At the corner of Seventh Avenue and West Thirty-fourth Street, I saw yellow Checker cabs with the words "Drivers Wanted" painted on the back. I noted the phone number and called during a break.

"Hello? This is Sichan Siv."

"Who?"

"Sichan Siv!"

"You have a hack's license?"

"What's a hack's license?"

"You have a driver's license?"

"Yes, I do."

"Whatever your name is, take this address down and come to take a test to get a hack's."

"Excuse me, do I need to study anything for the test?"

"No. Just shut up and bring your ass here as quickly as you can. I have a slot this afternoon at four-thirty."

I went to see the store manager and told him I needed to leave early. He did not ask for any details and I did not volunteer any. I took two subway trains to Queens and arrived at the test location exactly at four-thirty, completely out of breath. I saw a big man with a big stomach chomping on a big cigar behind a big cluttered desk. He wore a short-sleeved shirt tucked inside his pants, with a belt far below his belly. He had four pens in different colors in his shirt pocket. Before I finished introducing myself, he handed me a piece of paper and groaned, "Here! There is a table near the water fountain to the left. Bring it back when you're done!"

"Excuse me! How long do I . . ,"

"Didn't I tell you to shut up? Just take the goddamned test."

There was a series of questions, mainly about directions. One asked: "How do you get from the Waldorf-Astoria to the UN?" I had no idea where these places were, much less how to get from one to another. I probably checked the box that said, "Cross the midtown tunnel and take the New Jersey Turnpike south." This was the most difficult test I had ever taken. I might have answered all the questions wrong. At the end, I handed the piece of paper to the examiner and kept my fingers crossed. He glanced at the test sheet. He looked me over from head to toe, again and again. My heart was palpitating. He looked at me one more time. My legs were trembling when I saw him shaking his head and sighing. He finally said, "You passed!"

The parking lot on Thirty-first Street in Astoria, Queens, could be seen from the elevated track of the N train. I presented myself to the dispatcher, who handed me—through a tiny window—a trip sheet. He gave me the only instructions of my entire taxi career: "Write down the origin and destination of each trip. Pull the meter lever down at the beginning. Push it up at the end. Collect the fare. Keep the tips. Bring the record and the fares back to me at the end of the shift. And don't forget to fill the tank before you park the cab." I thanked him for the illuminating instructions and turned around. "Wait a sec. I'm not done yet. One more thing. Don't ever be late. You'll piss off the next guy. And you'll piss me off. And nobody pisses me off. Nobody. Now, go!"

In 1977, most New York City cabs were Checkers, which could easily accommodate up to seven people. The fare was twenty-five cents for the first fifth of a mile and five cents for each fifth of a mile thereafter. I drove during the day for a few weeks and then switched to the night shift when I learned that I would make more money at night. My paychecks varied between $100 and $150 per week. I carried all kinds of passengers: artists, businessmen, doctors, lawyers, teachers, and tourists. Six got into my cab at the Hilton on Fifty-third and Sixth. The one sitting in front shouted to his friends, "*Eh, les gars! Le chauffeur est cambodgien et il parle français!*—Hey, guys! The driver is Cambodian and he speaks French." I asked them where they wanted to go, and they said in one voice, "*Les ponts! Les ponts!*" They wanted to see the bridges, so I drove them down the FDR Drive, showing all the bridges over the East River in reverse order of what I saw from the plane when I had arrived in America the previous summer. I started with the Queensborough Bridge and then went under the Williamsburg, Manhattan, and Brooklyn bridges; I got off at Broad Street at the tip of Manhattan and took them to Wall Street and the World Trade Center and up the West Side Drive so that they could see Jersey City and the George Washington Bridge. I enjoyed playing tour guide and hearing their oohs and aahs of excitement. But my favorite fares were to the airport—usually less stressful, with a guaranteed fare back. During the break, I could catch up on some reading.

One particular incident from my time as a cabdriver stands out in my memory. It was summer, and summer in New York is hot. Women wear less and less. I would usually take a breather at Times Square to see the steady stream of colorful people and fashions parade by, as I munched on a hot dog and drank a soda. The Times Square of 1977 was nothing like the tourist attraction it is today—it was dirty, seedy, gritty, and sometimes dangerous. This one summer day, while leaning against the Checker, I saw two beautiful women giggling, floating down Broadway with their skirts flapping. A guy walked up to them. The women looked at him and giggled more. He followed them and kept on talking to them, but gave up at the next corner. He turned around and tripped over a trash bin. I laughed hard, but quickly turned my head away when I realized that he had seen me laughing. Suddenly, his face appeared before me with his nose an inch from mine. I bent backward over the Checker to avoid touching him and said in a soft voice, "Hi!"

"Do I know you? Have I seen your ugly face before?" he shouted at me, spraying saliva over my face.

"We may have met before, but I don't remember exactly where. I meet a lot of people in my line of work." I tried to lighten him up a little bit. But he still seemed to be mad.

"Don't try to smart-ass me. What the eff were you laughing about?"

"Nothing, really."

"Asshole!"

After hearing his good-bye, I stood up and saw him bump into a phone booth while trying his luck on an elegant passerby. My thoughts raced back to the Kabinburi prison in Thailand, and I mumbled to myself, "Nyce mitting you, Mista. Sankyou. Bang!"

Suddenly, he came back to me, put his middle finger in front of my eyes and shouted, "What did you say? What the eff did you say?"

"I didn't say nothing, man!"

"Don't you eff with me, dickhead!"

I jumped into the Checker and drove away, but not before seeing him hit the lamppost while trying to pick up another woman. Well, I thought after my heart stopped racing, at least I'd learned a few new words and more sign language.

In the evenings and at night, there were successive waves of cab users starting with the regular office workers at five PM, followed by the diners, the theatregoers, the partygoers, and the late-nighters. Most of them knew exactly where they were going and usually added a major landmark to the address. Besides, by using a special guide for cabbies, I could bring the passengers exactly to the front door at their destination, just by knowing their street address and doing a simple calculation. That was why the examiner did not really care whether I knew the difference between Grand Central Terminal and Penn Station. I was thankful he trusted that I could handle the job. In order to be a cabbie in New York City in 1977, you needed only good brakes, a strong horn, and basic sign language. I spent long hours behind the wheel and survived the Manhattan jungle with only one exception: a group of young noisy partygoers got into my cab and somehow managed to leave with the bag of my fares for the night.

At the end of my work night, I drove my own car from Long Island City back to Brooklyn. I was always dead tired when I reached my apartment at 1641 Ocean Avenue at sunrise. Before I took a warm shower and fell into a fitful sleep, I performed one last ritual: ironing my dollar bills and arranging them neatly. If I had to fold them, I did it with the portraits inside and kept the smaller bills outside. The idea was to spend small and save big. I kept that practice all along. At the teller's window, people in the line behind me got annoyed because I did not leave until I finished rearranging my bills. I got quite a chuckle when I saw a scene in the television movie *Barbarians at the Gate* where a housemaid ironed bills for her multimillionaire employer.

While continuing to look for a real job, I heard of the American Council for Émigrés in the Professions—a service organization offering aid in all aspects of resettlement. Located on East Forty-sixth Street, it had been helping refugees and immigrants from Europe. I assumed it would also help a refugee from Asia. I had an interview with Stephanie Ruskin, who contacted CARE on my behalf and arranged for me to see Lou Samia, a top executive at its headquarters on First Avenue. I had met him in Phnom Penh during the final months of the war in Cambodia. I remembered going to Pochentong, dodging artillery shells, to retrieve his passport, which he had left at the airport. But now he seemed to find me a nuisance, received me briefly, and did not make any offer to help. I reported back to Mrs. Ruskin about my visit. Some months later, the New York *Daily News* reported on the front page that Samia had been charged with embezzlement.

Shortly afterward, Mrs. Ruskin called me to ask if I would be interested in a temporary job with an artificial flower company. I told her that my mother used to have a natural flower business. I got the job. I started in the company's showroom on Fifth Avenue and then went to its plant near Teterboro Airport in New Jersey.

I went to a few employment agencies on Forty-second Street. At one place I overheard someone say, "We are not finding jobs for illegal immigrants who just got out of jail." I explained that I had come to America legally as a refugee, with "Employment Authorized" stamped on my papers. But the people at the agency were not convinced, having seen the words "alien" and "parole number" on my documents.

CHINATOWN

A friend told me that the Lower Eastside Service Center (LESC) on East Broadway in Chinatown was looking for a data coordinator. I did not know what the term meant, but went in anyway. The interviewer explained that it was another word for statistician and asked me if I knew anything about statistics. "I can hardly pronounce the word!" I said.

"Do you know how to add, subtract, multiply, and divide?"

"Yes, sir!"

"You can have the job and start next week."

One night after finishing my shift, I took my changer, trip sheet, and little shoulder bag out of the cab and closed the door. My eyes caught a leather wallet on the floor of the passenger compartment. There was a card with a name and telephone number. I called, and a man asked if I could bring the wallet to him the following day. I went to the Upper West Side, double-parked, rang the bell, and ran up five flights of stairs. The lucky passenger was waiting at the door. He took all the money in his wallet and gave it to me. I told him: "Thanks. But, no thanks!" He was more stunned when I added, "It was my pleasure."

Being a cabbie had been an interesting experience. I thanked my dispatcher, who looked slightly less mean than Danny DeVito's character in the television series *Taxi*. "I don't want to see your face here again. Ever." He slapped my back and shouted, "Now, get out of here!"

Before moving from a wheel to a desk, I gave myself a treat. I bought a copy of *A Guide to New York City Museums* and spent one whole week visiting as many museums as I could, sometimes two or three a day.

B eing a data coordinator was a simple job. I interpreted data and planned statistical studies, did surveys, and reported information to funding and sponsoring agencies, especially the New York State government. I got to know Chinatown very well and ate enough Chinese food to last two lifetimes.

One of my colleagues at LESC was begging me to share my experiences at her son's school. I was reluctant but finally accepted the invitation on May 19. It was my first public speech in America. The Cunningham High School newspaper, *The Mercury*, reported in its issue of June 1978 on my encounter with eighth graders:

Mr. Siv began by discussing geography. In addition to this he gave a great deal of interesting information. For instance, there have been no schools in Cambodia since 1975, when the Communists took over. Children from the age of a year are separated from their families and are sent to camps. There are no rich people in Cambodia, since the Communists took everything of value that the people had. Today, the majority of people work on farms.

Mr. Siv also described his life and how he escaped to the United States. When the Communist government came to power, Mr. Siv like all other Cambodians was forced out of the cities. He was told to return to his father's village and to live there. The Communists told the people that the Americans were going to bomb the cities, and if they wanted to eat they had to grow their own food in the villages. The Cambodians were given two sets of clothing. They consisted of two shirts and two pants. All Cambodian clothing is black.

After escaping from his village, Mr. Siv found a job near the border of Thailand. Then, he began to plan his escape into this country. Mr. Siv managed to jump from a truck, but his shirt was caught in a pile of lumber and he was dragged for a mile. He ran into the jungle and found his way into the country of Thailand. By the time he reached this country, he had encountered many hardships and many dangers.

While in Thailand, Mr. Siv was sent to jail and then sent to a refugee camp. He stayed there for three months and was finally set free, after writing to American government officials he had met through the organization CARE.

Mr. Siv now lives in Brooklyn and has a job as a statistician. He hopes to attend a graduate school in America. Mr. Siv does not know where his family is and he has not been able to contact them. He may never see them again, but he hopes that someday he will.

In 1978 CBS News received some footage from a Yugoslav television crew that had just visited Cambodia. The network turned it into a special hour-long program with Ed Bradley, "What's Happened to Cambodia?" Through the State Department's Cambodia Desk, CBS found me in New York. I was asked to help with the translation and interpretation. For several weeks, I spent many hours at the CBS studio on West Fifty-seventh Street going through various clips and transcripts. I was quite angry when I saw Pol Pot with an evil smile. I saw the U.S. embassy evacuation, which looked quite orderly. The program was broadcast on June 7, 1978. It was the first time I had seen Cambodia through the eyes of somebody else since I had left two years earlier.

Mrs. Ruskin, with whom I stayed in touch, called one day to let me know that the Lutheran Immigration and Refugee Service (LIRS) was looking for a social worker. I went for a few interviews at its headquarters and was offered the job.

MANHATTAN

I decided to move to Manhattan. I wanted to get a place where I would be able to walk to work and enjoy city life more. A real estate agent showed me two studios on East Ninth Street, between First and Second avenues. They were of the same square footage and on the same side of the building. One was $200 a month, the other $250.

"What's the fifty-dollar difference for?"

"Didn't you notice there is a tree in front of one window?"

"Fifty dollars a month to look at a tree?"

"When there is a tree, there are birds. It's very difficult to find birds in Manhattan. Unless you live on Central Park. Birds sing . . ."

"You have to open the window to hear the birds, and when you open the window you will hear the traffic on First and Second avenues, right?"

"Birds sing. When you look at the birds and focus your ears on their soothing songs, you won't hear anything else."

The rental agent was a good salesman. But fifty dollars a month—$600 a year—was a lot of money for me. I decided to choose the apartment without the birds.

The LIRS was actively involved in refugee resettlement through Lutheran sponsorships across America. A bookmark it sent out among educational materials read:

"I was a stranger and you took me in. Matthew 25:36."
They risked their lives to escape to freedom.
Now they wait in Southeast Asia camps for a sponsor.
Will your congregation give one of hundreds of refugee families
a future?

The leader of our advocacy group was Marnie Dawson, a very charming person, the daughter of a former president of *Time,* James Linen of Greenwich, Connecticut. Marnie and her husband Bob had lived in Thailand in the early 1970s. She encouraged me to speak out and to write about my experience—it would make me feel better if all came out, Americans would benefit from my story, and I could also help the advocacy program. I did not want to revisit the past. It was too painful. For two years, except for the time I spent with CBS, I had shut it out completely. Marnie did not give up and I began to give in.

My first speech was at a church in Basking Ridge, New Jersey. It was packed, and I was very nervous. The pastor introduced me as someone who had survived a holocaust. The audience gave me a big hand. Then there was complete silence. I smiled cautiously, walked to the podium, and began to speak so softly that the pastor had to come and adjust the microphone. As I stumbled along, I glanced at the people in the audience and saw that every pair of eyes was fixed on me. I became even more nervous. *This is not a Cambodian classroom,* I thought. *Oh, God! Please help me get though this.*

I did not know what I was saying but I remember ending with, "I am very thankful to be alive and to be in America." The audience stood up and gave me a sustained round of applause. The pastor gave me a hug. After giving a few more speeches at Holy Cross, St. Matthew's, etc., I became more comfortable.

Marnie later asked me to appear in a documentary, *Room for a Stranger,* and after a few takes, I survived the cutting room floor. She and I continued to stay in touch as we moved through various stages of our lives. She later invited me to speak at Christ Church, and at Brunswick School in Greenwich, where her son Alec was a student. When her father died, she asked me to be one of the ushers at the memorial service. Christ Church was packed with everybody who was somebody. I was a nobody who felt very special to have been part of the celebration of the life of a man who had done so much for Asia.

A few years later Marnie moved from LIRS to the Presiding Bishop's Fund for World Relief (PBFWR). She was establishing a new refugee program for the Episcopal Church and she needed help. So I joined her at the Episcopal Church Center at 815 Second Avenue to help resettle refugees from around the world.

New York was the place for everyone. There was the guidebook telling how to live on $500 a day before lunch, and there were the pretzel stands around the corner. There was always something to suit your taste. New Yorkers were generally friendly. I continued to find my acculturation fascinating.

On a Sunday afternoon in November 1978, a black man approached me at the corner of Thirty-third Street and Fifth Avenue. He said that he was from Soweto and needed help to find the Brownstone Apartments, where he had made a $100 deposit. I offered to take him to the nearby Empire State Building to find a phone book. There, he approached a woman with the same plea. She said she was a real estate agent but had never heard of that company. We both told him that he had been ripped off. He lamented that he had left his passport in a locker at the Port Authority Bus Terminal and that he had $500 with him at that moment. I told him nobody carried that much around. One could go to a machine, punch a few keys, and get some money. The woman suggested that I show him how it worked. The three of us went to a Citicard machine at Thirty-third and Fifth. I explained the whole procedure to him by punching my PIN number and withdrawing twenty dollars. "You see? It's easy to get your money." I took the money and put it in my pocket, feeling proud that I had educated someone who had come from a sad place. The woman recommended that I keep the man's money until they had retrieved his passport and returned. The man took a manila envelope and showed it to the woman, who examined its contents and confirmed, "It's $500 all right." The man put it inside my pocket with my twenty dollars and my ATM card. I told them to go directly to my apartment to get his money back.

We exchanged addresses and phone numbers. At the next store, I reached for my twenty dollars to pay for a purchase. There was no money and no card. In the manila envelope, I was horrified to see only shredded newspapers. I immediately reported the incident to Citibank and the police. Two officers came to my apartment. They called the Midtown South Precinct and let me speak directly to a detective. He told me that the two con artists worked together and that I was a victim of a con game.

"But I got the woman's address and phone number!" I was in denial.

"What are they?" the detective asked.

"Her address is 710 East Seventy-second Street and her phone number is 762-4242." A silent pause was followed by long roaring laughter on the other end of the telephone line. Still laughing, the detective managed to educate me more: "Seven Hundred Ten East Seventy-second Street would be in the East River, and the phone number also reads SOB HAHA."

I checked with Citibank one more time. My entire life savings had disappeared. "It's gone!" Not entirely. I still had forty-three cents left. That was November 19, 1978. *It could have been worse!*

THE CROCODILE AND THE TIGER

I was spending the Christmas holidays with the Charles family when we learned that communist Vietnam had invaded communist Cambodia.

Hanoi, angered by frequent border clashes with the Khmer Rouge and energized by its ambitious hegemony over the former French Indochina, launched a blitzkrieg with about 100,000 soldiers. In fifteen days the Vietnamese captured Phnom Penh and installed a puppet government headed by Heng Samrin, a former commander of the Khmer Rouge who had defected to the Vietnamese after having been marked for death by Pol Pot's troops.

Prince Sihanouk, rescued by the Chinese, came to New York to address the UN Security Council. The former prime minister Son Sann and head of state Cheng Heng attempted to get in touch with him at the Waldorf, but he had already escaped the Khmer Rouge watch and checked into a hospital, courtesy of the United States. He wanted to stay in the West indefinitely, but a meeting with Deng Xiaoping, who was on an official visit to Washington, changed his mind. He began to lead a struggle against the Vietnamese occupation.

On the ground in Cambodia, Khmer Rouge troops and cadres who ran into the jungle ahead of the invading army brought vengeance to the villages they accused of having collaborated with the Vietnamese. Refugees pouring into Thailand gave grim reports of starvation and disease. Food shortages had reached crisis proportions, and the lack of medical care resulted in thousands of deaths from diseases that were normally curable.

The Cambodian people were now caught between the crocodile and the tiger. Having been denied the very basic human right to life, they emerged from a decade of calamities too hurt to cry out in pain, and too weak to ask for help. Cambodian children stopped laughing when the Khmer Rouge came to power in 1975. At the beginning of the International Year of the Child in 1979 they stopped crying.

My initial reaction was mixed.

One tyrannical regime has toppled another tyrannical regime.

Will the end of the Khmer Rouge regime mean the beginning of true peace?

How can a nation be at peace if it is occupied by a historically annexationist neighbor? *It remains to be seen.*

There were only about fifty Cambodian families in the New York City area, compared with the tens of thousands in Long Beach, California, which had more Cambodians than France. In January

1979, a reporter for the *New York Times* came to interview me and a few other Cambodian refugees about life in America. At the end, I asked her if she knew Sydney Schanberg.

"He is my boss. He is the metropolitan editor."

"Please say hello to him for me."

"I certainly will."

I had become acquainted with Schanberg, his assistant Dith Pran, and other foreign correspondents in Phnom Penh at various functions where we all tried to exchange information to stay abreast of the rapidly changing situation. The following day, Sydney invited me to his office at the old *Times* building on West Forty-third Street. It was a hangar-like hall where everybody sat behind a typewriter at a cluttered desk.

"When did you get here?" he asked me.

"I arrived in Connecticut in 1976, and in 1977 I came to New York."

"Have you seen Pran?"

"Pran? I thought he came out with you on the helicopter."

"No. Only his family was evacuated by the U.S. embassy. They are now living in San Francisco."

"You came out with the convoy?"

"Yes. I decided to stay behind and Pran decided to stay with me. We went to the French embassy. I was trying to get him out with us but it did not work."

"I went to the French embassy with my brother, too, but they did not let us in. So where did he go?"

"The Khmer Rouge demanded that all Cambodians be turned over to them."

"He must have been killed, because Sirik Matak and others were killed shortly after they had been handed over."

"We don't know. The Khmer Rouge first asked for *lok thom*"—this term means big or important people. "That's why Sirik Matak and his family and others were handed over."

"How could the French let that happen? Why didn't they stand firm? And where is Pran?"

"I believe he is still alive. He may be able to disguise himself as a peasant and disappear for a while. You survived, and you look more like a *lok thom* than he does."

"True. But I am very lucky and my mother's milk is dear. If Pran's mother's milk is dear, he is still alive and he will make it to freedom."

After watching the two political conventions in the summer of 1976, I became more interested in America's political processes. I learned that one way to influence a policy was to make people know about your position on that particular issue. I started a sustained letter-writing campaign and gave speeches at every opportunity to keep the Cambodian issue alive. I wrote to New York's senators, the Republican Jacob Javits and the Democrat Daniel Patrick Moynihan; and to all the members of the Senate Foreign Relations Committee. On May 18 I received a response from the committee chair, the Democrat Senator Frank Church of Idaho:

> . . . I certainly agree with you that the Cambodian people have been subjected to "untold miseries" for many years, and deeply regret that their present condition is a tragedy. While the ability of the United States to influence this situation is limited, I believe that we must be alert for any opportunities that are available to ease the suffering of the Cambodian people. I shall keep this state of affairs in mind and hope that it will be possible for the United States to play a constructive role in improving conditions for the Cambodian people.

PARIS, *ENFIN!*

In the summer of 1979, I planned my first trip to Europe. Icelandic Air had a very cheap fare to Reykjavik and Brussels. From there, I would take a train to Paris using a Eurail pass and save a lot of money.

As a refugee, I had no passport but a travel document issued by the Department of Justice, called "Permit to Re-Enter the United States." I was so excited about my journey that I arrived at Kennedy Airport four hours before departure, only to learn that the flight was oversold but that I could instead go to Amsterdam. I was told that my visa would be valid for all Benelux countries.

In Amsterdam, I took a bus from Schiphol Airport to the central train station to store my luggage until my train departed. I put my travel documents, my Eurail pass, and my traveler's checks in a briefcase, which I set down on the floor for a few minutes. When I turned around, it was gone. I ran around like a headless chicken, looking everywhere. No sign of it. I filed a police report and began to ponder how I was going to get to Paris without papers. I took my chances.

The local night train arrived at the Belgian-French border before sunrise. The French police boarded the train to look at the sleeping and snoring passengers. I pretended to be asleep, keeping my face toward the wall. At the Gare du Nord, I noticed a few more police officers, holding German shepherds. I avoided eye contact with them, walked toward the taxi line, and took a cab to a cousin's apartment at Rue Saint-Antoine, near the Place des Vosges, where Victor Hugo used to live.

In Paris, I felt at home. I was not greatly awed by being in the City of Light. I had seen pictures of it all my life. It was part of my growing up. French culture had been in my blood since my childhood.

I spent the next few weeks at the U.S. consulate and the police prefecture to get my papers straightened out. A local staff member at the consulate gave me a piece of paper stamped with the address and phone number of the Immigration and Naturalization Service (INS) regional office in Frankfurt. I called the number: it was the Sheraton Hotel. The hotel must have received so many calls that the desk clerk responded to my brief silence with, "Are you looking for the INS?"

I reached the INS office, and the staff asked me to go to Frankfurt to get my new travel document. "How could I get to Frankfurt, if I could not even leave Paris?"

At the Préfecture de Police, I waited in an overflowing room with a long line of Africans to see a supervising official at the Service des Étrangers (service for foreigners). I explained my situation to her: "I am a U.S. permanent resident, had my papers stolen, and would like to get something to return to New York."

She said, "*Où voulez-vous que je mette le tampon? Sur votre front?*—Where do you want me to stamp? On your forehead?"

I went back to the U.S. consulate at the Place de la Concorde and asked to see the consul general. He told me to get a letter from my employer in New York, and he would ask the French authorities to issue me a *Certificat de Sauf-Conduit* (a safe-conduct certificate).

At the border between France and Luxembourg, the inspector did not recognize the document, although it had a Luxembourg visa. He had to make a few phone calls. My anxiety ran high at the airport when the officer there had to check with his superiors. After a few more phone calls, he let me board the plane. Since then, I always feel great relief on the last leg of any overseas trip and look forward to being home in America.

COLUMBIA

I began to send various applications to graduate schools. I wanted to get a master of business administration (MBA) and started to study furiously for the Graduate Management Admission Test (GMAT). I attended an MBA fair, talked to admissions officers, and sent about a dozen applications to top business schools. As a nonnative speaker of English, I was also required to submit the result of my Test of English as a Foreign Language (TOEFL). I had taken it on my arrival, while I was still in Wallingford, and had received marks in the high tier.

I worried about my GMAT. My scores came out in the middle

range. I was not used to answering hundreds of questions in two hours. In Cambodia, we were given this much time to write a single essay. All the schools I applied to turned me down, with their standard responses. Only Harvard sent me a personal letter. Its admissions committee had reviewed my application with great interest. They were impressed with my management experience in difficult situations in Cambodia and my ability to survive in hostile environments. But my quantitative skills were still inadequate, and it would be an insurmountable challenge for me to successfully complete the MBA. The committee suggested that I take some quantitative courses and reapply the following year.

Friends encouraged me to apply to a master's program at the Columbia School of International Affairs (SIA). One morning in January 1980, I received a call from the office of the SIA's dean, Harvey Picker. He would like to see me. I took the Broadway subway to the 116th Street station and walked across the main college plaza to the eastern side of the campus. The SIA and Columbia Law School buildings were next to each other. I took the elevator to the fourteenth floor and introduced myself to the secretary. Dean Picker extended his hand to me with a nice smile and led me into his bright office, which had a breathtaking view of Central Park, the Hudson River, New Jersey, and most of Manhattan. I surveyed his office quickly and saw no desk. I was curious as to how he got his work done. There was an interesting tall table. Maybe he worked standing up.

As we sat down, Dean Picker told me that I had been preceded by a slew of warm recommendations. On his coffee table, there was a pile of letters. He asked a question that I was not prepared for: "Why do you want to spend two years learning everything that you already know?"

I thought he was overly generous and struggled to find the right answer: I was going to spend the rest of my life in America, so it was important for me to have an American degree.

We chatted a few minutes more. He got up, shook my hand, and thanked me for the visit. "We'll be in touch with you!"

I had screwed it up! That was the kind of answer you don't want to hear, and I blamed myself. It was one of several typical rejections in job interviews: "We'll be in touch with you!" "We'll give you a call!" "You'll be hearing from us!" They all had the same meaning: "You are not the one we are looking for."

The following morning, the phone rang when I arrived at my desk.

"Sichan Siv. May I help you?" I answered the phone expecting another crisis from somewhere in the Midwest.

"How do you pronounce your name again?"

"See-jun Seev!"

"Sichan, this is Bob Randle. I'm an assistant dean at SIA. We will be happy to have you in our program. I also have some more good news for you. We are going to give you a full scholarship. And you can start next week!"

I was speechless. I could not believe what I was hearing. Three birds in my hand. I am accepted, with a full scholarship, in the semester to begin immediately.

"Hello? Are you still there?"

"Yes, sir."

"What do you say?"

"*Yessir!*"

"Great! There is an orientation on Tuesday. Plan to attend, if you can. I'll see you there."

Whew! I exclaimed with excitement as I put the receiver down: I am going to be a graduate student at an Ivy League school. I had been in New York for three years and had lived in two places: Ocean Avenue in Brooklyn and East Ninth Street in Manhattan. Never two without three. I wanted to have a real campus experience and decided to move to a Columbia dormitory. I got a room at Harmony Hall on West 110th Street (Cathedral Parkway).

DEATH AND DEVASTATION

The famine in Cambodia continued to haunt everyone's conscience. The cover story in *Time* magazine of November 17, 1979—"STARVATION Deathwatch in Cambodia"—as well as other media reports drove home the unimaginable suffering of a distant land. The crisis grew worse and worse every day. By the end of the year, it was estimated that 2.5 million Cambodians could face starvation. Everybody tried to do something to help. It was another reflection of the traditional American compassion.

The International Rescue Committee invited me to attend a ceremony in Shubert Alley, where the Broadway community under the leadership of the producer Joseph Papp and the actress Liv Ullmann raised nearly $200,000 for Cambodian relief. They presented the check to Leo Cherne, who had been leading the efforts to resettle refugees. Bob DeVecchi asked me if I would be interested in going to Thailand to work along the border. I told him that it would be too painful for me to go back so soon and be exposed to another tragic situation. I could be more helpful in the United States.

I started to pack up to move to the Columbia campus. Bob Charles called me to ask if I had any news about my family, because he had forwarded a letter from a refugee camp in Thailand. I opened the letter immediately and was shocked. My mother had been killed! I gave Bob the terrible news and told him that I would call him back.

The letter was from a childhood friend in Pochentong. He had been looking for my contact information since his arrival at Khao I Dang refugee camp. He went to Wat Koh and got it from the abbot who had ordained me. Without elaborating, he said that he was sorry to learn that my mother, my sister, my brother, and their families had been killed in Tonle Bati. Apparently, he went back to Pochentong after the Vietnamese invasion, and learned that none of my family had survived the Khmer Rouge.

I am completely dumbfounded. I am totally paralyzed.

My throat and mouth have become dry.

I cannot speak. I've lost my voice.

I am totally blind. I can see nothing, except darkness.

I cannot hear anything. I've lost my hearing.

Tears are streaming down my cheeks.

Never give up hope. Mae has been my hope. Now, she is gone.

I was devastated. It took several hours before I could pull myself together. I tried to have positive thoughts: At least she did not have to suffer very much. They did not have to suffer very much. Life had to go on.

The following day I went to a Thai *wat* in the Bronx and had my head shaved by the abbot. I was again the official mourner of my mother, sister, brother, nieces, and nephew. Not many people at SIA understood the meaning of a shaven head. Some of my classmates thought I had a new hairstyle. But Phil Oldenburg, who was an expert on South Asia and Hinduism, knew that there had been a death in the family. He came to offer condolences and asked me who it was. "*They* were . . ."

SOUTH PACIFIC

Sydney Schanberg alerted me that Dith Pran would be coming to New York to join the *Times* staff. He would be trained to be a photographer. Unlike CARE, news organizations seemed to take good care of their former Cambodian staffs. Sydney asked if I could provide some company until Pran settled in.

I took Pran around, showing him Manhattan, which I had come to know quite well from my days as a cabbie. We went to see Francis Ford Coppola's movie *Apocalypse Now.* I was quite spellbound and totally captivated by the story and scenes, especially the dangerous "Do not leave the boat" mission to Cambodia and Marlon Brando's character murmuring, "Horror, terror," as a way to control his followers, reminding me of the Khmer Rouge's subjugation of Cambodia.

I finished my first semester at Columbia without serious problems and earned a summer internship with the UN Development Program in Western Samoa, with SIA paying the airfare. I roomed and boarded with a Samoan family within walking distance so that I could really experience the local lifestyle. But the family members were more interested in practicing their English with me.

The islands of Samoa lie 1,800 miles north-northeast of New Zealand. The fertile land is covered with lush vegetation. It is a haven of sunshine and good life full of *fiafia* (feasting). The fun-loving islanders live along the coastline in their traditional *fales*, oval wooden structures covered by thatched roofs, but without walls. Hence, girls have to learn to change clothes without being exposed. The Samoan concept of the *aiga*—extended family—headed by the village chief, or *matai*, is the foundation of this devoutly Christian society. Take care of the *aiga* and everything else will follow. The rules of etiquette include spilling a few drops of the national beverage, *kava*, before drinking it; going around the edge of the mats in a *fale* when approaching your host; never stretching your legs out in front of you; always addressing a *matai* when sitting down; and always waiting for grace to be said before eating.

In 1980 Prime Minister Robert Muldoon of New Zealand came for an official visit and the Samoans rolled out their biggest reception for their former colonizer. I was invited to attend Muldoon's address to the *Fono* (parliament). Most members wore the traditional *tapa* cloth costumes. A few men came with an oily upper body, barefoot, wearing a skirt and a flyswatter. Dances were performed, and Muldoon was presented with an enormous roasted pig.

At a separate cultural show, I received a lei from the legendary Aggie Grey of James Michener's *Tales of the South Pacific* (she was the inspiration for the character Bloody Mary). I was extremely honored when she asked me to dance with her. The immigration director told me I was the first Cambodian to visit Samoa. The news spread around town. I was interviewed on the local radio and made the front page of the *Samoa Sun*.

Back at Columbia, I needed a new room on campus and rushed to the housing office to fill out the application. The young fellow behind the glass window looked at it quickly and asked me to correct a mistake: it should read "spring semester." I said, "It's correct. My application is for *this fall semester*."

The housing assistant barked at me, "For this fall semester? Are you kidding? Where the hell have you been, pal? You're two weeks late. There's nothing left." However, Columbia had a practice of giving preference in accommodations to students who had come from the farthest outside a fifty-mile radius.

"Wait a minute. You're from Cambodia. That's on the other side of the planet."

"You're correct."

"Sorry, pal. There's still nothing left. We've got nothing, even if you came from the moon; *nada!*" Another intern barked at me, "Why don't you come back in a few days? Maybe somebody will drop dead and you can move in as soon as the body has been removed. Give us your phone number and we'll call you."

"Please. I don't have a phone. I don't have anywhere to go. Please!"

The two undergraduate interns became softer. They went to a corner to confer. Minutes later, they were back.

"OK, pal. Here's what we're going to do. There's a room in Johnson Hall which has been reserved for a dumbhead from Arkansas. He was supposed to be here a few days ago. Maybe he was stranded behind when he left the road to take a leak. Maybe he dropped dead already. You can have his room. Here's the key. You're in luck, pal."

I grabbed the key and said, "Thank you, pals." *Never give up hope.*

The International Fellows Program (IFP) was an ancillary of SIA and functioned as an interdisciplinary graduate program to enable "gifted American students to combine their professional education with advanced training in international affairs." I wanted to get into the program but faced an insurmountable obstacle. It was reserved for U.S. citizens only.

I went to see the assistant dean, Bob Randle, who was IFP's director. I had established rapport with him from the beginning. I told him that I would be eligible for U.S. citizenship as soon as I had completed my five-year residency. Once sworn in, I would become a good American. Randle listened to me intently. As I waited anxiously, he gave me the final verdict, "You would be a great credit to the program." I was thrilled to get into IFP, where I met some very bright students from the business, law, and journalism schools.

Having been educated in the French system, I found Columbia quite challenging. There were dozens of pages of instruction just on how to use the libraries. In classes, I usually took notes and absorbed the information without asking questions or taking an active role in debates and discussions. Some of my professors were surprised that I did well at the finals. One wrote on my paper, "You did very well, especially for someone who was so quiet in the classroom."

WALL STREET

My first job after Columbia was with the Marine Midland Bank. The E train took me to its terminus at the World Trade Center. I squeezed through the masses of commuters and walked a few blocks to 140 Broadway, in the heart of the financial district. My duties involved financial evaluation and business analytical reports of multinational corporations as well as recommendations on credit facilities and loan proposals.

One fall evening in 1981, I walked down Nassau Street across from Federal Hall, where George Washington was sworn in as the first president of the United States on April 30, 1789. I heard heavy footsteps following me. They were catching up with me even though I walked faster. A black guy wearing a sweatsuit with a hood overtook me and turned around, holding a gun at my ribs.

"Give me your money," he ordered.

"I don't have any money," I pleaded with the robber.

"Give me your wallet. *Now!* Don't eff with me, asshole, or I'll blow your brains out."

A second guy behind me was pushing me with something hard and pointed. I saw no reason to bargain with these robbers and reached for my suit pocket.

"Slowly," said the guy in front of me. The minute he saw it was a wallet, he grabbed it, turned on his heel, and disappeared around the corner of Wall Street. I lost a few credit cards and about $100, the largest amount I had ever carried. *Piece of cake! It could have been worse!*

Over the years, all of us seemed to do well in our lives, except one fellow student about whom we read in the *New York Times*. He became a successful Wall Street lawyer, but for some reason ended up homeless and then died. This unfortunate twist of fate reminded me of a Cambodian story about how fate could be shaped and luck created.

Two boys went to see a fortune-teller about their future. The astrologer looked at their charts, examined their palms, and went into a contemplative mood. A few minutes later, he opened his eyes and reported his findings. One boy would have a hard working life; the other one would end up drinking from a silver bowl.

As they grew up, the first boy never stopped working hard. He got married and worked even harder to afford his children's education. He was able to provide a happy life for his loving family.

The second boy, believing that luck and fate would come in a silver bowl, did not study hard, failed his exams, and became a homeless drunkard. He wandered aimlessly, got lost in the jungle, and collapsed. A royal hunting party stumbled on him. The king ordered that he be given water from one of the royal silver bowls. The poor man died after drinking from the silver bowl.

FREEDOM FIGHTER

When Ronald Reagan came to Washington in January 1981, he was determined to improve the economy, build up defense, and defeat communism. Cambodia got more attention from the new administration.

The anti-Vietnamese resistance now entered a new phase. A Cambodian coalition was formed to fight the communist Vietnamese occupation, diplomatically and militarily. It included two noncommunist groups: Prince Sihanouk's National United Front for an Independent, Peaceful, and Neutral Cambodia (or FUNCINPEC, its acronym in French) and the former prime minister Son Sann's Khmer People's National Liberation Front (KPNLF). The hated Khmer Rouge's Democratic Kampuchea, headed by Khieu Samphan, was the third member. "Democratic Kampuchea" was a ludicrous name for a regime that was responsible for the deaths of 2 million of its own citizens. The coalition held the Cambodian seat at the UN.

Each time I heard "Democratic Kampuchea," it made me think of the following: the Japanese word for pumpkin is *kampocha*, as this vegetable was apparently brought in from Cambodia by the Portuguese. My favorite quiz question is: "What is 'rotten pumpkin' in Japanese?" The answer is "Democratic kampocha!"

It was very difficult for the noncommunists to be in a coalition with the Khmer Rouge, who had killed our families and friends. However, the fear of losing our country and its culture completely to a powerful neighbor surpassed the disgust and bitterness we had for the rotten Khmer Rouge.

Son Sann, whom I met through Cheng Heng in 1979, when we all went to the Waldorf-Astoria and knocked on the door of Prince Siha- nouk's suite, asked me to help represent the KPNLF at the United Na- tions. I hesitated at first, because the Khmer Rouge was part of the anti-Vietnamese alliance; but later I accepted his offer. Our team was headed by Penn Nhach. FUNCINPEC was led by Prince Sisowath Sirirath, a son of Prince Sirik Matak. Our job was not just to work the diplomatic corridors of the UN but to be the liaison with the U.S. government and the American opinion makers, media, academics, and public.

Nhach was a career diplomat and had once headed the Cambo- dian embassy in Cairo. He and I traveled around to explain the com- plex issue of the greater danger of a Vietnamized Cambodia and to ask for support. Unfortunately, Nhach died in Montreal of heart failure after having been in the position for one year.

In New York, we worked very closely with the United States and the Association of Southeast Asian Nations (ASEAN): Indonesia, Malaysia, Philippines, Singapore, and Thailand. Brunei joined in 1984. Their dip- lomats were instrumental in getting support for successive resolutions by the UN General Assembly, which demanded an end to the Vietnamese occupation of Cambodia. The annual exercise, which was always op- posed by Soviet bloc countries, received 91 positive votes when it was introduced in 1979. By 1989, the tally was yes, 124; no, 17; abstentions, 12; nonvoting, 6; total voting membership, 159. During the general de- bates, Prince Sihanouk made passionate and powerful statements.

Washington was a target-rich environment. With Reagan at the White House and a new conservative tide sweeping the capital, we were practically preaching to the choir. Both Democrats and Republi- cans had developed enormous sympathy for the plight of the Cambo- dian people. It was, however, important for us to be active on the front line of a never-ending educational process. Nobody could explain the problem from the heart as well as we could.

At the White House, my first contact was Chase Untermeyer, Vice President George Bush's executive assistant. Chase had a very impressive pedigree. He graduated from Harvard in 1968 with honors, served in the Pacific as a destroyer officer and aide to the commander of the U.S. naval forces in the Philippines, and worked for the *Houston Chronicle*. In 1976, the year I arrived in America, he was elected to the Texas House of Representatives from Houston. He was unassuming, low-key, and a good listener. President Reagan later nominated him to be assistant secretary of the navy.

In May 1983, I went to Thailand to visit camps that were under the administration of the KPNLF. For forty-five days, I traveled along the 400-mile border from south to north to east. I began in the southern region, opposite the Thai provinces of Trat and Chanthaburi. It was in this very hilly, thick jungle area that the KPNLF had been founded in October 1979. It was a mosquito-infested region, and malaria was all too common. I crossed the border from Thailand on foot after spending nearly three hours climbing a mountain. When I reached the Cambodian side at ten-thirty AM—this was a region outside the Vietnamese-occupied area—I knelt down and kissed the ground. It was May 18.

Although it was still dangerous to be traveling in a guerrilla war zone, I felt secure with an escort of Cambodian freedom fighters who risked their lives against a foreign occupying power.

The central region faced the Thai province of Prachin Buri and was the most populous outside the Vietnamese-occupied area, with some 100,000 Cambodians living in three different camps. The topography there was flat and therefore much more vulnerable to Vietnamese attacks.

The northern region was the most mountainous and was located at the top of the Dangrek Mountains, which constitute a natural border between Cambodia and Thailand.

The Cambodian population in those regions had a strong will to survive despite the difficulties and dangers of continuing Vietnamese attacks. Many suffered from malaria, measles, diarrhea, respiratory infections, and malnutrition. "The Communists destroy what we have built; we rebuild what they have destroyed," said a resistance leader. The UN Border Relief Operations and numerous NGOs and religious organizations had been providing a lot of help. It was quite an eye-opening trip for me.

In 1984 I broke out of my New York–Washington orbit and went on a three-month tour of Europe and Asia. In London, I visited the International Democratic Union and a few members of the House of Commons. I was surprised to see that members of Parliament—unlike members of the U.S. Congress—did not have elaborate offices or a retinue. I met the British MPs standing up in a hallway or sitting down on the marble stairs.

That November Ronald Reagan and George Bush were reelected in a landslide. At the UN, the diplomatic victories of the Cambodian coalition against the Vietnamese had little effect. We felt more and more that military muscle was needed to add pressure to the diplomatic success.

Bill Nojay, a lawyer friend from Rochester and a classmate from Columbia, volunteered to help out. We were trying to match our victories at the UN with victories on Capitol Hill. We descended on Washington regularly, making courtesy calls at the White House and the State Department. We kept them informed of our activities, but our focus was primarily on Congress. The greatest triumph was the passage of a $10 million authorization bill, spearheaded by Congressman Steve Solarz of New York, to provide assistance to the noncommunist resistance. A few days before the vote, Bill and I and Tommy Koh, who was the ambassador of Singapore and was one of Washington's most active diplomats, made our final assaults on the Hill. We contacted twenty-four congressional aides, especially those from the House International Relations Committee, to secure their support. It was only a decade after the Vietnam War had ended, and Washington was still opposed to any direct U.S. involvement in Southeast Asia, so we just wanted moral support and financial help.

Working on the Hill produced a different sensation from working at the UN. It was like dealing with 535 little missions, each with its own foreign policy adviser. They did not dance around the issue and had never heard of the old diplomatic adage that if a delegate said yes, he meant maybe; if he said maybe, he meant no; and he never said no. On the Hill, they said no all the time. On the tenth anniversary of the end of U.S. involvement in Southeast Asia, more Americans were prodded to take another look at Cambodia. Major U.S. newspapers, including the *New York Times, Seattle Post-Intelligencer, Wall Street Journal,* and *Washington Post,* began to advocate military assistance to the KPNLF and its noncommunist ally FUNCINPEC.

My brother, Sichhun, as a
police lieutenant, 1963.

Sichhun and Peou's
wedding, 1965.

Sichhun after his return
from Alabama, 1973.

San Chhuon, Kishore Mahbubani, me, Samnang and her groom, Sarin, and Sichhun,
1973. Everyone was killed, except Kishore, Samnang, and me.

Vice President and Mrs. Nixon with a daughter of King Sihanouk at Angkor Wat, October 30, 1953. (Richard Nixon Presidential Library)

Teaching English in a refugee camp, spring 1976.

Still in shock from a year in Cambodia's hell, spring 1976.

As a Buddhist monk in Thailand, spring 1976.

Christmas 1976 with Nancy, Bob, Julia, and Peter Charles in Wallingford, Connecticut.

June Magnaldi, Marnie Dawson, me, Nancy Charles, and Martha, Wallingford, 1988.

New York City's newest taxi driver, 1977.

With some of my Columbia classmates on a trip to Washington, D.C., 1981.

Learning how to be a cowboy in the Texas Panhandle, 1982.

With President Reagan and Vice President Bush at the thirtieth commemoration of Captive Nations Week in the Rose Garden, July 13, 1988. (Ronald Reagan Presidential Library)

My OPL colleagues and I in my office, 1989. (Ken Regan)

Larry Eagleburger and I at the UN in Geneva, 1989.

President Bush meeting Polish American leaders in the Oval Office, March 14, 1990. *To his left:* Robert Blackwell, me, Marlin Fitzwater. (George Bush Presidential Library)

Speaking for America, 2001–2006. (United Nations)

President Bush inspecting the elephants on my suit lining. (The White House)

I was apprehensive as we entered Cambodian airspace
on my first trip back.

Wearing my mother's *krama*, I offered robes to monks in
Tonle Bati where I nearly died on April 27, 1975. Phra
Kantasilo from Indiana looked on.

Martha and Cambodian officials at Pochentong Airport.
I was born less than a mile from here.

Martha's appetite for watermelon guided us to a discovery.

The truck driver's relatives on the steps of their traditional Cambodian house.

The 2006 Independence Day parade, Canadian, Texas: *This is a beautiful country!*

CHAPTER 13

TEXAS

It is difficult to say what is impossible,
for the dream of yesterday is the hope of today
and the reality of tomorrow.

—Robert Goddard (1882–1945)

I started to keep track of some important dates in my new life, which I would later label "most valuable dates" (MVDs). I immediately put two important ones on my list. Both were in 1976: February 13 was the day I began my escape, and June 4 was the day I arrived in America. For 1977, the MVD would be September 15. That was the day I met Martha Lee Pattillo.

THE FLOWERS

In New York in September 1977, while I was working on the Lower East Side of Manhattan, I called Martha Lee Pattillo at the suggestion of our friend Sam Oglesby. She invited me to her apartment for tea. The date was set for September 15. I stopped at a florist on Second Avenue and Forty-eighth Street to get a bouquet of flowers. When Martha opened her apartment door, she seemed to be very pleased to see the flowers and me together.

Martha had been born in Pampa in the Texas Panhandle about sixty miles northeast of Amarillo. She was the valedictorian of her high school class and went to the University of Texas–Austin, where she studied in the prestigious Plan II liberal arts honors program and majored in French. She continued at the Graduate School of Library and Information Sciences, where she obtained a master's degree. She did not say to me, "My dad is in the awl bidness!" Both of her parents were teachers.

She worked in Washington for a few years, bought a one-way ticket to Paris, and got a job at the Atlantic Institute. Then UNESCO offered her an assignment in Bangkok. She took a scenic route from Texas to New York. I told her I had taken an even more scenic route from Phnom Penh. We became very good friends, going out to restaurants, museums, and shows. When I worked on my graduate school applications, she was my personal editor; and she was the first person I called when I was admitted to Columbia. Her mother, Ellice, was visiting from Pampa and shared the news.

Despite our closeness, I dared not make the move. To me, she was the moon and I was the rabbit. The rabbit can only admire, but not touch, the moon, unless the moon descends to its level. I did open an account at the florist shop on Second Avenue and Forty-eighth Street and had flowers delivered to her on a regular basis. As time went by, our friendship became closer. In the early 1980s I was in great demand at a series of exhibitions on Cambodia, especially one by the National Geographic Society on Angkor. Martha and I spent more time together. In 1982, I invited her to Wallingford to meet the Charles family during the summer and she invited me to spend the Christmas holidays in Pampa. Both visits were wonderful.

Despite the way it may look or sound, the name Pattillo is not Spanish or Italian but Scottish; the Pattillos are dependents of the clan Macgregor. They originally came from Scotland's Fifeshire or Perthshire. Near Dundee, Robert Pittiloch recruited archer guards for the French service in 1423–1425. He accompanied them to France and became a commander. In 1452 he obtained letters of naturalization and was made lord of Sauveterre (Burgundy). He was known as *le petit roi de Gascoyne*. As Robert Pettillo de Clermond, he was one of the ambassadors accredited by James II to the kings of France and Castille. In the records of the Scots Guards he appears as Robin Petit Lo. The family changed the name from Pittiloch ("by the loch, or lake") to one more easily understood in French (*pas de l'eau*, "by the water").

They prospered and stayed in France; the Scots Guards were famous for their fidelity to the kings of France. As Protestants, they were protected by the Edict of Nantes, promulgated on April 13, 1598. However, after its revocation on October 18, 1685, their religious freedom was no longer guaranteed. During the subsequent persecution of the Huguenots (Protestants), they returned to Scotland and took refuge with relatives in Dundee. They changed their name again, to something more easily understood in Scotland: Pattillo, with several variant spellings.

In 1740 two Pattillo brothers, George and Henry, came to North America, to Nova Scotia and North Carolina; succeeding generations moving farther westward. Martha's grandfather, James Cuthbert Pattillo, was born in 1855 in Georgia. As a child, he came to Texas by covered wagon before the Civil War.

With this carefully documented genealogy, later generations maintained a strong interest in their family history and the French connection. Many had French names: Martha's father's name was Jean and an uncle was Le Roi. Martha is very proud to continue to carry the Pattillo name.

I met Ladd Pattillo through a colleague at LIRS in 1979, during his first trip to New York as a bond lawyer. I asked him if he knew Martha Pattillo. He said he had heard her name all his adult life and was dying to meet her. That evening I introduced the two Pattillos, who were unrelated.

Ladd called himself "terminally friendly." On my graduation from Columbia in May 1981, he sent me a round-trip ticket to Texas as a present. On my first visit to the Lone Star State, I flew to Houston, where he arranged for me to meet some of his friends, and to take a bus to Austin to see some of "God's country." It was an endless view of beautiful farms, rolling hills, and wildflowers along route 290. The serene landscape ended when the bus reached Austin in a heavy rainstorm. Ladd came to pick me up at the station and we plowed through the rain to his house in Westover Hills. On Mesa Drive, our car was briefly lifted off the ground by the water current, and we saw waves coming over the windshield. Fortunately, we made it safely home, where Ladd's wife Marilyn and their three children were waiting.

In their living room was a beautifully framed rubbing from Angkor, presented to Ladd by a Cambodian officer to whom he had given a lift at Fort Benning, Georgia, in 1974. It was a heartwarming presence. Ladd and Marilyn took me to all their favorite places in Austin and gave me a cowboy hat and a pair of boots.

THE COWBOY

In the fall of 1982, after a lot of paperwork and years of waiting, I went for a naturalization interview. The INS examiner asked me how many states there were in the United States (fifty), who makes federal laws (Congress), who my senators were (at the time, Alfonse D'Amato and Daniel Patrick Moynihan). Finally, he asked me to write something in English and asked if I wanted to change my name or add anything. That was the whole interview for citizenship. It had lasted less than thirty minutes.

On December 21, 1982, I was sworn in as a U.S. citizen in the Eastern District of New York in Brooklyn. We were given a package containing a congratulatory message from President Reagan.

Two dear friends—the best-selling author Eric Lustbader and his charming wife, Vicky—took me to a dinner at one of their favorite French restaurants on Twelfth Street for a celebration: "12/21 on #12!" I had met Eric two years earlier when he interviewed me for a book set in Cambodia. They gave me a cake, which I brought the following day to Texas. I met up with Martha in Dallas, and we flew to Amarillo with Martha's close family friends W. A. and Mattie Wave Morgan. They all had just come from Guadalajara, Mexico.

In the summer of 1983, Martha and I were both on assignments in Bangkok. On June 24, over a candlelight dinner at a Thai restaurant across the Chao Phraya River from the famous Oriental Hotel, I proposed and Martha eagerly accepted. We had known each other for six years now. Our strong friendship had bloomed into a steady romance. There was never an issue for us about this interracial union. Love has no boundaries. If anything, this was going to be a marriage *arranged* by us. We seemed to be perfect for each other.

We planned to have our wedding in Texas, but we were not sure whether it was going to be in Pampa, Martha's hometown; or Canadian, where Martha's mother was living in a nursing home. We thought that Christmas Eve would be the perfect date. We of course wanted Ellice to be at the wedding and asked her to choose the location. She said Pampa, at Martha's childhood church, the First Presbyterian.

We brought Mrs. Pattillo from Canadian and checked into the Coronado Inn. On Christmas Eve 1983, Pampa was one of the coldest spots in the United States. The temperature was seven degrees below zero; there was a foot of snow on the ground; the wind was blowing at twenty miles an hour; and it started snowing again. I carried Ellice in my arms from the car to the church and settled her in a wheelchair with layers of quilts. Our close friends packed the church. Many kept their coats on. There were flowers everywhere. As we walked down the aisle, I was thinking of *Mae*, Sarin, and Sichhun. They must be very happy to know that I now had a family.

The blizzard abated and we were able to drive to Albuquerque, Santa Fe, and Taos for our honeymoon. After Santa Fe, we stretched our honeymoon over a longer time by visiting Tampa, Boston, Washington, London, Paris, and Mexico City. In Paris, we dressed in traditional Cambodian wedding costumes. Having lived in Thailand for a few years, Martha was already familiar with the customs and tradition of neighboring Cambodia.

After the wedding, I felt very ecumenical: "Here I am, a Buddhist married to a Presbyterian. I came to America through a Catholic agency. I got jobs through a Jewish organization. I have worked for the Lutheran and Episcopal churches helping refugees of all faiths."

Through Martha, my new world continued to expand, to the Texas of the Panhandle: high plains of cattle ranches and oil wells. At the top of Texas, heaven and earth hug each other in an unobstructed 360-degree view. People say you don't go there unless you have to. Pampa is closer to five other state capitals (Oklahoma City, Santa Fe, Denver, Cheyenne, and Lincoln) than to Austin. It's said that there is nothing between Pampa and the North Pole except a barbed-wire fence, and two strands are down.

Texas is a state of mind. It's big, much bigger than Cambodia. Before joining the Union in 1845, Texas was an independent country. For a full decade, the United States and Texas exchanged diplomatic envoys.

It is difficult for us to visit our relatives and friends in one single trip. They are scattered all over the state, from Pampa in the north to Texarkana in the east and Bay City in the south, not to mention those in the big cities: Austin, Dallas, Houston, and San Antonio. It is 856 miles from Dalhart in the north to South Padre Island and 834 miles from Orange at the Louisiana border to El Paso in the Mountain Time zone near New Mexico. It takes at least two days to go across the state, and according to one popular saying, "The sun has riz, the sun has set, and here we is in Texas yet."

In Cambodia, all the western movies I saw were in French, including James Dean's *Géant*, John Wayne's *Alamo*, Kirk Douglas's *Le Dernier Train de Gun-Hill*, and Clint Eastwood's *Pour une Poignée de Dollars*. I always wanted to be in the saddle. The Panhandle was the perfect place to realize this dream. I had taken English-style horseback riding lessons at the Claremont Academy near New York City's Central Park. Now, I was riding western-style and was becoming a naturalized Texan! Ranches in Texas are measured in sections. Each section equals 640 acres. A small ranch probably has fifty sections or about 42,000 acres of land to ride in.

After Martha's mother died in 1984, we continued to visit the Panhandle at least once a year. Each time we fly to Amarillo, we have to go through DFW Airport. Besides New York and Washington, I believe that I have been to DFW more often than to any other airport in the world. People say that when you die, whether you go to heaven or hell, you change planes at DFW.

At a speech I gave at the Pampa Kiwanis Club, the chief of police told me in a slow drawl, "Well, the next time you are in Pampa give me a call. I'll buy you a cup of coffee!" Afterward, Martha turned to me and said that I might not realize the import of his invitation: "When the police chief of Pampa invites you to have a coffee with him, you've made it!"

THUNDER DRAGON

In 1987 Martha was sent by the UN Development Program (UNDP) to Bhutan to supervise setting up a library at Sherubtse College in Kanglung. I decided to accompany her. Getting there was quite an elaborate process and half the fun. There were only two ways to get to Paro, Bhutan's only airport—either from Calcutta in India or from Dhaka in Bangladesh.

In Bangkok, I called the Indian consulate to inquire about a transit visa, because the flights to Bhutan were very irregular. The consular officer assured me that I would not need one if I was going to be only in transit. He said that he had served at the Indian embassy in Thimphu for four years.

When Martha and I arrived in Calcutta, our Druk Air flight to Paro was canceled. We had to stay overnight at a nearby hotel and try our luck the following day. Martha had no problem, since she did have an Indian visa. I tried to explain my peculiar situation to the immigration officer, to no avail. I finally asked to see the supervisor and was brought to a nearby room. After I had waited on pins and needles for thirty minutes, the immigration chief showed up. A handsome Bengali, he wore a crisply pressed uniform and had a fine mustache. He looked very serious, and I began to worry. He said to me that he could let me leave for the hotel, but I would have to go to the immigration office in Calcutta if I missed the flight again. I said I would take my chances and thanked him profusely. In an even more serious tone, he said, "I have never done this for anybody. I am doing this for you because I trust you. You know why?"

"Because you find me a trustworthy person?"

He leaned closer to me and suddenly a nice smile appeared on his face. "Actually, I trust you because you and I have the same birthday." He slapped my leg, leaned back, and burst into a big laugh. I immediately joined him, laughing out loud. The chief pulled his ID out to show that he was telling me the truth.

Not to be outdone, I informed my new friend that my name in Sanskrit is "Srichandra Siva."

"Yes! Sichan Siv! Srichandra Siva! It's Lord Siva's Beautiful Moon! We are brothers!" Siva is one of the three divinities in Hinduism—the other two being Brahma and Vishnu. It is believed that Siva is both the creator and the destroyer of the universe.

The following morning, Martha and I returned to Calcutta's Dum Dum Airport. Our flight was delayed a few times. The airport restaurant had a Delayed Flight Services section where we spent most of our day. Finally, we were rounded up and boarded a few small cars to a high-wing twin-propeller plane. It was a Dornier seating sixteen to eighteen.

The flight from Calcutta to Paro was an unforgettable experience. It began over the flat plains of Bangladesh. The terrain became more and more mountainous as we got closer to the Himalayas. The Dornier followed valleys, and we suddenly noticed Bhutanese with their sheep on the mountainside at the level of our windows. As it made the final approach, we saw red chiles being dried on the rooftops. Welcome to Druk Yul, the Kingdom of the Thunder Dragon, as Bhutan is known in *dzongkha*.

Half the size of Indiana, this predominantly Buddhist country is mountainous in the north, with peaks reaching to 24,000 feet; and has plains and river valleys in the south. Sandwiched between India and China, the two most populous countries on earth, the 1.4 million Bhutanese had lived in relative peace and followed their centuries-old customs. The country has remained untouched, well preserved, and wild. It is indeed Shangri-la on the top of the world.

Martha and I were in Bhutan on September 15, 1987, the tenth anniversary of the day we had met in New York. Sam Oglesby, who had introduced us, was our host. After a few wonderful days enjoying one of the most beautiful places on earth, Martha left for a three-day road trip across the 124 miles from Thimphu to Kanglung in the far eastern part of the country. I left for the two-hour drive to Paro. There was only one other passenger on the Druk Air flight to Calcutta: a young Bhutanese man. After we took off, he asked me if I wanted to have some coffee.

"There is no flight attendant?"

"There is a thermos of coffee, and everything is at the rear seat. We are supposed to help ourselves."

So we did. My travel companion told me that he was going to Oxford for a master's program and that he was the first Bhutanese to be the recipient of such a scholarship. As we continued our conversation, I kept looking through the plane window and wondered how many places were left on the planet that had such natural beauty. My journey to Druk Yul, Kingdom of the Thunder Dragon, was simply otherworldly.

THE CAMPAIGN

The year of my first direct involvement in a presidential campaign was 1987. It was a good opportunity for me to try to understand American politics better. On my arrival in America in 1976, I had been attracted to the Republican Party. I shared its core principles of family values, less taxes, and a strong defense. After I had been sworn in as a U.S. citizen at the Brooklyn courthouse in December 1982, I immediately registered to be a Republican.

Through a number of friends, I came into touch with Bruce Gelb, who, along with Walter Curley, would be heading the New York campaign for George Bush. Having signed on as a volunteer, I helped raise money and plan strategies in the Big Apple. I spent endless hours on the phone to round up national support for my candidate. At the same time, I got an eye-opening education on the fast-paced world of U.S. elections. I volunteered early enough to be exposed to the complete, complex, challenging process of a presidential campaign. This I would call MPP: money, politics, and policy. I learned that grassroots outreach was among the most important strategies in a successful campaign. And regardless of the level of involvement, a supporter must be familiar with various positions of the candidate, and be willing to speak out in his or her defense.

After a few visits to Washington in the early 1980s, I got myself on the mailing list of Reagan's White House and began to receive invitations to various programs. It was quite a thrill to get mail from the White House, especially an invitation. Sitting in Room 450 of the Old Executive Office Building (OEOB), I marveled at the White House staff, who seemed to do everything to perfection. *Wouldn't it be wonderful to work at the White House?*

As time went by, I was slowly moved by the White House staff from the back of the OEOB auditorium to an assigned seat front and center. Then I was recognized. On December 10, 1984, Assistant Secretary of State Elliott Abrams introduced me at the Human Rights Day commemoration at the White House.

But nothing could top the Rose Garden ceremony on July 13, 1988. Every year the White House organized this event, and the president would proclaim the third week of July "Captive Nations Week," dedicated to all the countries that had fallen to communism since the end of World War II. In 1984, I attended the event in the East Room. In 1988 I was promoted to the dais.

It was the ultimate privilege for me to be chosen from millions of ethnic Americans to participate at the thirtieth commemoration ceremony. I was told to stand at the extreme right, and therefore I was the first to greet President Reagan and Vice President Bush when they came onto the dais. I thanked the president for everything he had done for Cambodia. He smiled and gave me a very firm handshake. To the vice president, I said, "You have my support." "Thank you, sir," was his response.

Such an honor put me on cloud nine. I was surprised to realize how hot heaven could be. Imagine standing for forty-five minutes on a stage under ninety-degree sun in a dark suit, in front of 250 people and the media, and for thirty minutes of that time in the company of the president and vice president of the United States, with additional spotlights on your face. It went, however, very quickly. It was a most memorable moment.

Four months later, my candidate, George Bush, was elected as the forty-first president of the United States. He carried forty states, including California, with a total of 426 electoral votes. In the Northeast, New York and Massachusetts went to Governor Michael Dukakis.

PART IV:

ON BEHALF OF
THE PRESIDENT

*There is nothing more fulfilling than to serve your country
and your fellow citizens and do it well.*

—George Bush

CHAPTER 14:

41 AND 41

During the Monday of the Martin Luther King holiday weekend in January 1989, I went to my office at the Institute of
International Education across the street from the UN to catch up on
some work. Around mid-morning, the phone rang. I did not pick it
up—nobody knew I had come to the office. About fifteen minutes
later, it rang again. I looked at the phone and decided to ignore it. After another fifteen minutes, there was another call. Somebody was
quite persistent, as if he or she knew I was there. I picked up the phone.
It was Mary Kate Grant, an old friend of mine who used to work for
Congressman Hamilton Fish IV of New York. She had just spoken
with Martha, who had told her I was at the office. Mary Kate asked if
I could go to Washington to meet with David Demarest.

"David who?"

"David is the communications director of the transition. He is
likely to keep that job at the White House."

"When do you want me to be there?"

"Tomorrow at ten o'clock, if possible."

"I'll be there," I said to her right away. And I was very glad that I
had answered her phone call.

On Tuesday, January 17, I took the shuttle to Washington. I met with Demarest for about thirty minutes. He explained to me the organization of his communications shop at the White House, which would include speechwriting, research, media relations, and public liaison. The transition team was looking for somebody to handle national security issues at the Office of Public Liaison (OPL). After a friendly conversation, he told me that he would have to check with John Sununu, the governor of New Hampshire, who was coming in as chief of staff. He introduced me briefly to Bobbie Kilberg, who would be my counterpart for domestic issues.

Chase Untermeyer, who was the personnel chief for the transition, had come across my résumé when Demarest asked for a recommendation. Had David asked a few days later, Chase might have filed my paper away and forgotten it. Timing is everything.

FROM GEORGE TO GEORGE

Martha and I had planned to attend the inauguration, which would be our first. It was a "George to George" bicentennial celebration: from George Washington to George Bush.

Friday, January 20, 1989, was a beautiful day in Washington. The capital and the rest of the country were in a celebratory mood. We participated in the celebration, giving great attention to every single detail of the ceremony. *This is history.*

Chief Justice William Rehnquist swore George Bush in as the forty-first president of the United States.

In his inaugural address, the new president talked about unity, diversity, generosity, a new breeze, and candor and said that America's strength was the force for good. He said that freedom was like a beautiful kite which could go higher and higher with the breeze, and that challenges were great, but will was greater. He introduced hopefulness and meaning.

President Reagan, with a sixty-five percent approval rating, saluted his successor from the steps of his helicopter. The new president returned the salute from the steps of the Capitol. *It was an incredibly peaceful transfer of power.*

The theme of the inauguration was "peace, prosperity, and independence." Our seats were in front of the White House, next to the presidential reviewing stand. I was in awe, seeing the president and Mrs. Bush getting out of their limousine to walk and wave. I was aiming my camera at him when he got to his seat. Martha exclaimed in excitement: "Sichan, look. He is waving at you." I put my camera down and we both waved back at him. I had no idea that I would be working for him in just a few weeks. *Is it possible?*

The parade was simply beautiful. Bob Hope and Chuck Yeager served as grand marshals. Military units, marching bands, beautifully decorated floats, horses, men, women, boys, and girls. A Grumman Avenger (a torpedo bomber of the type flown by the president in World War II) rolled by. Everything, everyone was beautiful and cheerful. I couldn't keep track of all the good things. We stayed almost until the end but then had to change into a tuxedo and evening gown for the later festivities.

The inaugural committee assigned us, residents of the Big Apple, to the New York ball, held with a few other states. We were entertained by Lester Lanin and his orchestra. The floor was packed. We could hardly move our arms and legs, much less dance. Lanin distributed hats and tapes to the revelers, who went wild. President and Mrs. Bush and Vice President and Mrs. Quayle dropped by and thanked us for our support.

On Monday, January 23, Nick Hayes rang me up to say that the White House was looking for me. I called the White House and was told to go in and process my paperwork. There I met my new assistant, Charles Bacarisse, a young political appointee, who had stayed on from the Reagan White House. He seemed to know everything. He showed me my new digs, Suite 128 of the OEOB.

I was quite moved to see "Sichan Siv" in the White House tele-phone phone directory dated January 21, 1989. It seemed that just the other day I was running for my life in the jungle of Cambodia, and now my name was listed with Brent Scowcroft and the like. I was speechless.

TRISKAIDEKAPHILIA

My first day as deputy assistant to the president for public liaison was February 13, 1989. This was the culmination of a series that make thir-teen my lucky number.

During the thirteen years from February 13, 1976, to February 13, 1989, I counted among the important dates May 13, 1981, the day I graduated from Columbia; and July 13, 1988, the day I met both Presi-dent Reagan and Vice President Bush.

My mother was born on April 13, 1913. April 13 is when Cambo-dians and Theravada Buddhists celebrate the new year and when Thomas Jefferson was born in 1743.

Many Christians, however, consider the number thirteen a bad omen, because there were thirteen people at the Last Supper before the crucifixion of Jesus. Some people do not travel or sign deals on the thirteenth. Others will not have thirteen people to dinner. And many tall buildings have no thirteenth floor.

America's history is full of thirteens. First, there were the original thirteen colonies. The American flag has thirteen red and white stripes, and the seal of the United States has thirteen olive branches, stars, and arrows. During the battle of the Alamo, the Texans held out for thirteen days before they were massacred by the forces of the Mexi-can general, Santa Anna.

Apollo 13 was launched on Jefferson's birthday in 1970, and al-though it almost became a disaster, it instead became a monumental example of extraordinary teamwork.

In ancient times, the Romans associated the number thirteen with omens of death and destruction, but the Egyptians believed that thirteen was the number of steps to immortality.

As for me, I am happy to turn the fear of the number thirteen, triskaidekaphobia, to triskaidekaphilia.

Thirteen years to the day after I began my escape from the Cambodian nightmare, I walked into my new office at the White House—as the president's new deputy assistant for public liaison, the first Asian to be appointed at this level.

ON BEHALF OF THE PRESIDENT

The Office of Public Liaison (OPL) was founded by President Eisenhower to function as a conduit between the president and the American people. Most voters were organized into associations or federations with representative offices in Washington. They were there to lobby Capitol Hill as well as the administration, starting with the White House. The OPL officers maintained contact with these various constituencies of ethnic groups, bankers, doctors, farmers, lawyers, teachers, truckers, women, and so on to inform them of the president's policies, especially those that affected their constituents. At the same time, we listened to their concerns and relayed them to the president and other White House colleagues.

After being sworn in, I sat down in the high-backed four-wheeled leather chair and took a few deep breaths.

"Is this really happening to me or am I dreaming?"

"Am I really at the White House working for the president of the United States?"

"Could it be possible that thirteen years ago I was fleeing hell on earth, and now I am a presidential aide?"

"Only in America!"

I awoke from my deep thought when Charles Bacarisse knocked

on the door and handed me "George Bush's Marching Orders." They
included the following:

- Think big.
- Challenge the system.
- Adhere to the highest ethical standards.
- Be on the record as much as possible.
- Be frank.
- Fight hard for your position.
- When I make a call, we move as a team.
- Work with Congress.
- Represent the United States with dignity.

This president was an avid note writer. He liked to stay in touch
with his fellow Americans: if the people take time to contact us, we
must find time to respond. I told my colleagues that we must make every effort to return phone calls within twenty-four hours and corre-
spondence within one week.

It had been twenty-four years since my last visit to the USIS library in Phnom Penh in 1965. At seventeen, I was a master of U.S.
geography and history, which I had learned in French. Now it was time
to take a refresher course, in two of my favorite subjects, this time in
English. Besides knowing all the state capitals, the longest rivers, the
largest lakes, the highest peaks, and the names of presidents in order
from George to George, I needed to know, among other things, who
said what. One of my favorite activities was reading inaugural speeches.
Actually, I did this more to practice my delivery than merely for the
sake of reading.

I used a music stand that belonged to Martha when she was a
member of the Pride of Pampa band at her high school, playing clari-
net and oboe. Although my audience consisted of one person—
Martha—I pretended that there were thousands of people. I practiced

what I called a "Z 180" delivery: starting at the farthest corner on the left, moving across the audience to the farthest corner on the right, cutting from there to the nearest corner on the left and finally to the nearest corner on the right. Each of these three moves had to be broken into increments of sixty degrees each. This meant that I had to lower my eyes for a few seconds to read what I was going to say before the next sixty-degree stop. At this point, I would reverse the Z, moving from right to left—hence, a "Z 180" delivery. This enabled me to maintain regular eye contact with my audience. Martha's job was to take note of my mispronunciations and to guess whose address it was. Obviously, I had to skip passages that would give away the identity of the speaker. Besides, I avoided following the historical chronology of the presidencies.

"On behalf of the president" became a standard opening remark for me in countless briefings, meetings, and other events that my colleagues and I organized at the White House. Each time I uttered those five words, I had an enormous sense of pride. I felt I was extraordinarily lucky and blessed to be working for George Bush and speaking on behalf of the president of the United States.

ONLY IN AMERICA

Invitations began to pour into my office. My assistant, Charles Bacarisse, who knew Washington better than I did, usually gave me his recommendations: "yes, no, maybe."

On March 20, I went to the Kennedy Center to attend a military event. The program began with the national anthem. We all stood up, and I was blank. I did not know how to sing "The Star-Spangled Banner." The following day, I discreetly inquired and made enough copies of our national anthem to have it everywhere: in my office, at home (on the refrigerator, in the bathroom, on the bedside table), in the car, in my pocket. For some time, I would practice singing "The Star-Spangled

Banner" every morning before going to work. I was probably one of the few Americans who did that every morning.

Now I was ready to sing, and eagerly awaiting another military invitation. In June the Marine Corps commandant, Al Gray, invited the president and Mrs. Bush along with the White House senior staff to the summer drill at the corps barracks in Washington. In one of the exercises, when the marines threw their rifles into the air for the others to catch, one missed and the rifle fell to the ground. The president sent a warm handwritten note to the poor marine who had missed. He was later invited to the White House. It was an impeccable review overall and close to perfection.

My good friend Chase Untermeyer became director of presidential personnel at the White House. Chase had known the president before he was a congressman. Always loyal and trustworthy, he was the perfect person to hold that job. One day, he called and asked if I would like to go to Geneva for a few days as cochair of the U.S. delegation to a refugee conference. Without knowing who the other cochair was, I said yes. Chase then informed me that Deputy Secretary of State Lawrence Eagleburger and I would lead the delegation.

At the Palais des Nations in Geneva, I recognized Jean-David Levitte, an old friend who was France's permanent representative. I tapped his shoulder, and he was very surprised to see me.

"Sichan! *Qu'est ce que tu fais là?*—What are you doing here?"

Without responding to his question, I smiled and presented my business card. Under the embossed gold seal of the United States, it read: SICHAN SIV, DEPUTY ASSISTANT TO THE PRESIDENT, THE WHITE HOUSE. Jean-David was stunned. He looked at the card one more time and exclaimed, "*Tu es à la Maison Blanche?*—You are at the White House?" He continued slowly in English: "This is great! This is America! You know, Sichan, had you gone to France, you might not be still driving a taxi in Paris, but working for Mitterrand would be beyond imagination. You've made it. Only in America!"

"*Merci*, Jean-David; coming from you, this is the ultimate compliment."

We gave each other a hug and walked in the same direction to our seats. In French and in alphabetical order, *États-Unis* and France are close to each other. In fact, our refugee policies were also similar. Ironically, Britain, our strongest ally on all fronts, was in an awkward position with us, because of a thorny issue in Hong Kong involving Vietnamese boat refugees.

After two days, I flew back to Washington with Eagleburger on a government Gulfstream. We stopped in Gander for refueling. I walked to the gift shop as an Aeroflot Ilyushin was rolling slowly onto the tarmac. It was a flight from Moscow to Havana. I stopped to watch the disembarking passengers. Seeing how they were dressed, I wondered whether they were going to win the cold war.

Can people be judged by their appearance? Obviously not. As the French used to say, *L'habit ne fait pas le moine*—"The habit does not make a monk." But in this case it may!

As I rode the White House car from Andrews Air Force Base back to the office, I was grateful not only that I had survived, but that I had prevailed so far because of *Mae*'s message of hope. And because I had managed to make my way to a country where such hope—along with lots of hard work—can make the most improbable dreams come true.

Only in America!

CHAPTER 15:

THE WHITE HOUSE

I cannot say how overwhelmed I was to walk to the northwest gate of the White House on February 13, 1989, to report for duty. I kept asking myself how it was possible for somebody like me to make it that far in what felt like such a short time. It must have been a combination of luck and fate. My White House years were a fascinating period when I could see how the world of Washington power politics looked through the eyes of a former refugee.

POWER TO SERVE

For a few months, until Martha was able to move from New York to join the World Bank in May, my world consisted of a sliver of Washington between a rented furnished studio, a twenty-five-minute walk away, on Massachusetts Avenue to 1600 Pennsylvania Avenue. I usually got to the office around seven-thirty AM and did not leave until twelve or thirteen hours later. Each day went by very quickly. I always felt privileged each time I reached the White House gate, either on foot or by car.

Martha and I both had new experiences. Having lived in New

York City for twelve years, we had never owned a car. I hadn't owned one since I had a beat-up old Toyota when I was driving a cab and living in Brooklyn! Unless you are rich enough to have a driver, having a car in Manhattan is an extra burden, financially and otherwise. The New York City public transportation system is quite effective.

In Washington, we needed a car. So we went to get a loan and were faced with the typical questions.

"Have you ever owned a car?"

"No."

"Do you have any debts?"

"No."

"If you have never owned a car and you have no debt, it's very difficult for us to establish a credit history. Sorry, we cannot help you."

I could not believe it! It was ridiculous that you had to be in debt in order to borrow money. And this was for a measly $10,000. We went to a second place, and the only question the staff asked was, "When?"

This little incident reminded me that in the real world some people do not care whether or not you have the trust and confidence of the leader of the free world. If you don't fit their template, you are out of luck.

People view power differently. In many developing countries, power is synonymous with financial benefits, or corruption. Here in America, I define power as the ability to solve problems, to serve and help people, and to make things better for them. I was given the privilege of serving, and I planned to serve. For me, the person I was serving was George Bush, the forty-first president of the United States, and through him the American people. I set out to be his representative to the public interest groups, to the American people, and not the other way around. I was determined to avoid clientitis by all means.

I was reminded of the analogy of the monkey. The higher he

climbed, the more he showed his behind. Although I was close to the most powerful person on earth, I preferred to keep my body, from head to toe, as low as possible so that nobody could see my behind.

One has to admit that the words "White House" do carry incredible cachet. For starters, your phone calls are always returned. Second, you receive a lot of attention.

PERSONNEL, POLITICS, AND POLICIES

The White House commissioned officers are the assistants to the president, deputy assistants, and special assistants. In the spring of 1989 there were thirteen assistants, twenty-four deputy assistants, and forty-four special assistants.

All the assistants had their offices in the West Wing. Most of these offices were half the size of mine in the OEOB. If proximity was important, I could get to the Oval Office in sixty seconds!

Among the people who went to work for George Bush, I was the one who had traveled the longest and on the most tortuous road before reaching the White House. Unlike many who had known the president for a long time, I had met him only once and had been with him for just thirty minutes on July 13, 1988. Among my colleagues, I was a complete outsider with the least knowledge of Washington. However, I was familiar with the president's domestic, economic, and foreign policies, which I supported wholeheartedly.

I relished in the fact that I had not known a single human being when I arrived in America thirteen years earlier. Along the way, I had made many friends, and I was married to a very lovely and supportive wife. Everywhere, people seem to stand ready to "adopt" me, and I have always remained very "adoptable and adaptable."

I thought I knew everything that the president stood for. But it was only an iota compared with what many of my colleagues knew. Some had been in his campaign full-time. They had known each other since then, or even before. A few had been with the president when he was vice president or in his other previous incarnations, including CIA director, Republican National Committee chairman, and congressman.

I was not sure how I would be received at the Bush White House.

At the OPL, my domestic counterpart was Bobbie Kilberg, who had been in the White House during previous Republican administrations. She knew all the key players in Washington and had a fine grasp of politics. She once told an interviewer that she could trust me with her life. I thought it was an extraordinary compliment. She was Jewish and I was Buddhist, so the Bush White House had a "Buddhish" leadership in its outreach office. There were fifteen people in OPL, which was much smaller than it had been in the Reagan White House, when it was headed only by women, including Elizabeth Dole before she was appointed secretary of transportation. Bobbie and I had our weekly meeting in my office with the entire OPL staff, a group of highly motivated, hardworking people. We were very lucky to have such strong and effective support in our office, which was managed by Susan Denniston. She and Bobbie were really the mothers of OPL.

Rose Zamaria had been with the president longer than anybody else. She was as tough as nails. I was always scared of her. One evening, Martha and I came from a reception, swung our car door open, and accidentally punctured a tiny hole in the left rear light of a nearby car with Florida plates. I did not know it was Rose's car until Charles told me that I'd better start praying. I called Rose immediately and offered to pay for the repair. I thought she was going to scream at me, but she was very appreciative of my candor, saying that she would never have noticed the tiny hole if I hadn't told her. Evidently, not many people walked around every day looking for tiny damage to their vehicles. We became good friends. Although she never went out speaking, she did accept my invitation to address a group of people who wanted to hear from someone who had known the president longest. During the rededication of Ellis Island, Rose and I were the only two White House staffers to accompany Vice President and Mrs. Quayle: she as a descendant of Italian immigrants, I as a former refugee.

I had been trying to get the most coveted status symbol, a "staff pin" that gave the wearer full access to presidential events anywhere. I had been stopped in West Virginia when the president went to present the Teacher of the Year Award to a teacher in Slanesville. I had been stopped at the Waldorf when I was on my way to a meeting between the president and Prince Sihanouk of Cambodia. The local secret service agents did not recognize me or my "guest pin." I reported this to Rose, and she was able to give me a staff pin. It helps to know people in high places!

The first White House romance and wedding I witnessed involved Chase Untermeyer and Diana Kendrick, who worked in the counsel's office. When we learned that they planned their honeymoon in Nepal, Martha and I suggested Bhutan, which was even more exotic, and offered to accompany them. So we provided our first and only guided honeymoon tour, joined by our friend Julia Chang Bloch, who was ambassador to Nepal.

The media found out very quickly about my presence at the White House. New York *Newsday* got the first scoop and had a big spread the day after I was sworn in: "From Cambodia to the White House, Ex-Cabbie Is Liaison to Bush." Then came the *Washington Post*, the *New York Times*, wire services, radio (Jim Bohannon), and TV (Charlie Rose). *People's* six-page story, "Escape from the Inferno," on March 27, 1989, detailed the nightmare of blood and violence I had experienced. *Parade* ("I Survived on Hope," July 8, 1990), *Reader's Digest* ("The Rebirth of Sichan Siv," February 1991), and many others recounted the story of a man who fought his way through hell in order to find freedom and love on the other side.

SACRIFICE AND PRIVILEGE

A few days after I arrived at the White House, I received a memo listing various perks, including access to the White House tennis court and mess. This was a dividing line between the senior staff (assistants and deputy assistants) and the special assistants. Although the special assistants had access to the mess, they could eat only in the staff or ward rooms, not in the wood-paneled executive dining hall next to the Situation Room. That was reserved for cabinet members and the senior White House staff, and the host had his or her name carved on a navy-style pewter plate. This stems from a tradition that the military provides support services to the White House: the army drives the cars, the air force flies the planes, the marines fly the helicopters, and the navy runs the mess. The tennis court was quite a place, invisible from outside, with incredible views of the White House when you were serving on one side of the net and of the Washington Monument when you were serving on the other side.

The presidential boxes at the Kennedy Center were used for representational purposes. I never had anybody say no to dining or playing tennis at the White House or attending a performance in a presidential box. These perks were available in a bidding process. The highest-ranking person had the first go on their use.

Kathy Wills—whom we called ROTUS, for "receptionist of the United States" because she was the first person to greet visitors in the West Wing—was in charge of scheduling the perks. She was so diligent that she would call me up if she did not hear from me for a long while.

On March 2 (Texas Independence Day), I rushed back to the White House after a nice lunch with Julia Chang Bloch. That afternoon, OPL organized a presidential event in the East Room to honor fifty-three teachers selected by the National Endowment for the Humanities. A few minutes before the events, Tim McBride, the president's personal aide, told me that the president wanted to see me in the Green Room. The minute I walked in, the president shook my hand and said he wanted to welcome me to the White House. He was happy that I was there and wished me all the best. Meanwhile, David Valdez, the chief photographer, took a few pictures. It was an awesome moment. I had been at the White House only two weeks, and the chief executive sought me out to welcome me. Amazing!

On April 10, I was to take Miss Universe and Miss USA to meet the president. While waiting in the West Wing reception area, I was amused to see many of my male colleagues stop by to say hello. In the Oval Office, after the usual courtesies and the photo opportunity, the president turned to me: "Sichan, you didn't get a picture with me. Let's go over there and have one!" We stood before the portrait of George Washington, as the still photographer and video cameraman recorded the memorable event. The president told me that he had read "that powerful story" about my life, in *People*. He added: "It's a wonderful tribute to your perseverance. I am very happy and proud to have you at the White House." His guests looked at him with admiration for taking time to care about his staff. I was ecstatic to have his picture with me in my office so soon. This is a sign of trust, confidence, and loyalty.

The president liked to mention his staff at every opportunity. On April 2, 1990, in remarks to the National Association of Broadcasters in Atlanta, he illustrated his point on Voice of America by telling my story:

> To fully appreciate what these broadcasts mean, you need only ask someone who listened to them. Sichan Siv . . . lived through the horrors of the killing fields. And he's told me that when the Khmer Rouge took control of a village the very first items they

confiscated were the radios, for if they respected and feared any-thing, it was the power of free information. But even under the threat of death, men and women like Sichan Siv were so hun-gry for news from the outside world that they would turn on a hidden transistor radio at the lowest possible volume and then put it up flush to one ear. We take free news broadcasts for granted in America, but some people risked death to hear the truth. And some people still do, and we're not going to let them down.

CHAPTER 16:

AMERICANS FIRST

I n my outreach to ethnic communities across the country, my message had been, "We are all Americans first and everything else second." We came from every part of the world because we believe in American values. Out of many, into one! *E pluribus unum!*

For a few decades, Americans of Asian and Pacific ancestry have grown faster than any other segments of the population. Their profiles as an ethnic group are diverse and impressive. They are Buddhists, Christians, Jews, Muslims, and Hindus. They speak different languages, eat different foods, and wear different clothes. Despite their diverse cultural identities, Asian and Pacific Americans are united in a common belief in education, family values, hard work, self-sacrifice, and freedom.

This ethnic diversity—one of America's greatest strengths—stems from earlier immigration patterns and admissions of refugees since the 1970s. As a result, there is widespread demographic dispersion of Asians throughout the country. They can be found as a vibrant part of nearly every U.S. city from Stockton in California to Lowell in Massachusetts. Earlier Asian immigrants made enormous contributions to America, from building the transcontinental railroad to winning the

Nobel Prize and becoming CEOs of major corporations. Thousands exemplify their significance with proud service in the armed forces. Those who gave their lives symbolize commitment and dedication to the bravest aspect of America—defending the values on which this nation stands.

They have faced many problems across the land: hate crimes, youth gangs, university admission quotas, and glass ceilings. But they work seven days a week, often at two jobs, with high hopes and a strong determination to make it in America. They run groceries, drive taxis, work at filling stations and fast-food restaurants. They are also doctors and lawyers; social workers and teachers; musical geniuses and astronauts. Among the refugees of the 1970s and 1980s, Haing Ngor of *The Killing Fields,* a Cambodian, became the first Asian to win an Oscar. Vietnamese graduated from the service academies. And in 1991, a Hmong graduated from West Point.

They are seen on television screens all around the country as news anchors, meteorologists, and sportscasters. One (Dr. David Ho) became *Time*'s Man of the Year in 1996. They constitute about one-fourth of the winners in the Westinghouse science talent search every year. Some who could hardly speak English when they reached America went on to win spelling bees. They win all kinds of championships for the United States, from Olympic skating (Kristi Yamaguchi and Michelle Kwan) to the French Open (Michael Chang) to sumo wrestling (Konishiki "Dump Truck" Yasokichi). They hold public office, from school board to courthouse to city hall to state legislature and state house, and to the U.S. Congress.

For a number of years, the president of the United States had designated one week in May as Asian Pacific American Heritage Week. In 1990, President Bush extended the celebration to the whole month of May.

I thought that a presidential event outside the White House would be appropriate to recognize the contributions of Americans of Asian and Pacific ancestry. After much research and preparation, we settled on Mile Square Regional Park in Fountain Valley, California. John Tsu, a veteran Republican leader, and Elizabeth Szu were spearheading the efforts. Miss Universe 1988, Porntip Nakhirunkanok, whom I introduced to the president shortly after I arrived at the White House, was the emcee.

The community leaders put on an impressive show. Some 60,000 people participated. They set up booths displaying arts and handicrafts from Asia and the Pacific. They held a contest for the best booth, and Cambodia won the first prize. President and Mrs. Bush had a photo op with the welcoming committee and the cast members of a performance of classical and folk dances.

After Air Force One took off from Los Angeles, I spent a brief moment in the plane's computer room writing a memo to the president summing up the Fountain Valley event. A few minutes later, I got a copy of my memo with the president's handwritten response. He was very happy with the "Asian Pacific Salute."

We had two stops before Andrews Air Force Base: Grand Junction, Colorado, and Milwaukee, Wisconsin. After working nonstop for one week, I thought I deserved a few hours' break and decided to treat myself to some relaxation at 31,000 feet. Nobody in the staff cabin was watching television; everyone was listening to music, reading, writing, or taking a nap (which I came to call a "power break"). The movie program listed among the selections *Predator 2*. I loved Schwarzenegger's movies, especially the first *Predator*, and thought he was in the second one. I picked up the phone and was startled when the operator recognized me: "Yes, Mr. Siv. What can I do for you?"

I put my headset on, lay back in the comfortable armchair, and enjoyed the movie. When we landed at Grand Junction, I picked up the phone and before I uttered a word, the operator said: "Yes, Mr. Siv, I'll stop the movie for you." On the way to Milwaukee, the same procedure: "Yes, Mr. Siv, I'll start the movie for you."

The Boeing 747 stopped rolling on the tarmac at Andrews at exactly ten-forty-five PM, as specified in the president's schedule. Talk about precision. I got up at the same time as my seatmate, Secretary of Education Lamar Alexander, who asked, "What movie was it, Sichan?" Lamar had apparently seen action sequences but could not hear without a headset.

"*Predator 2!*"

"As secretary of education, I am going to ban this movie tomorrow," he said, deadpan.

On November 12, 1991, George Bush became the first sitting president to address the Asia Society. Founded in 1956 by John D. Rockefeller, the society's mission was to strengthen ties between the United States and Asia through educational and cultural programs. Its annual dinner had been the organization's most important event. It brought together Asian and Americans from academe, the arts, business, and government. In October, the society held a symposium in Los Angeles, "The Asian American Experience: Looking Ahead," during which I spoke about the president's position on education and other issues of interest to the community, including U.S. policies toward Asia and the Pacific, as well as the role of ethnic Americans in the U.S. policy-making process. There were about 1,000 participants, mostly of Asian and Pacific ancestry.

In preparation for the fiftieth anniversary of Pearl Harbor, I called a meeting of our national security communications task force. I also invited a few members of a unit that became famous during World War II, the Japanese-American 442nd Regiment. For its size, this unit, whose slogan was "Go for Broke," was the most decorated in America history. Throughout the discussion, many people used the term "Japanese-American." Then one member of the regiment raised his hand and said, "We are not Japanese-Americans. We are Americans of Japanese ancestry." We took note of that, and the president's speech in Pearl Harbor was very well received.

It was important for people to know that they had been part of the whole process. They were with us when we took off, and we were together when we landed. Throughout my years at the White House, the Asian and Pacific community, from Susan Allen in Washington to Florence Fang and Frank Jao in California, was mostly supportive of the president. So were the other ethnic groups. That was why I was continually on the phone, staying in touch with the leaders; and traveling around the country giving speeches to explain the president's policies. To be in the real America was a fun part of the job. I was in Portland, Maine, one weekend and in Portland, Oregon, the next.

As White House commissioned officers, we were on call twenty-four hours a day. On Sunday, January 13, 1991, I was at home, about to have brunch with Martha, when the deputy chief of staff, Andy Card, called to suggest that I meet with Baltic American leaders. They were coming to Washington from various states. So, with a bowl of *pho*—traditional Vietnamese noodle soup—on my lap, off I went. I might be the first and only person to have eaten Vietnamese noodles while driving to the White House to meet thirteen Baltic Americans. They expressed their concerns about the Soviet military crackdown in Vilnius, Lithuania, which caused thirteen civilian deaths. I immediately reported to Andy about the meeting. I found Condoleezza Rice—who was then the director of Soviet affairs for the National Security Council (NSC)—in the Situation Room with a football game on television. Condi had alerted me that the president would speak about the situation on his arrival from Camp David that afternoon. The remarks were well received by the community.

The Iraqi invasion and the occupation of Kuwait under Saddam Hussein took up a lot of our time. It was a major campaign: militarily, diplomatically, politically, internationally, and domestically.

One day in December 1990, I got a call from Amnesty International. It was delivering, hot off the press, a manuscript on Iraqi atrocities in occupied Kuwait. I forwarded the eighty-two-page report quickly to the president through Jim Cicconi. I did not expect him to read such a thick report, but it became the document most often mentioned by the president. He still talks about that report.

BATTLE OVER CHINA

I spent more than 1,000 days at the White House, working for the president of the United States. But if you ask me to name the best day of all, there's simply no contest: January 25, 1990.

After the Chinese government's bloody repression of a peaceful student demonstration in Tiananmen Square in June 1989, American public opinion was overwhelmingly against extension of most-favored-nation trade status for China. But the president had decided to keep the channels of communication open: the Chinese who traded with us were the engines of reform and the future of China, and human rights would always remain an important component of our dialogue. He had vetoed a congressional censure of China, and now Congress was trying to override the veto. We lost the House to a strong opposition led by Nancy Pelosi, a well-meaning and fiercely determined congresswoman from California. Our hopes were on the Senate.

Criticizing China's abuses by means of a congressional declaration or a newspaper editorial was surely an appropriate response. But to rush a piece of legislation through Congress that affected the status of more than 40,000 Chinese nationals who were then in the United States would undoubtedly result in a stinging loss of face within the Chinese government.

Because U.S. strategic interests in Asia depended heavily on keeping open the lines of communication with China, President Bush had early on rejected the congressional slap as a mistake. That was why he had vetoed the measure within a few weeks of its passage, in late 1989. And it was why he had then called on everybody to help prevent the Senate from overriding his veto with a mandated two-thirds majority.

Fully engaged in that effort, I had spent most of December and January working eighteen hours a day to educate the public on the subtleties and nuances of the issues—in the hope of persuading millions of reasonable citizens around the country that America's real interests depended on working quietly backstage with the Chinese, in order to reform the abuses.

President Bush proposed to use a more flexible Executive Order to extend the stay of the students as well as scholars and scientists, rather than the proposed legislative action. Intent on explaining my president's correct position on this matter, I hosted dozens of meetings and seminars with Chinese-American community leaders, college educators, elected officials, and business executives, all around the country. I talked myself hoarse, as I repeatedly urged them to let their congressional leaders know that they understood the complexities of the Chinese situation, and that they adamantly opposed the quick fix.

Although I was prohibited from lobbying Congress myself, my job was to do my very best to educate the American public at large on this extraordinarily complex issue, and thus to do what I could to protect true American interests in Asia, along with the president's indisputable right to shape U.S. foreign policy.

My own inner struggle to come to terms with the issue had been sharp, even agonizing at times. As a survivor of the Cambodian genocide whose mother, sister, and brother had been brutally murdered by the communists, I felt as much as anybody else the abuses of human rights that had taken place at Tiananmen Square. There was no question that the Chinese tactics—firing on unarmed students in order to enforce a rigid ideology with naked steel—needed to be denounced as despicable and beneath contempt. But contempt did not provide us with a license to ignore political reality. What was needed here was the intellectual discipline—and the emotional courage—to think our way through the dilemma, rather than merely venting our outrage through angry public relations gestures. Such discipline was painful, of course, as I had learned once again, only a month or so before.

Everywhere I went, I was well received. People asked all kinds of questions. However, some could be outright hostile, and I had to take the bull by the horns. At a briefing in San Francisco, a group of angry Chinese students criticized the president's position on the veto by insisting that the abuses at Tiananmen Square should not be tolerated anywhere, ever.

I roared into the microphone: "You want to talk about human rights? Do you know that my mother, sister, brother, their children—all of them were clubbed to death by the communists? And you know what? Today I support the inclusion of the Khmer Rouge in the UN peace process—because there is no other way to ensure the peaceful stability of Cambodia!"

They had immediately fallen silent, as I went on to point out that you cannot allow emotions to overwhelm your powers of analysis—not if you hope to act in ways that protect the deepest, widest-ranging interests of freedom-loving people everywhere, rather than merely let off steam. This was the backdrop against which I had been laboring non-stop for months, as the showdown over the veto approached.

Now, as I piloted our Ford Escort station wagon through the streets of Washington on that bitterly cold morning in January 1990, I couldn't help wondering. Did we have the five or six key votes that would be needed to prevent the two-thirds "override" majority in the Senate? Or would the president's veto go down to ignominious defeat, and trigger some very frightening international consequences for dear old Uncle Sam?

It was too close to call.

As the Escort—the faithful Ford that we'd named "Friendly" in honor of my first restaurant job in Connecticut—rumbled down E Street toward West Executive Drive and parking space number 74 at the White House, I found myself counting the Senate votes for the hundredth time. And they didn't add up. No matter which way the vote went, I knew the margin would be razor-thin.

Humming "The Star-Spangled Banner" as I waited for the inevitable identity check at the White House gate, I began to fantasize about using a crystal ball to foresee and a magic wand to influence the vote that would be cast that day. Chuckling, I left the car and climbed the stairs of the OEOB. Was I about to lose my mind, along with the vote? But these private little jokes ended fast, the moment I strode into Suite 128 and looked at the magnificent photo of the temples at Angkor Wat, along with the accompanying picture of the tiny refugee girl from Cambodia.

I had hung those pictures on the wall for one reason: so that I would never forget my major task here in Washington—to work ceaselessly, with all my heart and soul, to help struggling people and poverty-stricken refugees like that little girl.

In a very real way, her fate and the fate of millions like her hinged on this administration's ability to solve international political problems such as the episode in Tiananmen Square.

Frowning with anxiety, I sat down at my desk and dug into the huge pile of paperwork that had accumulated overnight.

But the peace and quiet didn't last long. Within seconds, the interruptions began.

"Sichan Siv. May I help you?"

And so it went, hour after hour, phone call after phone call, until, sometime around three PM, the door to my office burst open and I suddenly confronted the flushed, excited face of my top aide, Charles Bacarisse.

"Sichan, are you watching C-SPAN? They've begun to tally the votes!"

Within a few seconds, I was hypnotized by the television screen. Meanwhile, I was doing my best to keep up my end of the conversation with an important visitor, our cousin Robert McKinney. Robert, a very successful entrepreneur, had a distinguished career serving under Eisenhower as assistant secretary of the interior and under Kennedy and Johnson as ambassador to Switzerland and the first U.S. representative to the International Atomic Energy Agency. He was also the publisher of the major daily paper in Santa Fe, the *New Mexican* ("The West's Oldest Paper").

"I hope you'll pardon me, Robert," I kept mumbling as I gazed over his shoulder at the flashing vote board. "I seem to be a little distracted today."

I could feel my pulse speeding up, as the votes for Bush inched up toward that magic one-third mark. Were we going to make it?

"Well, Sichan," Robert was saying, "I think you laid out the options on China clearly enough. But I was wondering . . ."

Suddenly, the door was thrust open. It was Bacarisse again. This time, he was shouting and waving his arms like a traffic cop at rush hour.

"I just got the word from Legislative Affairs—it looks like we may have the votes!" I sat there, gaping at him. "Look at the screen!" he snapped. Robert and I both whirled around and saw the televised vote board lighting up again and again with the numbers that told the tale: veto sustained!

I rose to my feet and fought back the impulse to grab Martha's cousin in a bone-crushing hug. We've done it! The presidential veto had carried the day—by the breathtakingly narrow margin of only three votes.

The next thing I remember clearly was Bacarisse telling me that David Demarest had just invited us all to a champagne reception in his West Wing office.

Scrambling with Bacarisse along the ornate, high-ceilinged hallways toward Demarest's office, I realized all over again: somehow, the naked duck-chasing kid from Pochentong had managed to land himself one of the most exciting jobs on earth.

And my excitement grew as the champagne corks popped and the bubbly fizzed, and a few of us were suddenly instructed to head for Bush's private quarters on the second floor of the Executive Mansion. There, the president thanked us personally for what the pundits were already calling "the first major legislative victory of this administration."

I was soon standing in the reception area with Washington's policy makers, including Vice President Dan Quayle, Secretary of State James Baker, White House Chief of Staff John Sununu, and congressional leaders who had fought for the president on the veto. And Brent Scowcroft and Bob Gates.

Grinning, the president of the United States stuck out his right hand. "Hello, Sichan. Thanks for a job well done!"

In that terrific moment, I felt that I was accomplishing what I'd gone to Washington for. I was protecting Cambodia, for one thing—since the Chinese had always been the major force involved in helping us to sort out the incredibly violent and complex factions that were at work there. The ultimate irony was that the trouble had started with the communists—Chinese, Soviet, and Vietnamese.

And now, we could continue our efforts to encourage the People's Republic as a negotiator and mediator in that tormented corner of the world.

And second, I knew that I had been able to assist a president who was working as hard as he could for true statecraft, by recognizing that maintaining a good relationship with the Chinese was vital to achieving our national goals throughout Asia and the world.

For me, this was a key moment in my long journey from Pochentong to Pennsylvania Avenue—because it symbolized the way I had been able to put aside my own personal feelings for the larger good of the country to which I now belonged.

As I walked back to rejoin Friendly the car, on that wonderful evening in 1990, I also knew that I had been able to honor my mother's memory. How proud she would have been to know that her youngest son had helped to make history in the United States!

And how pleased she would have felt, to know I had done something that day—something small, perhaps, but also something very real—to defend and protect Cambodia, which both of us had always loved.

On the Cambodian new year, Saturday, April 13, 1991, Martha and I drove from Pampa to Amarillo, trying to find a Laotian Buddhist temple, on the way to an art auction to benefit the High Plains Epilepsy Foundation. I had never known that there was a Laotian community in this part of the country. From my experience with refugee resettlement, the largest concentration of Hmong and Laotian refugees were in Minnesota and California.

But my mind was at the White House. Before I left Washington a few days earlier, I recommended to David Demarest that the president receive the Dalai Lama of Tibet, who would be visiting the nation's capital the following week. I suggested that he be received at the Executive Mansion to avoid the appearance of giving him official recognition, and therefore antagonizing the Chinese. I argued that such a reception would tremendously increase the president's popularity with Asians, Buddhists, and the human rights community.

Martha and I found the temple and went in to pay our respects to the monks. They and most people who attended the new year's celebration had heard of me. They were excited to have somebody who was from the White House, and who looked like them, at their daylong ceremony. April is usually a hot month in South Asia and Southeast Asia. Cambodians, Burmese, Laotians, Thais, and others who celebrate the same new year normally splash water on each other as a sign of blessing. In the Texas Panhandle, April is still cold, but the Laotians kept the tradition. I found it amusing that many preferred to shiver under the chilly splash than avoid it.

I got hold of Doug Paal, a staff member at the NSC, and learned that if the president were to see the Dalai Lama, it would have to be on either Monday or Tuesday. I asked my new assistant, Jim Schaeffer, to inquire discreetly about the Dalai Lama's schedule, without giving any impression that he would be invited to meet the president at the White House.

Back in Washington, on April 15 I hosted a luncheon for a group of close friends and colleagues in honor of the new Cambodian menu at the White House mess. During the previous two years, I had eaten everything that was on the menu. The new food chief was a young lieutenant named Tony Mauro. I proposed that we should expand the choices to include some exotic dishes, such as Cambodian food, and he accepted immediately. One evening, he and I went to a Cambodian restaurant in Virginia. I ordered eight different dishes for him to try. He liked every one of them. The following week he sent one of his chefs to work at the restaurant for a couple of days. A week later, Tony called to suggest a tasting session. The dishes came out beautifully. After I made a few minor suggestions, Tony and I found a special date for the historic occasion: the new Cambodian Year of the Ram, 2534. I proposed Monday, April 15. Tony circulated advance notice to mess members and printed a special menu. The mess was decorated with some of Martha's and my Khmer art and handicrafts, including beautiful silk and silver.

Most of the people who dined at the mess tried the Cambodian dishes and liked them. The presidential photographer David Valdez and the president's personal aide Bruce Caughman gave me thumbs-up. Brent Scowcroft, who ate in his office, liked the chicken. Overall, it was a smashing success. For the first time in the history of the United States, the White House mess had featured Khmer dishes on its menu.

At the end of the day, I finally got the green light: "The President and Mrs. Bush will receive His Holiness the Dalai Lama at the Residence tomorrow at six PM." In anticipation, I had already sent a memo to the West Wing to meet the usual three PM deadline in order to have it included in the president's briefing book for the following day.

The Dalai Lama, who received the Nobel Peace Prize in 1989, was on a lecture tour in the United States. He was going to deliver the invocation at the National Endowment for Democracy Award Dinner on April 16 with the vice president in attendance. He was also scheduled to meet with congressional leaders later that week. He had been a staunch supporter of a peaceful, nonviolent approach to achieving independent national status for Tibet and continued to lobby world leaders to support Tibet's drive for independence.

The United States had no intention of changing its policy, which recognized Tibet as part of China. However, we were providing $500,000 in aid to help resettle Tibetan refugees in India and Nepal. In addition, Voice of America started broadcasting to Tibet in late March 1991. There had been no reaction from the People's Republic, and there had been no indication as to whether the broadcast had been jammed.

On April 16, 1991, I brought His Holiness the Dalai Lama to meet the president at the private quarters. As the elevator doors opened, Barbara Bush greeted us. Seeing the saffron robe of our holy visitor, Ranger, one of Millie's puppies, started to bark loudly. Mrs. Bush said, "Quiet, this is His Holiness." Ranger stopped barking and began to wag his tail. After the meeting, the president and Mrs. Bush walked us toward the elevator. Ranger ran into it before everybody else. The president smiled at me, "Sichan, are you taking Ranger with you?"

"What do you want me to do with him, sir?"

"Oh, just let him run. He knows his way around."

We followed Ranger to the diplomatic entrance. I showed the Dalai Lama my picture as a Buddhist monk. He noticed that I was a Theravada monk, which is slightly different from his Mahayana sect. To my great surprise, he asked if he could keep the photo. Then he said, "Would you like to autograph it for me?" I was on cloud nine for a long time. I saluted His Holiness with a *sampeah*—two palms put together in front of my face and head bowed slightly, while Ranger barked his farewell to our honored guest. When I turned around, Ranger was gone, frolicking on the South Lawn.

The meeting, which was the first between the president of the United States and the Dalai Lama, irked Chinese officials but created enormous elation elsewhere. I reported the reactions to the president. He wrote back: "Sichan, thank you for handling this matter so well. I'm glad you were at the meeting. GB."

Drawing on the experience of China's most-favored-nation status, I decided to establish a White House communications task force on national security issues, which I regularly chaired. It was an interoffice and interdepartmental operation that addressed the public communications angle of our defense and foreign policies. The outfit was very useful in rolling out such issues as the annual national security strategy of the United States, on which I worked closely with the NSC staffer Mike Hayden, who went on to become director of the CIA.

CHAPTER 17:

RETURN TO CAMBODIA

President Eisenhower spent most of September 1958 vacationing in Newport, Rhode Island, returning to Washington at the end of the month. On the last Sunday, he attended services at the National Presbyterian Church and went fishing. On Tuesday, September 30, he met with Prime Minister Norodom Sihanouk of Cambodia and hosted a luncheon in his honor.

In six decades of his political career, the Cambodian leader had more direct dealings with Republicans than Democrats. The meeting between Eisenhower and Sihanouk was preceded by visits to Cambodia by the Republican governor of New York, Thomas Dewey, in 1951; Vice President and Mrs. Nixon in 1953; and Secretary of State John Foster Dulles in 1955. Dewey had always wanted to visit Angkor and got his wish after he narrowly lost to the Democrat Harry Truman in 1948. King Sihanouk sent his Packard limousine to take Dewey around Angkor and was the host at a lavish French dinner and at the royal ballet in Phnom Penh.

The king had tried to reach out to the White House before. He sent an elephant—a symbol of commitment, loyalty, and strength—to President Truman as a gift. Unfortunately, the elephant, named Harry by the crew of the cargo ship, died off the coast of South Africa near Cape Town.

Kennedy was the only Democratic president Sihanouk met; but he maintained good relationships with other Democrats, especially Dean Acheson, who won the Preah Vihear Temple case for Cambodia over Thailand at the International Court of Justice; and the Senate majority leader, Mike Mansfield.

It was not until the administrations of presidents Reagan and Bush that the prince was able to meet again with the occupants of the White House.

The Bush administration had played a leading role in the two-year Cambodia peace process that concluded in October 1991. After Vietnam announced on April 5, 1989, that it would complete the withdrawal of its occupation forces from Cambodia by September 30, France and Indonesia convened the Paris Conference on Cambodia (PCC). My old friend Charlie Twining, director of Vietnam, Laos, and Cambodia Affairs at the State Department, asked if I could join the U.S. delegation, to be headed by Secretary of State James Baker. I checked with David Demarest and Andy Card, who gave me the green light but suggested that I should break the monthlong stay in Paris and be at the White House for a week. The NSC staffer Karl Jackson and I flew on Secretary Baker's plane with his top aides, including Dick Solomon, Margaret Tutwiler, and Bob Zoellick. We stopped in Shannon for refueling in the wee hours. In the transit lounge, as many others yawned and dozed off, Bob was reading a book on Cambodia.

We arrived in Paris at dawn and were whisked to the InterContinental, where I was given a suite. We moved in motorcades everywhere. It was a big change for me from ten years ago when I was taking a bus or the Métro between the U.S. consulate and the police prefecture, trying to get out of Paris. After Secretary Baker left, I was demoted to a single room at a tourist hotel.

Twenty delegations participated at the PCC: the UN secretary-general; the five permanent members of the UN Security Council (the United States, the United Kingdom, China, France, and the Soviet Union, which later became the Russian Federation); the six members of the Association of Southeast Asian Nations (Brunei, Indonesia, Malaysia, Philippines, Singapore, Thailand); Australia; Canada; India; Japan; Laos and Vietnam (Cambodia's other two neighbors); and Zimbabwe as chairman of the Nonaligned Movement. Cambodia was represented by four parties, seated according to their ages: Son Sann, Prince Sihanouk, Khieu Samphan, and Hun Sen.

The United States supported Prince Sihanouk as the person around whom a political settlement must be achieved and had for several years provided nonmilitary assistance to Cambodia's noncommunist resistance. The endless meetings at the Klebert Center were held with France's hospitality: exquisite food and great wine. We worked hard. Our objective was to seek an acceptable formula, addressing both external and internal aspects of the Cambodian-Vietnamese conflict. Despite our efforts, no agreement on sharing power could be reached. Sergio Vieira de Mello of the UN High Commission for Refugees (UNHCR) urged us to maintain Cambodian repatriation as a key component of a comprehensive settlement.

The American delegation and I decided to go out for a pizza. I guessed we were trying to get ready for our regular diet back home after our exposure to haute cuisine. The following day I flew back to Washington. On September 2, I was in Austin to address the Cambodian National Convention, where I reported about the PCC and also mentioned other issues that were important to the eight-month-old administration: keeping the economy strong, seizing international opportunities for peace, investing in our future, and working for a kinder, gentler America.

At a lunch in New York, Dick Solomon and I discussed shifting the Cambodia process to the five permanent members of the UN Security Council (P5). I later went to listen to the president's address to the UN General Assembly and saw many old friends. In motorcades through Manhattan, my memory flashed back to twelve years before, when I was making my way behind the wheel of a yellow Checker cab. Now people lined the streets, clapping, shouting, and waving with a look of curiosity and awe on their faces. One guy was in his bathrobe. It was an amazing scene.

At the Wall Street landing zone, I could not figure out which helicopter was Nighthawk III, the White House helicopter I was supposed to be on. I stood there, confused by the noise of the helicopters and the flashing lights of the motorcade until John Gardner shouted at me to follow him. There was a breathtaking view of New York City, my hometown, with the bright lights of the World Trade Center and lower Manhattan in the foreground. In minutes, I was on Air Force One—perhaps the world's most famous plane—on the way to Washington. *Awesome!* It took us two years, two months, and twenty-two days to reach a comprehensive agreement on Cambodia.

On March 9, 1992, I joined the highest-level U.S. government mission to Cambodia since 1975, before the largest UN peacekeeping deployment in history. I knew my return would be emotional and decided to do some meditation the day before at the Wat Bowornives quarters of Phra Kantasilo. He was an American monk from Anderson, Indiana, and secretary to the supreme patriarch of Thailand, whom I had met during an earlier visit.

We flew to the Gulf of Thailand and turned left toward Phnom Penh. It was a longer and unusual route, and the navigation chart had "Aircraft infringing upon Non-Free Flying Territory may be fired upon without warning" written all over it.

"We are entering the Cambodian airspace," said the aircraft commander. My heart began to beat faster. I stood up in the big cockpit of the U.S. Air Force C-130 and looked outside through the windows.

The sky was blue with some scattered white cotton clouds. Underneath, I saw mountains covered with a thick jungle canopy. I had been sitting in the cockpit with Dick Solomon since we left Don Muang Air Force Base, outside Bangkok. The rest of the nine-member delegation was in the main cabin—four from the State Department, two Pentagon officials, and the director of the POW/MIA National League of Families.

Sixteen years earlier, I had crossed to Thailand from Cambodia on foot after having survived a bloody year under the Khmer Rouge, when typical days included eighteen hours of hard labor and communist lectures, with only one meal. I had managed to fight back waves of devastating grief as I summoned up memories of the world I had lost—the world of a loving family that my mother, Chea Aun, had nurtured in a society blessed with a rich culture and an ancient civilization. Those things were now gone forever. I had no tears left to cry. Sixteen years earlier, I left as a refugee. Now I was returning as a deputy assistant to the president of the United States. I had mixed feelings about this trip. I did not know how I would react to what I would see.

My flashbacks were interrupted when we landed at Pochentong, where I was born and lived until April 17, 1975. I had taken off and landed at Pochentong so many times that I could easily pinpoint my house from the air. I was looking for it as we were landing, but could not locate it. The village seemed to be overcrowded with shelters and temporary buildings.

The airport terminal, the VIP reception hall, and the tall control tower, however, looked the same. The ride from Pochentong was overwhelming. The four-lane boulevard lined with flame trees looked smaller than I remembered. The traffic was heavy with bicycles, motorcycles, cars, buses, trucks. Everybody seemed to be trying to inch along the crowded road, both sides of which had been overbuilt. There was no zoning.

After a seventeen-year blackout, I recognized hardly anything. I was numb.

We had a series of meetings with UN officials, including Sergio de Mello, who had the enormous task of planning the repatriation and resettlement of 370,000 Cambodian refugees.

On the Cambodian side, we called on Prince Sihanouk, who hosted a luncheon for us at Khemarin Palace. He thanked us for the U.S. role in the peace agreement and our commitment to making it work. He told us he was no longer in the "antiimperialist" (Ho Chi Minh, Nasser, Nehru, Sukarno, Tito, Zhou Enlai) mode of the 1950s and 1960s. He was getting older and had become wiser. In the beautiful Royal Palace, he was surrounded by an interesting cast of characters: his stern and out-of-place bodyguards were North Koreans; his kitchen staff (chefs, cooks, butlers, waiters) were Chinese; his doctors were Chinese and Thais; and his speechwriter was French.

We met separately with the noncommunist resistance leaders as well as those in the Cambodian People's Party. As soon as we sat down at the prime minister's office, Hun Sen turned to me and said, "I would like to welcome His Excellency Siv Sichan back to Cambodia." We later flew to Siem Reap to visit a refugee reception center and a UN post, where we were briefed about the UN's deployment plan in the region. During a short break, we went on a quick tour of Bayon and Angkor Wat. The banyan tree where my mother and I had a picnic in 1959 and where I encountered Khmer Rouge soldiers in 1975 was still there. It seemed ageless.

The C-130 crew asked me help communicate with the towers at Phnom Penh and Siem Reap. I had always wanted to fly an airplane—after all, I did grow up next to an airport. After arriving in Washington in 1989 and working in a high-pressure job, I looked for a way to depressurize myself. I went for serious, and long, training—I had little spare time—at a flying school in Manassas, Virginia. The town became briefly infamous after a woman cut off her husband's private

part, which she considered an instrument of torture, before returning
to its glory as the site of a major Civil War battle. I had gotten my pi-
lot's license and the C-130 crew knew all about it.

Our call sign was Repat (as in repatriation) 02, but the Cambodian air traffic controllers never got it right. Phnom Penh called us
"Repair 02" and Siem Reap called us "Hotel 02." I created quite a com-
motion among the Siem Reap air traffic controllers when I asked them
in Khmer for permission to circle Angkor Wat. This was very unusual,
since the international language of the skies is English! The view from
the air was unbelievable. The crew left me an autographed navigation
chart as a souvenir of my return visit with them.

HANUMAN

After the delegation left, I visited my father's native village, Hanuman,
in Tonle Bati district of Takeo province, about an hour south of Phnom
Penh.

Most countries in Asia have a version of the Hindu epic story, the
Ramayana. The Cambodian version, known in Khmer as *Ream Ker*, is
shorter and represents only some parts of the original Indian story. It
was one of the books prescribed in our Khmer literature course and
was studied at length in my youth. Each time I am in Hanuman, I remember an episode of my years at Sisowath. Here is the gist of the
Ream Ker story.

Preah Ream (Rama) loses his right to succeed his father, King
Dasaratha, on the throne as a result of a palace coup engineered
by his stepmother. He is banished to the jungle with his wife
Seda (Sita) and younger brother Preah Lieak (Lakshmana).
Krong Reap (Ravana), the demon king, falls in love with Prin-
cess Seda, kidnaps her, and takes her to his palace in Lanka.
Preah Ream asks Hanuman, the white monkey general, to raise

an army of monkeys and attack Lanka. After a bloody war, in
which countless monkeys are slaughtered, Preah Ream is able
to free Seda but continues to doubt her faithfulness. Seda is
hurt and proves her innocence by walking over a fire. The husband and wife reconcile and return to the kingdom, where
Preah Ream is crowned king.

In the final exam, the teacher of Khmer literature asked us to write
an essay giving our opinion of *Ream Ker*. I said that it was immoral to
sacrifice so many lives for the whim of a prince. Preah Ream was using
Hanuman and the monkeys for his own glory. And he did not even
trust his wife.

Before returning our papers, the teacher told the class, without
making any reference to my conclusion, that *Ream Ker* could be a love
story, a husband's dedication to his wife. But most of all, it was the
story of a war between good and evil.

"The objective of a war is to win. It does not matter what it takes.
There is no substitute for victory. You win, you live. You lose, you die."

He walked back and forth on the platform in front of the blackboard without looking at us and continued: "The monkeys are soldiers.
They execute orders without asking questions. They represent the best
of what dedication and devotion are all about. It's an honor for them to
die for their master. Hanuman is the ultimate symbol of the servant's
loyalty to his master. Preah Ream asks him to build a bridge to Lanka;
he moves mountains to do it. No job is too big for him. No task is too
difficult. And nothing is impossible!"

Cambodian teachers used different methods to discipline us after
caning and whipping were banned. They called students to go and retrieve the papers from the front of the classroom. Some teachers called
from the bottom grades, others from the top grades. This one had fun
waging a psychological war with us. He mixed the papers so that we
could not tell where we stood in the rankings. I was sure I had failed

because my argument was opposite of his. My idea was rebellious. At seventeen I had become a nonconformist.

"Siv Sichan!" I stood up on hearing my name and walked to the front. I saw "12 over 20" in red ink on the top of my paper, a passable grade. *He could have flunked me for disagreeing wih him. It could have been worse.*

On Friday, March 13, 1992, exactly sixteen years and one month after I began my three-day trek across the jungle toward Thailand, I visited the scenes of the crimes. I returned to my father's native village; it was an emotional return for me to be at Hanuman and Tonle Bati. I had many happy memories from my childhood, but the Khmer Rouge had turned the village into horrifying killing grounds.

It was a bittersweet moment. Living conditions were much worse in the provinces than in Phnom Penh, where one could find almost everything from Russian caviar to portable generators. A most heartrending realization for me was that despite two decades of untold misery in a series of human calamities, the Khmer people were able to maintain their "Khmerness" with friendly smiles, kindness and gentleness, and a caring and affectionate attitude. They had, however, changed their traditional greeting from "Have you eaten?" to "How many do you have left in your family?"

At Hanuman, I met many surviving distant relatives. They had aged tremendously. The village had changed. It looked poorer than in 1960s. I could not recognize any house, rice field, or pond. It was dry, hot, and humid. Only the palm trees seemed to have stayed still and stood tall during these horrendous years.

I was taken to a Buddhist monastery south of the village and shown a huge pile of skulls and bones in a *chedey* (funerary monument) in front of the *preah vihear*. I was sick to my stomach.

Finally, I was at a dry rice field farther south. The villagers believed that my mother, sister, and brother had been killed there, clubbed to death by the Khmer Rouge. Completely speechless and overwhelmed with sadness and sorrow, I had a Buddhist memorial service performed on the spot.

Back in Hanuman, more villagers came to gather around me. They called me "the man of golden bones," a Khmer expression meaning somebody with a lot of luck.

A few days later I had another memorial service at my village monastery at Pochentong, where I also visited my family's house. This was a bigger service, and a lot of people participated. An old woman knew my mother. Having lost her sight, she reached out with both hands to touch my face. She wanted to feel how much I had changed. I noticed tears in her eyes.

On March 18, 1992, as I entered the Oval Office, the president said, "Sichan! How was your trip?" In an earlier handwritten note, he had said, "Call me when you get back from Cambodia. I want to get a good debrief on what I'm sure will be an emotional return."

"Yes, sir. As you said, it was an emotional return."

For sixteen years in America, the thought never crossed my mind that one day I would return to Cambodia, let alone as a presidential assistant in a government aircraft. Back at my office, I was in shock. In a few days, I had taken probably the longest emotional and physical journey: from the killing fields of Cambodia to the office of the most powerful person on earth, by various means of transportation, including one used by six presidents of the United States (Kennedy, Johnson, Nixon, Ford, Carter, and Reagan). I felt even more blessed and lucky because my boss was George Bush. Despite his enormous burden as leader of the free world, the forty-first president never for a moment lost his unique personality: the ultimate altruist! He was not only a great president, but an even greater man.

NO MATTER WHAT HAPPENS

After confronting the killing fields, I realized that I might have come full circle. The greatest tragedy for me was that my mother died in brutal circumstance, murdered by the communist death machine.

I never saw my mother again.

Her spirit did not perish with her. *Mae* was full of sacrifice and wisdom. She told me, "There are three kinds of children that make their parents sad and unhappy. The first one is a stillborn child. The second is a child who dies after he or she is born. The third is a child who has no education. The first two make their parents sad for a period of time. The third one makes them unhappy for the rest of their lives."

She told me, "Happiness is something you cannot keep unless you give it away."

She also said, "Hate ends not with more hate but with love. And from that we take hope. Without love and hope, our lives will be empty. Love triumphs over death and destruction, if only one can hold on to hope, endure the pain, and wait for the light."

I found that light, when the villagers praised me for my survival, freedom, and success in America, and told me that they thought of me as "the man with the golden bones," a very blessed and lucky man. *I am indeed, because I never gave up hope.*

SOLDIERS OF DEMOCRACY

Those of us who had worked in the shadow of Reagan's ideals know that an election does not a democracy make. Cambodia is a case in point. In May 1993, after twenty-three years of turmoil—a period that began with a war against the North Vietnamese and Vietcong forces, followed by the genocidal rule of the Khmer Rouge and ten years of Vietnamese occupation—Cambodia was dying and wanted an immediate end to its suffering. Ninety percent of registered voters went to the polls. The FUNCINPEC won the UN supervised election, but the CPP, which still maintained a larger force, threatened a coup and civil war. It bullied its way into the government, which had showed some signs of promise at the beginning. There were efforts to support economic growth and political stability. The currency was stabilized at about 2,500 riels to a dollar. Newspapers sprang up, and progress was made in human rights. Both the International Republican Institute (IRI) and the National Democratic Institute (NDI) did an excellent job of promoting democratic change. So did other NGOs and international development agencies in their social and humanitarian work.

PART V:

ON BEHALF OF THE UNITED STATES

Being who rules over the universe, who presides in the councils of nations, and whose providential aids can supply every human defect, that His benediction may consecrate to the liberties and happiness of the people of the United States a Government instituted by themselves for these essential purposes, and may enable every instrument employed in its administration to execute with success the functions allotted to his charge.

—George Washington

CHAPTER 18:

THE PRINCIPLES

January 20, 2001, was a cold, drizzly, snowy day. Martha and I sat in the reviewing stand in front of the White House long enough to watch most of the parade and left in the late afternoon to change for the ball. We planned to attend three balls that night. We started at the armory and went on to the Texas ball at the Convention Center. Outside, the snow fell, heavier and heavier. By the time we got to the third ball, at the Woodley Park Sheraton, around the corner from our home, the younger crowd was taking over the dance floor with blasting rock and roll music.

I had been so confident that George W. Bush was going to win the election of 2000 that I went to Wayne's Western Wear in Pampa and asked the owner for a cowboy hat that would go with formal attire. He sold me a Resistol "Midnight" model. We decided to have our photograph taken in front of the inaugural logo, with me in my black hat and tuxedo, and Martha in a beautiful black and gold dress. The hat became so popular that the next person in line borrowed it for a picture with his guest, as did the next, and the next. We waited around for a long time before all the guests were through borrowing Midnight.

GENEVA

Most of us who had worked in the campaign wanted to serve in the new administration. Some had already started in the transition. Others, like me, expressed our interest to the transition team by submitting our CVs and résumés.

In early March, the White House personnel officer Monica Kladakis asked if I would be interested in serving as a delegate to the Fifty-seventh UN Commission on Human Rights (CHR) for six weeks in March and April in Geneva. I said yes on the spot, and went to the State Department to fill out numerous forms for clearance. Before leaving for Geneva, I had an official interview on March 13 with Stuart Holliday, Monica's boss at the White House, for a possible position in the new administration. We discussed the Peace Corps, the United Nations, and USAID.

The CHR has been the most politically charged body of the UN. Its fifty-three members, elected by the UN Economic and Social Council (ECOSOC), represent a mixture of democracies and dictatorships.

I made friends with the owner of a Cambodian restaurant and was allowed to cook some of my favorite dishes. At the end of the CHR session, I invited the U.S. delegation to the restaurant and cooked a three-course dinner for them. The menu included a Khmer salad of cabbage and chicken, stir-fried chicken with ginger, and the classic *samlaw machu* soup with fish, pineapple, and tomatoes. All my colleagues seemed to enjoy the dinner. Not only did they survive my cooking, three were appointed ambassadors.

After the CHR, I flew to Asia for some business meetings and stopped in Los Angeles on my way back. There, on May 7, I got a call from Ambassador John Negroponte, who suggested lunch two days later at the University Club.

John had been nominated by the president to be the chief U.S. representative to the UN. I met him for the first time in New York at a conference at the Asia Society when he was deputy assistant secretary of state for East Asian and Pacific Affairs in the Carter administration. In our brief encounter, I found him friendly and personable, and I stayed in touch with him over the years. In 1989 I invited him to attend the White House Cinco de Mayo event in the East Room, even though he had not yet been confirmed by the Senate as ambassador to Mexico. I called on him in 1994 when he was ambassador to the Philippines and attended a dinner that he and his charming wife, Diana, hosted.

At the University Club, John told me that with the president's blessing, he would like to consider me a member of his ambassadorial team. At the lunch and in subsequent conversations, he always ended with: "We will have a lot of work, but we shall have fun."

After the president signed off on my nomination, there was more paperwork to fill out. And I began to prepare for the confirmation hearing. The preparations included a "murder board," a mock hearing with a dozen of my future colleagues acting like senators asking tough questions.

For months, I had been studying a thick briefing book that the State Department had prepared for my hearing. It seemed to contain every foreign policy issue under the sun. During the murder board, my future colleagues, who were experts in their areas, asked all kinds of questions. Some were intended to make me angry, or to draw me into very complex and controversial issues such as abortions in China or the possible return of the United States to UNESCO. I managed to remain calm, cool, and collected. I responded to the questions in such detail that one of the board members told me at the end that I had overstudied the issues.

CONFIRMATION

On September 11, 2001, I was on the way to the Metro station when it was reported that smoke was billowing out of one of the towers of the World Trade Center. I joined a few dumbfounded people around a television set at the International Republican Institute and suddenly, before our eyes, one tower crashed. It was an awful sight. We screamed!

I miraculously reached Martha by phone and told her to go home immediately. Martha's office at the World Bank was just one block west of the White House. Mine was three blocks east of it. If there were another plane, the White House would be the most likely target.

Martha and I found each other at home. And for the whole day, we were glued to the television set. We called friends and relatives to find out if they were all safe and sound and to tell them that we were at home. Most of the time, we heard only a busy signal.

John Negroponte's hearing had been scheduled for the following day but was postponed for one day. I went with my former White House colleague Dan Nichols to give John some moral support. The full Senate Foreign Relations Committee (SFRC) was in session, presided over by Senator Joe Biden of Delaware. It was a difficult hearing for John. A few senators, especially Barbara Boxer of California, grilled him on his role as ambassador to Honduras, about twenty years earlier. And he had been confirmed numerous times since then.

John made it out of the committee and reported to the full Senate with only three negative votes. All Democrats, of course!

Tom Korologos gave me a few important tips for handling the confirmation hearings. He recommended that I appear very humble and deferential, ready to give short, polite, and persuasive answers. His "eighty-twenty" rule dictated that a nominee must not talk more than twenty percent of the time and must let the senators, who can ask any kind of questions, speak for the rest of the time. He reminded me that if I did not know an answer, I should take a drink of water. It would give me at least one minute to think and would keep my mouth less dry.

On November 8, four of us appeared before the SFRC: Christopher Burnham of Connecticut, nominated to be assistant secretary of state for management; Eric Javits of New York, to be ambassador to the conference on disarmament in Geneva; Richard Williamson of Illinois, to be ambassador to the UN for special political affairs; and myself. The hearing was in the subcommittee on international organizations, chaired by Barbara Boxer. Chris, having been a treasurer of Connecticut, was the only one with presenters. Both were democratic senators from his (and my other) home state, Connecticut: Christopher Dodd and Joe Lieberman.

During the hearing Dodd was particularly pleased to note that I had started out in Connecticut. I told him that if I did well in my life, it was because I began in the Constitution State. He raised one fist and said, "Yeah!" Each of us was asked to make a five-minute opening statement. I was the last to speak. It was a love fest. Each of us received only one question. Mine was on HIV-AIDS.

John Negroponte had written to Senator Biden urging my speedy confirmation, saying that it would be very helpful to have me in place when the General Assembly began on November 10. He told me that I should plan to be at the U.S. Mission to the UN (USUN) that day for the president's visit.

On November 9, Martha drove me to Union Station. As I got out of the car, Tony Banburry of the NSC, who speaks Khmer fluently, reached me on my cell phone: I had been confirmed by the full Senate. When I arrived in New York, he reported that the president attested to my appointment at six PM.

On November 10, just moments before the president arrived, John Negroponte swore me in on the twelfth floor of the U.S. Mission, in front of the presidential flag and the American flag. I became the twenty-eighth U.S. ambassador to ECOSOC.

It was the crowning moment of a long and arduous process of some 237 days from the official White House interview to the time I took my oath of office. This included much complicated paperwork on background check, top security clearance, and financial disclosure. It then picked up speed: thirty-six days from the time the nomination reached the Senate and an amazing record of thirty-one hours from hearing to appointment.

The United States usually has five ambassadors accredited to the UN: the chief of mission, the deputy chief, and the ambassadors for ECOSOC, for management and reform, and for special political affairs.

The United States was present at the creation of the UN. It is the host country and the largest contributor. The United States and United Nations have the same first name. The country and the organization share many of the same principles: people, peace, freedom, and common welfare. Our Constitution and the UN Charter start with almost the same words: "We, the People . . ." and "We the peoples . . ."

The ECOSOC is one of the five principal organs of the United Nations. The other four are the United Nations General Assembly (UNGA), International Court of Justice (ICJ), United Nations Security Council (UNSC), and Trusteeship Council. The ECOSOC carries out the UN mandate to promote higher standards of living and respect for human rights, as well as solutions to international developmental, economic, social, and health problems from cradle to coffin. It has enormous reach within the UN system. It oversees the integrated and coordinated follow-up to the UN cycle of major conferences and summits. It reports to the General Assembly, which elects ECOSOC members each fall.

The United States has always been a member, but it must run for election to ECOSOC (unlike Security Council). The president and vice presidents of ECOSOC (chosen on a rotating basis from regional groups) are collectively known as the "Bureau," serving for a year. The U.S. and other permanent members of the Security Council do not (with rare exceptions) serve in UN bureaus.

The substance of ECOSOC's work is handled by its fourteen subsidiary organs, such as the Commission on the Status of Women and the Commission on Human Rights. They meet in the spring, so as not to overlap with UNGA. Each has a bureau and a secretary. The ECO-SOC elects countries to serve on these bodies, which all report to its Substantive Session, held in July and alternating between New York and Geneva. In addition to reviewing the work of ECOSOC's subsidiary bodies, the Session also includes High-Level, Coordination, and Operational and Humanitarian segments.

The ECOSOC holds a spring meeting with the boards of the World Bank, International Monetary Fund, World Trade Organization, and more recently, UN Conference on Trade and Development. It meets during the year for resumed organizational sessions to conclude unfinished business and for ad hoc issues. It elects members to the executive boards of the UN funds and programs, such as the UN Children's Fund, and almost always operates by consensus.

The ambassador to ECOSOC also represents the United States at the General Assembly and Security Council and serves as overall U.S. coordinator for General Assembly affairs, as well as development issues and humanitarian crises. This section at USUN oversees seventy percent of the UN budget.

Documents of the UN are published in the six official languages: Arabic, Chinese, English, French, Russian, and Spanish. Only a few countries have Chinese or Russian as their official language, yet the amount of documents is the same as for the more widely used languages, such as English, French, and Spanish. It is a waste of effort and resources.

CHARM, CHAMPAGNE, AND CHANDELIERS

Representation is a key part of a diplomat's job. You have to entertain and be entertained at numerous breakfasts, lunches, cocktail parties, receptions, and dinners. We lobby each other for resolutions, which are the end result of long negotiations. We ask each other for support of our candidates and candidacies for elections. Often, we are "drinking and eating for our country." In addition to good suits, one must have a strong liver and a good stomach.

Despite our status as an economic and military power, the United States does not have an unlimited budget. This is why I adhered strictly to the theory of the "biggest bang for the smallest buck." I wanted to do something different and add an exotic flavor to the world's largest diplomatic community.

After Philadelphia, New York became the young nation's capital. George Washington was sworn in as the nation's first president at Federal Hall at the top of Wall Street. Within walking distance stood Fraunces Tavern at the corner of Pearl and Broad streets, built in 1719 for the wealthy merchant Stephen Delancey. In 1762, the innkeeper Samuel Fraunces purchased the tavern and turned it into a fine dining establishment. It became a place where the city's elite gathered. George Washington was such a frequent guest that in 1783 he used the tavern for his farewell address to fellow officers of the Continental Army. The tavern was rented by the U.S. government as its first building, and housed the departments of War, Treasury, and Foreign Affairs. Thomas Jefferson worked there as the first secretary of state. He managed two embassies and ten consulates with a staff of five and an annual budget of $25,000.

Most of my colleagues had never been to Fraunces Tavern. They were surprised to find it easy to get there from the UN, down the FDR Drive—faster than going across town. I regaled them with the history of the financial district and the tavern's historic connections. Colin Powell also chose the tavern to host a dinner for his counterparts in G-8.

Diplomatic receptions can be very boring and stuffy. To lighten things, I took a clue from my Asian colleagues. The ASEAN ambassadors always had karaoke at their regular get-together. Brunei's ambassador, Serbini Ali, who chaired their club, invited me to join them. I went prepared with some old tunes from the 1960s. I felt relieved that I did not embarrass the United States in the singing forum. Indonesia had the most sophisticated system and a live band. I quickly formed a most exclusive diplomatic quartet: Brunei, Indonesia, Japan, and the United States. The first two started the singing receptions; Japan invented karaoke. When hosting a function, I alerted the three other members of the quartet to get ready to warm up the audience. The Japanese ambassador, Yoshiyuki Motomura, who could be taken for Elvis because of his incredible voice, had an officer singing "YMCA" in Japanese. He brought the house down.

CHAPTER 19:

THE GOOD, THE BAD,
THE UGLY

The United States contributes twenty-two percent to the regular UN budget, followed by Japan and Germany. They and just over a dozen countries pay nearly all of the UN bills. Regardless of financial contributions or population, each member has one vote. You may call it representation without taxation.

CONVEY, CONVINCE, CONVERT

The UN is sometimes a place where people speak and nobody listens. And the smaller the countries, the longer the speeches.

I cut the introductory diplomatic niceties and went straight to the heart of the issues in our statements. I usually kept them to less than 900 words.

Here are the "Siv Rules for an Effective Speech":

- Use short sentences (fewer than fifteen words per sentence). Use direct action verbs. Use "I congratulate you" instead of

> "I would like to take this special opportunity to have the pleasure of congratulating you . . ."

- Spell out "U.S." and other abbreviations. Put acronyms in parentheses following the spelled-out words, especially for later use in the statement.
- Do not repeat words (unless for emphasis).
- Include one presidential quote, whenever appropriate.
- Use the Listerine effect: deliver bad news first, if any; conclude on a forward-looking, positive, upbeat note.
- Reading copy—double-spaced, Times New Roman, 20-point font size, with numbered pages; fewer than nine pages for a 900-word statement.
- Post on USUN Web site within one hour of delivery.

I also had a one-page rule, which I had learned from my White House years: if you want anybody to read what you write, keep it short. Keep letters, memos, and talking points to one page. Talking points may include no more than four bullet points per issue. Additional background may be attached. I also strongly recommended that all cables be kept to seven paragraphs and that all reporting be done within twenty-four hours.

The highlight of 2003 was Martha's and my twentieth wedding anniversary on Christmas Eve in Pampa. First, we stopped at the Big Texan in Amarillo (home of the free seventy-two-ounce steak if eaten in one hour). We spent a beautiful afternoon in Palo Duro Canyon, America's second largest, and were later the guests of Neva and Robert Burks. In Santa Fe and Taos, where we had spent our honeymoon, we visited our cousins Robin and Meade Martin. On Christmas Eve, we made a grand entrance into Pampa with a stop at the seventy-five-year-old Coney Island Cafe. After visiting the graves of Martha's parents, we did our traditional western-wear shopping before joining friends for a special dinner. At eleven PM we all went to the First Presbyterian Church for the candlelight service, to celebrate our anniversary. After midnight, we left with Lilith Brainard and her family for Canadian, Texas, where we had a wonderful Christmas with all seventeen of them. I spent the next three days working on one of their ranches. I finished my basic cowboy training without losing an animal in the cattle drive or falling off my white horse, Sydney.

At dinner at Dyer's BBQ in Pampa, the Brainards presented me with a Lazy B Ranch jacket—equipped with a cell phone pocket—and other cowboy gear for my "graduation." The *Pampa News*, the most widely read paper in the top of Texas, did a front-page above-the-fold story: "UN Ambassador Visits Panhandle!"

Upon my arrival in New York in 2001, I joined the Buddhist ambassadors club and the International Vesak Festival. Vesak is the most sacred Buddhist holiday, marking the triple anniversary of Buddha's birth, his enlightenment, and his passing. During my tenure, the event was hosted successively by Burma, India, Sri Lanka, and Thailand. I took the opportunity of mentioning that I was a Buddhist monk, and we all knew that U Thant, who became secretary-general after Dag Hammarskjold was killed in a plane crash, was a Buddhist.

On April 13 (the Cambodian new year and Thomas Jefferson's birthday) of 2004 I received the actor Richard Gere, a long-time supporter of Tibet and the Dalai Lama, in my office. I briefed him about our position on human rights in China, recounting my speech in Geneva, which drew retaliation form the Chinese ambassador. We then walked two blocks north under a heavy rain to Dag Hammarskjold Plaza, where a group of Tibetans were conducting a hunger strike that was overwhelmed by the heavy presence of news cameras and journalists. We received Buddhist greetings and were presented with traditional scarves. Gere asked me to speak first, but I deferred to him, knowing that everybody was there to see him. He told the Tibetans that his own heart was very involved in their struggle and that he would continue to see them as his brothers and sisters: "Your fate is my fate." He then introduced me as a great American who had survived the killing fields. I told them as a fellow Buddhist that I considered the rain as a blessing. I added that we were concerned about the situation in Tibet; this was why we decided to introduce a resolution at the Commission on Human Rights.

The United States was the only nation that delivered a country-specific report on human rights, one that identified the bad and the ugly. These violators of human rights are like arsonists trying to join a firemen's club. They wanted to be members of CHR, not to promote the issues but to defend themselves. It was ridiculous that countries such as Cuba and Sudan were members of CHR. I walked out on their elections.

Fidel Castro's Cuba was the first among ugly equals. Besides trying to derail every human rights resolution, Havana promoted a resolution on the trade embargo in an attempt to blame its economic woes on the United States, and to divert attention from its abysmal human rights record. The embargo, imposed after the large-scale illegal expropriation of American properties, had been kept in place by successive administrations in order to maintain pressure to restore freedom and democracy in Cuba. Cuba's trade with other countries was affected not by the embargo but by its poor credit rating and the communist regime's failed economic policies.

In November 2003 I delivered, in Spanish, the U.S. statement on the trade embargo. At the end I switched to English: "In the 1980s, President Reagan reflected on U.S.-Soviet relations by using a Russian quote: *Doveryai, no proveryai* ["Trust but verify"]. On communists and dictators like those in Havana, I say, *Nikogda ne doveryai, vsegda proveryai* ["Never trust, always verify"]. The best day for Cuba will be when the Cuban people open their ears and hear the truth, when they open their eyes and see freedom, when they open their mouths and say *Viva Cuba libre!* Cuba's best day is when the Cuban people have terminated Castro's evil, communist, dictatorial regime and said to him *Hasta la vista, baby!"* This lightened the General Assembly. Our delegates in the U.S. seats, including a former congressman from New York, Ben Gilman, had a big laugh.

If January 25, 1990, was my greatest day at the White House, then March 1, 2004, was my happiest day at USUN—not because it was my birthday, but because my lovely friend Doro Bush Koch arrived to serve as a delegate to the UN Commission on the Status of Women (CSW). Doro brought a different perspective, being the daughter of one president and the sister of another. I introduced her to many of my UN colleagues, especially female ambassadors. They were all quite impressed with Doro's friendliness and down-to-earth personality.

At a luncheon I hosted for her and the U.S. delegation, Doro gave a memorable speech, recounting a story about the national security adviser, Condoleezza Rice. Once, when Rice went to a dinner in Mexico with President Bush and Secretary of State Colin Powell, Powell noticed that she had a huge run in her stocking. Rice said that she had to change. This was almost certainly the first time in history that the president of the United States and the secretary of state had ever waited while the national security adviser changed her hose.

CHAPTER 20:

THE AMBASSADORS

The member countries of the UN usually send their best diplomats to New York. For those that cannot afford to have many embassies around the world, the UN is one of their most important posts. Ambassadors to the UN, officially known as permanent representatives, are at the top of their career or are very well connected at home. On finishing their assignments, many go on to become ambassadors to Washington, foreign ministers, or prime ministers. Some have had those posts before coming to the Big Apple. A few are kept in New York because they are political rivals of the leaders at home.

On arriving in New York on November 10, 2001, I made courtesy calls on my colleagues. I offered to go to their missions, unless they suggested a different place, usually one of the UN lounges, because their missions were small or far away, or because they were having meetings at the UN. For me and my colleagues at USUN, it took about five minutes on foot to get there. We only had to cross First Avenue.

As our relationships warmed, I laid down some markers: there had been a change of administrations in Washington; the fact that we had done something in the past did not necessarily mean that we were going to do the same thing the same way; we were not going to go along just for the sake of getting along. But I promised my colleagues as much cooperation and support as I could. "We may disagree, but we should not be disagreeable." I reached out to everyone except the untouchables: Cuba, Iran, Iraq, North Korea, and Libya. These were the countries whose delegates we were not supposed to socialize with. We could only work with them. Iran was chairman of G77, a group of some 130 developing countries focusing on economic issues. I met with the Iranian ambassador during some crucial negotiations. We had better dealings with Iran's chairmanship than with that of Venezuela, which followed Iran. Iraq and Libya were later taken off the list and replaced at one point by Burma (Myanmar) and Sudan. I exchanged kisses on the cheeks with the Libyan ambassador when we saw each other. My colleagues were stunned when I showed up at Libyan receptions. Such is international diplomacy.

The big or rich countries organized lavish receptions on their national days. Sometimes, they brought symphony orchestras, folk music, and incredible art exhibits to New York. But the small and poor countries could not afford any of this. With a calendar of national days on hand, I called the ambassadors to offer congratulations and invited them for tea or coffee in the delegates' lounge. I made a practice of never asking for anything on my first call. Such outreach went a long way in developing and strengthening personal and professional relationships. Also with me all the time was a list that I had developed, containing crucial information about the 192 member countries of the UN.

Most missions have only one ambassador. Some have two. The big ones have four or five. The United States has five: we are the host country for the UN and the largest contributor in addition to being a cofounder. Still, we have fewer ambassadors than the Dominican Republic, which has eight.

Except for the chief of mission who had twenty-four-hour use of an armored limousine, the other four ambassadors could use cars only between nine AM and five PM, if they were available. Attending evening functions at elegant ambassadorial residences on Fifth and Park avenues, I usually arrived in a yellow cab and hailed another one to get home. My colleagues from other countries got into their shining chauffeured sedans. Occasionally, I got a ride from one of them.

I later asked to drive the U.S. mission vehicles myself. Here I was, a former cabbie, and I ended up giving my colleagues a ride home after diplomatic receptions. These vehicles were equipped with police lights and sirens, which could be used in an emergency. My former White House colleague Rob Portman, a congressman from Ohio, and his family came to visit me once. As I was driving them to Penn Station, a car cut so close in front that it almost hit the mission van. I turned the emergency horn on, and the children got all excited.

There were nearly 250 ambassador-ranked diplomats at the UN. It was difficult to remember everybody's name. The safest thing was to call them "ambassador" or, better yet, "excellency." You can never go wrong that way. When using "excellency," I tried to refrain from thinking in Khmer, because of its resemblance to a Khmer word meaning "piece of shit."

Among the ambassadors, Singapore's Kishore Mahbubani was the one I had known longest. We reminisced about the time we were together in Cambodia, and the Saturday breakfast club. I had learned how to make our favorite Phnom Penh noodles, and we invited many of our colleagues to his residence for an unusually informal "sit-eat-move" noodle breakfast. We wanted to re-create the atmosphere of Phnom Penh, but without the heat, humidity, or flies. I made about sixty bowls of noodles that day. Waiters in tuxedos came into the kitchen to give their orders to the cook: "Ambassador, one bowl with broth! Ambassador, one more bowl without broth!" Everybody enjoyed the noodles, or at least seemed to enjoy them. A few of our guests went on to become foreign ministers, and all are still alive and well.

Each ambassador had an interesting personality. Russia's Sergey

Lavrov, a chain-smoker, had a spat with Secretary-General Kofi Annan, who banned smoking at the UN in accordance with New York City's codes. Lavrov defied the ban, saying the secretary-general did not own the building, and walked around with his own ashtray: he later became foreign minister. This incident and Madeleine Albright's opposition to Boutros Boutros-Ghali before she became secretary of state seemed to start a new trend: if you wanted to become foreign minister, you challenged the UN secretary-general.

Egypt receives one of the biggest grants of U.S. foreign aid. But its record of voting with the United States was abysmal. Its ambassador, Ahmed Aboul Gheit, was, however, a friendly person. He once hosted an *iftar* dinner for John Negroponte and myself with all the Muslim ambassadors, to mark the end of Ramadan. He also became foreign minister.

The United States has a practice of not trading or revealing votes. At a meeting of the Community of Democracies with the undersecretary of state, Paula Dobriansky, the Ecuadorian ambassador, Luis Gallegos, stood up and asked us to revise our position.

"Sichan, everybody is exchanging votes. You do not tell anybody how you vote; you do not trade votes. When are you going to change that practice?"

"Yes, Luis, you are correct. We are the only country that is doing that. I like it. Everyone in my government likes it. I strongly believe that it is a good practice for us and that it should continue. Thanks for asking this excellent question." I slowly added, paraphrasing Humphrey Bogart's last line in *Casablanca*, "Luis, I think this is the beginning of a beautiful friendship!"

The twelfth floor of the U.S. Mission burst into roaring laughter.

CHAPTER 21:

THE CARAVAN

RELIEF, REHABILITATION, RECONSTRUCTION

Of all the travels I did for the United States, none topped the trip to Iraq. It was quite an eye-opener for me. In September 2004 I flew in a C-130 from Kuwait to Mosul. I was sitting in the cockpit with the crew and an army general. The minute the aircraft entered Iraqi airspace, the crew put on bulletproof vests and helmets. Taking that as our cue, the general and I immediately put on ours.

At Baghdad International Airport, I was met by my control officer and security detail and we boarded a Blackhawk helicopter for the Iraqi capital.

I went to see John Negroponte in his empty office; then we went to lunch in the huge embassy cafeteria. John suggested that I take two of the plastic forks. I had spaghetti and meatballs, probably the best I've ever had. After a few bites, one fork broke. I guess John ate there frequently.

During the thirty-one-hour visit, with an overnight stay at the ambassador's residence, I had in-depth consultations with Iraqi leaders. I was impressed by their commitment to bring their country back from the brink. I told them that my country of birth, Cambodia, had gone through death and destruction. It was recovering slowly but surely, because it had a solid cultural foundation of a few thousand years. Iraq's culture went back farther—after all, the land between the Tigris and Euphrates rivers was the "cradle of civilization." I had no doubt that it would recover.

I was even more impressed with our military and civilian personnel, who were working hard trying to help Iraq steady its caravan to democracy and prosperity. They did their job with total dedication and enthusiasm. I could never forget the sight of two U.S. Army guys jogging in 120-degree heat.

Before I left for a Security Council mission to Africa, I sent an e-mail to John Negroponte thanking him for his hospitality and also for taking the time to write a recommendation for one of our USUN officers. All of them worked very hard, and I was lucky to have a very good team, despite the fact that working at the UN in New York could be a hardship post for American diplomats: there was no diplomatic immunity; our salaries were not tax-exempt; and, except for a few, there was no housing allowance. And New York is probably the most costly city in the country. Those who go to USUN to benefit from the best multilateral exposure are usually single or rich, or they have relatives in the city.

I n December 2004 Martha and I were in the Texas Panhandle for the holidays. I usually spent my time working as a hand at the Lazy B Ranch—my way of relaxation after endless hours of diplomatic negotiations at the UN. It was there in Canadian that I learned about the Asian tsunami. Back in New York, I met my colleagues from donor countries and the UN to map our strategy.

The United States was the first to respond to this tragedy. The U.S. government pledged $350 million. That amount did not include our military assets with the Abraham Lincoln Carrier Battle Group— twenty-seven ships, forty-five aircraft, fifty-seven helicopters, and 15,000 personnel.

We delivered about 12 million pounds of supplies. At a conference on small island developing states in Mauritius in January 2005, I announced that the United States would support international efforts to develop a global early warning system for tsunamis as well as a range of other natural disasters. By March 1, 2005, the American people had contributed over $1 billion to more than 130 U.S. nonprofit agencies, according to the Indiana University's Center on Philanthropy.

As an American ambassador, I also had the opportunity to be a host to all kinds of visitors at the United Nations. On Texas Independence Day, March 2, 2005, I received a group of French students from the École de la Légion d'Honneur, a prestigious girl's school open only to descendants of the legion's medalists. The girls wore their beautiful uniforms with white gloves. We spoke in English and French. At the end of my presentation on U.S. objectives at the UN, I quizzed them on Franco-American relations, and gave some prizes for correct answers. They knew about Franklin, Jefferson, and Lafayette, but I was able to stump them with some tricky ones.

On June 25, 2005, I delivered a statement at the UN's sixtieth-anniversary celebration in San Francisco. It was a great honor for me to follow in the footsteps of previous illustrious speakers: presidents Truman in 1945, Eisenhower in 1955, and Johnson in 1965; Secretary of State Shultz in 1985; and President Clinton in 1995.

The sixtieth anniversary had great personal significance for me, as my life was closely intertwined with the UN. As a child in Cambodia, I had waved a flag to welcome Secretary-General Dag Hammarskjold. Many of us were inoculated by UNICEF. Among my Asian and Buddhist brethren, there was a strong affinity with Secretary-General U Thant in the 1960s.

In the following decade, the UN played a key role in maintaining peace and security. However, in 1975 the Khmer Rouge turned Cambodia into a land of blood and tears, and the UN was powerless to stop the genocide. Only five countries spoke out against these violations of human rights: Australia, Canada, Norway, the United Kingdom, and the United States. In 1976 I was under the care of the UN High Commissioner for Refugees.

Martha and I agreed that the sixtieth session of the General Assembly should be my last. Some 180 heads of state and government descended on the East Side neighborhood of Manhattan known as Turtle Bay. President and Mrs. Bush hosted a reception for these dignitaries at the Waldorf-Astoria. Martha and I were the first to welcome them after protocol officers brought them to the reception.

The general debate is the time when heads of delegation deliver their official statements. The U.S. practice requires the presence of an ambassador at the seat when the speaker is a head of state or government or is from a member of the Security Council. I listened while working on something else. My cell phone vibrated with a text message from the Colombian ambassador, Maria Angela Holguin: *Qué idioma habla*—"What language is he speaking?" I looked toward the podium and saw Prime Minister Hun Sen of Cambodia. "Khmer" was my response.

By the end of 2005, I would have been at my ambassadorial post for four years. I would have managed U.S. participation in five sessions of UNGA and numerous conferences.

I began a tally of diplomatic faux pas. I could not think of a major disaster. Only three incidents came to mind.

First, I had kissed a female foreign minister on both cheeks, thinking she was the wife of the ambassador. The ambassador later was promoted to an even more important post. I was not certain if I had anything to do with it.

Second, I had introduced the Latvian ambassador as the Czech ambassador, because both of them were wearing bow ties. Actually, there were five of us who wore bow ties at the UN: the ambassadors of Czech Republic, Latvia, Samoa, and Spain, and myself. Although most of them sported a bow tie all the time, I wore one only on Tuesdays and Thursdays; I had more neckties. I became interested in bow ties because of a convincing point made by my good friend Nitya Pibulsonggram, who was the Thai ambassador to the UN and Washington before becoming foreign minister. He offered me the following wisdom: "If you spill something at dinner, you will have to send the necktie to the cleaner. It could be as expensive as buying a new one. But if you wore a bow tie, only the shirt goes to the cleaner." It makes sense, doesn't it?

The third incident occurred when a number of my USUN colleagues and I were invited to a karaoke dinner by the Chinese Ambassador, Zhang Yishan, at his residence overlooking the UN and the East River. The United States and China disagreed on some issues, especially human rights and population, but our relations were too important to have these issues overshadow strategic views. Zhang and I always had a very good working relationship. Our dealings had been frank, yet cordial.

Zhang alerted me that the dinner would be a U.S.-China session. No other country had been invited. I obliquely assumed that this might be in response to the informal karaoke quartet I had set up with Brunei, Indonesia, Japan, and the United States. I told my colleagues to be prepared. Some of the Chinese delegates were very good singers. Zhang, his wife, and the Chinese mission staff welcomed us very warmly.

It was going to be informal, and we were advised to take off our jackets. We were treated to the best Chinese dishes and delicious wine. Before the real fun began, I stood up and walked to the karaoke machine to admire the elaborate equipment. One of my colleagues pulled me into the corridor. I thought there was another emergency or crisis.

He whispered in my ear that the back of my pants had a split seam right at my rear, big enough to see my white underwear underneath. Who was it who said, "Always wear clean underwear, in case you have an accident?" I immediately put my jacket on again. Throughout the evening, our hosts encouraged me to be less formal: "You're welcome to take off your jacket." I told them that I sang better with my jacket on.

The United States was at a slight disadvantage. We could sing only in English, but our hosts could do songs in both English and Chinese. It was a really fun evening—food and songs added new dimensions to modern diplomacy.

As I looked back, I felt that overall I did not do so badly: three unnoticeable faux pas in 1,825 days. I could live with it.

My greatest satisfaction was our solid record of winning every election we ran for at the UN. Our excellent USUN team and the strong support from Washington and our overseas missions had made this possible.

CHAPTER 22

TWO THOUSAND SIX

THE FIRST MONTH AND SEVENTEENTH DAY:
THE DEDICATION

I suddenly woke up from a flashback after hearing my name mentioned in one of the speeches. Martha and I were participating in an impressive dedication ceremony for the new American embassy in Phnom Penh, on Ben Franklin's 300th birthday.

Franklin was eighty-four when he died in 1790. The second and third presidents of the United States, John Adams and Thomas Jefferson, both died on July 4, 1826—the nation's fiftieth Independence Day. They were, respectively, ninety-one and eighty-three.

In Cambodia, older people usually give a blessing to younger ones by saying, "May you live to be 120!" As a child with no concept of how long 120 years were, I usually responded simply: "Thanks. You too!" Asia is the world's largest and most populous continent, with many ancient cultures and civilizations. There, life is divided into cycles of twelve years each. The most important birthday is the sixtieth, because it marks the end of the fifth cycle and the highest point of one's life. And ten life cycles equal 120 years.

The first U.S.-owned complex in Cambodia in fifty-five years, the embassy was a new post-9/11 "standard embassy design" and cost $60 million, nearly equal to the U.S. bilateral assistance budget. Despite its security features—which were the highest in Asia and on which all future embassies would be based—the architecture was elegant, airy, and welcoming. The $3 million landscaping made the embassy blend well in this old section of the Cambodian capital.

The new embassy compound covered an area of 6.2 acres and had almost 30,000 square feet of floor space. Workers, including 1,500 local hires, logged about 3 million hours and consumed more than sixty tons of meat, 121 tons of rice and vegetables, and almost 49,000 gallons of bottled water. The chancery design included native plants and a facade made of 5 million pounds of Carrara stone from the same Italian quarry that Michelangelo used for his sculptures. Its construction pumped $18 million into the local economy, and resulted in five marriages between American workers and Cambodian citizens and at least three Cambodian-American offspring. One American, nicknamed "Gravy," married the Cambodian cook at his favorite restaurant—a match made in culinary heaven.

The embassy, which boasted a collection of about 100 original works by American and Cambodian artists, hosted a reception in my honor with over 300 guests. I also took the opportunity to give a speech to more than 500 university students, entitled "*E Pluribus Unum:* The Power of Unity."

We called on King Sihamoni and met with Prime Minister Hun Sen, who announced the release of some human rights activists.

THE SIXTH MONTH AND NINTH DAY: THE FIFTH CYCLE

In June, Martha and I flew to Bangkok at the invitation of the Thai government to attend the sixtieth anniversary of King Bhumibol's accession to the throne. The king, currently the longest-serving monarch

in the world, had reigned for five life cycles. The United States and
Thailand have more than 170 years of solid friendship since the Treaty
of Amity and Commerce in 1833, the first such treaty signed between
America and an Asian country. On December 30, 2003, President
George W. Bush designated Thailand as a major non-NATO ally. The
U.S. Congress adopted a resolution commemorating the historic event.

Bangkok declared a five-day holiday and banned vehicular traffic
from most of the city. There were twenty-five monarchies present at
the jubilee.

THE SIXTH MONTH AND EIGHTEENTH DAY:
THE PAST IS PRESENT

From Bangkok, we took a fifty-minute flight to Siem Reap. We decided to retrace the last leg of my escape route thirty years ago. I
wanted to find the family of my guardian angel and the mysterious
monk, who were instrumental in my survival under the Pol Pot regime and my escape to freedom. This, I believed, would help close
the loop of a thirty-year odyssey. I did not expect much. Since my
first return to Cambodia along the Thai-Cambodian border in 1983
and my trip to Phnom Penh in 1992, each time I was in the country
I always inquired about Chim Chun and the monk. The results had
been zero. I was still hopeful. For the first time, I would be in Sisophon, where I met both of them in 1975–1976, the first year of Cambodia's nightmare.

We spent a few days at Angkor, visiting the exquisite temples, and
seeing a sunrise at Angkor Wat. We admired the serene beauty of the
enchanted forest from the Elephant's Terrace near the Bayon, the
center of Angkor Thom. The late-afternoon sun made the treetops
golden. We said hello to my ageless banyan tree. It is the first one on
the left, closest to the steps of the western causeway of Angkor Wat.

We can never get enough of Angkor. It is always magic, pure and simple!
We ran into a mahout we had met on a previous trip. He introduced

us to his elephant partner, Srey Lorm, a gorgeous thirty-five-year-old female.

On June 17, we arrived at Sisophon in the late morning and went straight to the railroad station. I walked back and forth on the platform, trying to recollect the happy memories of my visits to my sister Sarin in the late 1950s and early 1960s. The yellowish station looked the same although run-down because of poor or no maintenance. It seemed smaller than I remembered. The Khmer words *Serei Sophorn* were still painted in black on both the north and the south sides of the station. People with merchandise were waiting for the once daily train from Battambang.

Under the scorching sun, Martha and I walked the half mile between the station and the downtown area. We looked for the wooden row houses that had lined both sides of the street when Sarin lived there. We found only one left. I was not sure whether that was the one where my sister and her young family were living nearly half a century ago.

In the afternoon, we went to Wat Svay Chas to call on the top monk, So Hul. He was in charge of 214 monasteries in Banteay Meanchey province, carved out of the old Battambang province to give birth to a new one with Sisophon as its capital. He told us that he could think of only one monk who fit my description. Unfortunately, that monk had died in 2001. His niece, now a nun at the temple, had built a memorial in honor of her uncle. The venerable So Hul pointed to me the *kod* where she was living, on the riverbank.

Our conversation with the nun revealed more striking coincidences with the mysterious monk. It seemed that we were now on the right track to identify him.

We rushed to Svay Chek, about thirty minutes north of Sisophon on route 69 on the way to Banteay Chamar. We first looked for the chief of the Svay Chek commune, but his house was locked. His neighbors did not know when he was coming back. We then went to the district office and found two men wearing shorts and *krama* working under an office awning. It was Saturday afternoon and all offices were closed. The two men were there to catch up with some work; pieces of paper were fluttering all over the table. They invited us to sit down, giving the best chair to Martha, and I told them the objective of our visit.

"We are looking for a man named Chim Chun who is originally from the Svay Chek area. I met him in late May 1975, when we both were prisoners of the Khmer Rouge. If he is still alive, he should be in his late sixties. I am confident that that is his real name and that he has returned to his native village. The only background information I have on him is that he was a bus and truck driver in Lon Nol's time and that his mother's house was in the old Khmer style, on the east side of route 69 near some big trees in the area. But that was 1975."

The two overworked, underpaid civil servants said that they had been transferred recently from other provinces and did not know many people. They suggested that we try the commune chief, who might have some information. In the meantime, we should talk to the people who lived in a few old Khmer-style houses on the northern side of Svay Chek. We should also talk to the village chiefs of Treas, a few miles to the north; and Tabaen, a few miles to the south, all on route 69.

We spent a few hours talking to those families but still had no lead. We stopped at the house of the commune chief again, but it was still locked. We decided to head back to Sisophon before it got dark. I had to see the primary school where I spent my first night after getting through the Khmer Rouge security cordon, and the secondary school-cum-hospital where I spent nearly two weeks waiting to die, but recovered.

On the way back, a few miles south of Svay Chek in the village of

Tabaen, Martha noticed some women selling watermelons, which we wanted to have for dessert that night. While Martha practiced her Khmer by shopping, I casually asked an older seller if she knew a Chim Chun. After I gave her the background information, she said she knew a woman whose brother was a truck driver before the Khmer Rouge, but she was not sure if he was the right person. I told her that we would be back the following morning and would appreciate it if she could inquire further.

Back in Sisophon, we went to the secondary school on a hill. People were taking advantage of the remaining sunlight to play a final game of basketball and volleyball. I recognized the location of the ward where I had lain, waiting to die, in the Khmer Rouge hospital. The structure of the building had changed.

At the primary school, only two wooden structures still stood. We walked from there to the river through the back alley. I showed Martha where I used to take a bath. The area around the school was overbuilt, with houses constructed almost on top of each other.

Sunday, June 18, 2006, at six o'clock in the morning, while Martha got dressed, I took a *motodup*—motorcycle taxi—to the railroad station. There was a train with old ramshackle cars waiting to be loaded with the various goods I had seen the day before.

I looked at the wooden row house one more time, and tears started running down my cheeks. I suddenly missed my sister Sarin more than at any other time in my life. She was so gentle, so caring, and so sweet. She was always very happy to see me. I remembered that *Mae* took me to see her at the maternity clinic each time she had a baby. She usually waited to eat until I arrived so that she could share with me the nutritious meals reserved for new mothers.

When I visited her and her family in the provinces, she immediately asked me about school, our family, and the latest news from Pochentong and Phnom Penh. Coming from the capital, I was expected to know everything. She took me around to introduce me to her friends and neighbors. She took me to Aranyaprathet—the Thai town just across the border from Cambodia, where I later spent a few months in a refugee camp and in a Buddhist temple.

Being fifteen years older than I was, she seemed very proud to say, "My baby brother Sichan." She was very giving and a perfect extension of *Mae*. She seemed to love me more than she loved anybody else. She saved my life with her *sdao* medicine in April 1975.

I was now wondering if she knew that I loved her as much as she loved me. The more I thought about her, the more tears came down. For some reason, I felt that she loved me more than Sichhun did. Or maybe they both loved me the same, but as a man Sichhun did not want to show his emotion.

The motorcycle driver, sensing that I was choking behind him, looked discreetly at me through his rearview mirror. I wiped my tears, and the blowing wind helped dry them before we arrived at the next destination.

From the railroad station, I went back to the Svay Chas monastery. I found the nun, and the final clue to the real identity of the mysterious monk. His name was Barn Phlong. He was born in 1906, the fifth of six boys. His parents had sent him to the Buddhist monastery at Makak in 1918, when he was twelve. Having children educated at the Buddhist temples was an old Cambodian custom. The parents would ask the abbot to do whatever he pleased with the boy, and "leave us only his bones to cremate."

Phlong was ordained a monk thereafter.

The nun who was his niece said that he was the last monk to leave the temple after the Khmer Rouge began to force everyone out of all the towns and cities. And he managed to return to Wat Svay Chas a few times by boat. The last two times were probably when he met me and when he collected the offerings I left for him. He was arrested and disrobed by the Khmer Rouge, who spared his life only on learning that he knew about traditional medicine. They put him in charge of their collective pharmacy, looking for plants, roots, and leaves to make *thanam Khmer*—Cambodian medicine.

After the Vietnamese invasion in 1979, Phlong wanted to return to monkhood, but his niece told him that she would not be able to take care of him properly when he got older and sick: a woman could not touch a monk. He decided to remain a layman and continued teaching *Vippasanna* meditation. He died in 2001 at the age of ninety-five. His disciples printed 500 copies of his biography and some of his teachings and distributed them as memorial books. There were pictures of Barn Phlong on the wall of his niece's *kod* and in a booklet of which she was kind enough to give me a copy. I did not clearly recollect his face after meeting him only briefly three decades ago, but my earlier calculation had been correct. He was in his sixties when we met. He was truly a wise man, and his wisdom has remained with me. Yet for thirty years I had been thinking that he never physically existed.

The rain stopped when we finished the conversation. I left some contributions with the nun in honor of Barn Phlong. We exchanged the *sampeahs*. I hopped back onto the motorcycle taxi behind the driver, and he returned me to the Golden Dragon Hotel.

Martha had never been to Battambang, so we decided to go there for breakfast. We took national route 5 eastward and arrived at Cambodia's second largest city in less than one hour. We ate and then toured the city a little bit, including its bustling market, and returned to Sisophon.

It had been raining and we were concerned that the women selling fruit might not be there at the side of the muddy road. We arrived at Tabaen at eleven AM. Sure enough, they were there. The minute I got out of the car, my contact informed me that Chim Chun's youngest sister was waiting with an older sister at their house near a big tamarind tree just a few hundred yards south.

We all went there. As we exchanged the *sampeahs*, I recognized the bone structure of the two sisters' faces. It was strikingly similar to Chim Chun's. They spoke Khmer with the same heavy northwestern accent as their older brother. Phin, the younger of the two and the youngest of Chun's siblings, answered most of my questions and told most of the story. It was the first time that I learned about Chun's family.

There were six of them, with Chun being the eldest. Phin, who was now fifty-one lived with Chun and his family when she was a young girl. Amazingly, they all survived the Khmer Rouge. Perhaps their peasant background helped them adapt better to the extreme hardship all Cambodians were submitted to. A few years after the Vietnamese invasion, Chun went to Thamaw Puak to collect money from people who owed it to him and his wife. On the way back, he was killed with one of his children in a bus accident. His wife died of an illness in 2003. All of their five remaining children were still alive, but Phin had lost touch with them.

I thanked Phin and her sister for all the information and asked them to try to find Chun's children. "I'll be back!" I gave them a lot of goodies and we left for Banteay Chamar.

Somewhere north of Treas near the Kapik Bridge, I asked the driver to stop. That is, according to Phin, where Chun was killed. I lit a candle and incense on the west side of route 69 and prayed for Chun's soul so that he might rest in peace.

We reached Banteay Chamar shortly after midday. We went directly to the northeast corner of the moat of the twelfth-century temple. It was there that I had taken my last bath in Cambodia on February 13, 1976, a few hours before my fateful leap from the logging truck. What had been a small village of a few houses had become a lively market area.

After touring the temple, we headed back to Thamaw Puak. There were rice fields and villages on both sides of route 69 south of Banteay Chamar. I talked to a small group of villagers playing cards under a house on stilts. They informed me that they had moved from other provinces as part of the government's community development programs, which provided some land for them to cultivate. No wonder I could not recognize the area.

I found one big bend on the road. Was this where I jumped off the logging truck on February 13, 1976, in search of freedom? It was north of the single bridge between Thamaw Puak and Banteay Chamar, which had been planned, designed, and built by the U.S. Army Pacific and the 412th Engineer Command.

As we drove away from the bend and the bridge, I tried to digest the enormous changes that had taken place during the past three decades.

In 1976, I was the loneliest person on earth. I had no family, no friends, no neighbors, no one to rely on, and no one to trust. I had no place to call home, no land to call a country, and nowhere to go, except death. But I had my mother's wisdom. I had hope and was lucky to have survived one of the twentieth century's worst nightmares.

Three decades later, the jungle had given way to rice fields. I was blessed to have a new country, a new home, and a new family. I felt as if I were in the concluding scene of Steven Spielberg's *Saving Private Ryan*, when Ryan returns to France to visit the grave of his savior.

I had now lived in America longer than in Cambodia. I had held more jobs, met more people, and made more friends. But as a common saying went, "You can take a person out of Cambodia; you can't take Cambodia out of him."

So am I Cambodian or American?

I am an ABC.

An American by Choice.

An American Born Cambodian.

I am blessed to have freedom and opportunities and I am proud to maintain an ancient cultural heritage.

THE SEVENTH MONTH AND FOURTH DAY: THE PARADE

A few days after our return from Asia, Martha and I fly to Texas. At DFW Airport, I feel very much out of place. No one else wears a cowboy hat, yet. This is the town J. R. Ewing made famous, with his flashy business suit and hat.

No. Not one gentleman has serious headgear. Plenty of baseball caps, but no cowboy hats. No kidding.

I tell Martha that I will give her a two-dollar bill if she finds another man with a hat before I do. My eyes start searching while we move from one terminal to another. Finally, I spot one at gate D7. The only other wearer of a cowboy hat at DFW is even better dressed than I am. His blue jeans are nicely pressed and his boots are shining. He wears a navy blue suit jacket over his cowboy shirt.

In Amarillo, we join our friend Neva Burks at the Big Texan for our steak ritual. I stop at the honor roll that lists the latest champs with date, name, age, weight, amount of time taken to wolf down the steak, and their comments.

The big winner is number 8847 on May 13 (my lucky number), 2005. He is a nineteen-year-old Korean from Seoul. He weighs 165 pounds (my weight the day I became a U.S. citizen on December 21, 1982) and consumes his prize in thirty-six minutes. Can you imagine eating a seventy-two-ounce steak with all the fixin's—baked potato, roll and butter, shrimp cocktail, tossed salad—in a mere thirty-six minutes? His comment was *Go Duke!* Some of the others on the blackboard are *Bring me one more. I'll be back. I'm still walking. What's for dessert? U.S.M.C. No problem. Feel good. Whoa!*

I salute all the champs for their culinary achievements and join Martha and Neva to get my regular dose of steak. I feel very much at home in the Texas Panhandle. All gentlemen keep their hats on while eating.

Like many small towns in America, Pampa has lost quite a bit of population over the years. More than 24,000 were living there when I visited the first time in 1982. Now, there are only 17,787 residents in the top of Texas. Even Miami (pronounced "Mayama"), the only town in Roberts County with one flashing traffic light, has lost population. There used to be 813 people. The number has gone down to 588.

Our tradition in Pampa includes getting flowers for the graves of Martha's parents in the cemetery across from Pampa High School and stopping by Wayne's to check out any new items for the Sivs' wardrobes. We drive by the First Presbyterian Church, where we were married on Christmas Eve in 1983.

The minute we arrive at the Brainard townhouse in Canadian, an hour northeast of Pampa, we hear, "Sichan is here! Sichan is here!" We are immediately surrounded by the Brainard grandchildren. The first thing they tell me about is the death of my favorite horse, Sydney, whom I have been riding for many years. He died on Memorial Day weekend at the ripe old age of twenty-four.

On July 4, we assemble on the grounds of Canadian High School. Our entry in the Independence Day parade is called the "Lazy B Express." Martha rides in a wagon with the Brainard grandchildren pulled by two enormous mules named Bonnie and Clyde. Toughie, my new mount, and I follow them. He is on foot, I am on his back.

With a population of just over 2,000, Canadian, Texas, is swollen with visitors this day. They line both sides of the street from the high school through downtown to watch the parade. The crowd gets thicker as we approach the courthouse.

The organizers of the parade were smart to put the police cars and the fire trucks ahead of everyone else and far away from the horses. The blasting sirens could easily scare the animals and send them bucking and running. It reminds me of a story of the Khmer army in the twelfth century. The elephants and the horses had to be separated from each other. The horses were scared of the elephants: they were very big, yet they didn't make any noise. The elephants were scared of the horses: they were so small, yet so noisy.

The biggest challenge for me is to watch out for children who run to the street to pick up candies and sweets thrown by those in front of me.

Thirty years ago I was in Jeffersonville, Vermont, as a spectator for my first American Fourth of July. Now I am *in* the Fourth of July parade in Canadian, Texas, on horseback. The view is certainly different at nine feet up.

In the afternoon, we go to the rodeo grounds to participate in the 118th annual rodeo, America's oldest. In 1888, Panhandle cowboys and families came in wagons and by horseback to Canadian, their new railroad and cattle capital, to have the area's first Fourth of July celebration. It became a tradition.

I ride in the rodeo "grand entry," escorted into the arena by two cowboys—one carrying the American flag and the other the flag of Texas. The announcer jokes about ambassadors not knowing how to ride a horse. He adds that *this one seems to be doing OK.*

He does not know that the previous year, I had a terrible riding accident that left me with eight broken ribs and a broken collarbone. A few friends and I were at the end of an hourlong ride in Caumsett Park on Long Island, near Teddy Roosevelt's Sagamore Hill, when we decided to canter. The thoroughbred horses picked up speed very fast. Mine, whose name was Tembo ("elephant" in Swahili), swerved suddenly to the left. I, as a good Republican, went to the right and was thrown to the ground. I could not breathe. None of us had a cell phone, and one rider had to gallop to the nearest house to call an ambulance. While lying on the ground in agony for one hour, I wondered why it took one of the wealthiest communities in America so long to get an ambulance. The first person to arrive on foot was a park police officer. He shouted, "Who is it?"

"Sichan Siv!" my fellow riders shouted back in unison.

"Who's he?"

"He is an American ambassador to the United Nations!"

"Ambassador? From which country?"

"United States of America!" The heavyset officer, out of breath, leaned over me and asked the same questions.

The ambulance finally found a way to get through the park and to me, one hour later. I was brought to the emergency room of Huntington Hospital, only fifteen minutes away. I spent a few days in the intensive care unit in a very expensive bed that could do all sort of things at the press of a button.

In the meantime, Martha alerted my very able assistant, Connie Padovano. There was an outpouring of get-well wishes from many people, including the two presidents Bush. Most of the messages were funny and everyone tried to cheer me up, although laughing, coughing, and sneezing were quite painful. Andy Card told me not to take it out on the horse. Jack Danforth advised me to find a more graceful way to exit a horse. Al Kamen of the *Washington Post* reported the accident, and the news spread. Dick Solomon sent an e-mail: *What a way to get sympathy. I always respect you as a man of integrity, but this latest scam is just too much!*

I have been visiting Texas for nearly a quarter of a century. July 4, 2006, is the first time I have been to a live rodeo, instead of watching one on television. The program includes riding (bareback, bull, saddle bronc, barrel racing), roping (breakaway, calf, team), steer wrestling, and mutton bustin'.

No event stirs up more excitement than bull riding. I marvel at riders who manage to stay on top of the animal for eight seconds, which must seem to be a lifetime to them. As an armchair rodeo junkie, I regret not having a chance to meet the 1,800-pound Bodacious, called by critics the meanest beast and by fans the greatest bull. It's democracy to have different opinions, even about a bovine. It's freedom to say whatever is on one's mind.

In the evening, we are back at the rodeo grounds to watch the fireworks.

I have really come full circle. I reflect on my brother Sichhun's words in Alabama in 1973 and my thoughts in Vermont in 1976.

I say to Martha: *This is a beautiful country!*

Acknowledgments

The greatest blessings in life are having a loving family, having wonderful friends, and having good colleagues. I have been lucky to have all of them. They helped me write this memoir. In fact, everyone whom I came across has had a role in it. I am thankful to have met these good people. Some are mentioned in this book. Others are not. Many have died, some in tragic circumstances.

My mother, and my sister and brother and their families who were killed; the army sergeant, the fisherman, the truck driver who told me to "stay on the road"; the mysterious monk who counseled me to "follow the moon and the sun" to find freedom—I owe all of them an eternal debt of gratitude. And those who trusted me by giving me jobs—from the apple orchard supervisor in Connecticut to the taxi examiner in New York and two presidents of the United States—I thank them profoundly for the opportunity to live the American dream.

In between, Harvey Picker, then dean of Columbia University School of International Affairs, admitted me to the program; and Helen Maguire Muller offered me a full scholarship. They provided a turning point in my academic and professional life.

I learned from my colleagues at the White House, the U.S. government, the private sector, nonprofit circles, and the diplomatic world.

I benefited enormously from their expertise, advice, and friendship, in the United States and elsewhere around the globe.

Many people have offered me hospitality while I was writing the book. Bob and Nancy Charles's eighteenth-century home in Wallingford, Connecticut, my birthplace of freedom, stands out. The idyllic landscape I saw in the summer of 1976 still looks the same.

I have no records of my family. Everything was destroyed. All pre-1976 photos were gifts from friends and relatives. Joe Connors was superb with his photographic work, as was Fred Canpolat. The staff of the George Bush Presidential Library in College Station, Texas, were very helpful.

Golden Bones was brought to the publisher's attention through the kindness of Yue-Sai Kan, Ijaz Malik, and Melik Kaylan.

My beloved wife, Martha, is a wonderful editor; one cannot ask for more. She reads everything diligently and edits meaningfully. Chase Untermeyer, Bill Nojay, and Bill Canary most generously offered critical comments on the manuscript.

At HarperCollins, my editor Doug Grad is of unsurpassed literary wisdom. His editorial guidance was complemented by the excellent team under the leadership of the publisher, Jonathan Burnham. They include, among others, Jamie Brickhouse, Susan Gamer, Josh Marwell, Nina Olmstead, Kathy Schneider, Emily Taff, and Campbell Wharton. All contributed in their own way to make *Golden Bones* what it is.

To one and all, thank you from the bottom of my heart for undertaking this project together. You have my golden wishes for the best!